Contents

Bibliography	**15**	
Bibliography	**19**	
Educational Journey	27	
Bibliography	**39**	
The Personal Journey	50	
Bibliography	**59**	
Bibliography	**67**	
The Activist Emerges	73	
The Rise to Prominence	**97**	
The Rise to Prominence	97	
Making Waves in Politics	100	
International Advocacy	125	
Media and Public Recognition	147	
Bibliography	**157**	
A Legacy of Advocacy	**175**	
A Legacy of Advocacy	175	
The Future of LGBTQ and Disability Rights	177	
Recognitions and Honors	202	
Bibliography	**219**	
Bibliography	**223**	
Life Behind the Activism	227	

Bibliography	**233**
Bibliography	**249**
Unauthorized	**255**
Unauthorized	255
The Controversies and Backlash	259
The Unfinished Life of Paula Lupi	280
Index	**301**

Childhood in Lisbon

Paula Lupi was born in the vibrant heart of Lisbon, Portugal, a city that pulses with life, culture, and a rich tapestry of history. From the narrow, winding streets of Alfama to the bustling squares of Baixa, her childhood was steeped in the sights and sounds of a city that thrived on diversity and resilience. Lisbon, with its picturesque views of the Tagus River and its iconic trams, served as both a backdrop and a character in Paula's early life, offering her a unique blend of opportunities and challenges.

1.1.1 A Bustling City Filled with Opportunities

The opportunities presented by Lisbon's dynamic environment were abundant. The city was a melting pot of cultures, where influences from Africa, Brazil, and Europe converged. This diverse atmosphere played a crucial role in shaping Paula's worldview. She was exposed to various art forms, languages, and traditions, which ignited her passion for social justice and advocacy. The streets were alive with music, from fado to contemporary pop, and these sounds became the soundtrack to her formative years.

1.1.2 Paula's Supportive and Loving Family

At the core of Paula's childhood was her family, a steadfast support system that nurtured her spirit and encouraged her individuality. Her parents, both educators, instilled in her the values of empathy, education, and activism. They often engaged in discussions about societal issues, fostering a home environment where questioning norms was not only accepted but celebrated. This foundation of love and support empowered Paula to explore her identity and advocate for those around her.

1.1.3 Early Signs of Activism and Advocacy

From a young age, Paula exhibited signs of activism. Whether it was defending a classmate being bullied or organizing neighborhood clean-ups, her innate sense of justice was evident. These early experiences laid the groundwork for her future endeavors. She often recalled a pivotal moment in her childhood when she stood up for a friend who faced discrimination. This act of bravery not only solidified her commitment to advocacy but also illustrated the power of individual action in the face of injustice.

1.1.4 Discovering Her Own Identity

As Paula navigated her childhood, she began to grapple with her own identity. Growing up in a society with rigid expectations regarding gender and sexuality, she often felt the weight of societal norms. The journey of self-discovery was fraught with challenges, yet it was also a time of profound exploration. She sought solace in literature and art, finding inspiration in the works of authors and activists who challenged the status quo. This exploration of her identity was not just personal; it became a catalyst for her future activism.

1.1.5 Navigating Societal Expectations and Challenges

Lisbon, while vibrant and diverse, was not without its societal challenges. The expectations placed upon Paula by her peers and community often clashed with her emerging identity. She faced moments of isolation and misunderstanding, particularly as she began to question the norms surrounding gender and sexuality. These experiences, though painful, were instrumental in shaping her resilience. They taught her the importance of standing firm in her beliefs and the value of community support.

1.1.6 Finding Solace in Music and Art

In the face of societal pressures, Paula found refuge in music and art. These creative outlets became her sanctuary, allowing her to express her emotions and experiences. She immersed herself in the local art scene, attending exhibitions and performances that celebrated diversity and challenged societal norms. Music, particularly, became a powerful tool for self-expression, with artists like Aldina Duarte and David Carreira inspiring her to embrace her identity fully.

1.1.7 The Influence of Her Diverse Friendships

Paula's friendships played a pivotal role in her development. Growing up in a diverse neighborhood, she formed bonds with individuals from various backgrounds, each bringing their unique perspectives and experiences. These friendships nurtured her understanding of intersectionality, illustrating how race, gender, and sexuality intersected in complex ways. They provided a safe space for her to explore her identity, share her struggles, and celebrate her victories.

1.1.8 Starting to Question Norms and Prejudices

As she matured, Paula began to critically assess the norms and prejudices that permeated her surroundings. She questioned the stereotypes and biases that often dictated behavior and attitudes within her community. This questioning was not merely intellectual; it was deeply personal. Paula recognized the impact of these societal constructs on her life and the lives of those around her, fueling her desire to advocate for change.

1.1.9 Developing a Strong Sense of Justice and Equality

Through her experiences, Paula developed a robust sense of justice and equality. She became acutely aware of the disparities faced by marginalized communities, particularly within the LGBTQ and disability spheres. This awareness ignited a passion for advocacy that would define her life. Paula's sense of justice was not limited to her own experiences; it extended to all those who faced discrimination and injustice, compelling her to take action.

1.1.10 Laying the Foundations for a Lifetime of Activism

Ultimately, Paula's childhood in Lisbon laid the groundwork for her lifelong commitment to activism. The combination of her supportive family, diverse friendships, and exposure to societal challenges shaped her into a formidable advocate for LGBTQ and disability rights. The experiences she gathered during these formative years would serve as the foundation for her future endeavors, empowering her to become a voice for those who often went unheard. As she reflected on her childhood, Paula recognized the profound impact it had on her journey, shaping her into the passionate activist she would become.

Childhood in Lisbon

Paula Lupi was born and raised in the vibrant city of Lisbon, Portugal, a place where history and modernity collide in a breathtaking tapestry of culture and diversity. From the narrow cobblestone streets of Alfama to the bustling markets of Baixa, Lisbon is a city that breathes life into its inhabitants, offering both challenges and opportunities. For Paula, her childhood in this lively metropolis was marked by the interplay of familial love, societal expectations, and the early stirrings of activism that would define her life.

1.1.1 A Bustling City Filled with Opportunities

Lisbon, with its rich history and picturesque landscapes, served as the backdrop for Paula's formative years. The city was not just a place of residence; it was a living entity that shaped her worldview. The vibrant colors of the azulejos, the sounds of Fado music echoing through the streets, and the aroma of pastéis de nata wafting from local bakeries created an environment ripe for exploration and creativity. In this dynamic setting, Paula found herself surrounded by a plethora of opportunities that would later fuel her passion for advocacy.

1.1.2 Paula's Supportive and Loving Family

At the heart of Paula's childhood was her family, a source of unwavering support and encouragement. Her parents, both educators, instilled in her the values of empathy, justice, and resilience. They fostered an environment where open discussions about identity, culture, and societal issues were commonplace. This nurturing atmosphere allowed Paula to express her thoughts and feelings freely, laying the groundwork for her future activism. The importance of family cannot be overstated; it served as a safe haven where Paula could explore her identity without fear of judgment.

1.1.3 Early Signs of Activism and Advocacy

Even as a child, Paula exhibited signs of her future activism. She was often found advocating for her friends who faced bullying or exclusion at school. Her innate sense of justice compelled her to stand up for those who were marginalized, even if it meant putting herself in uncomfortable situations. This early engagement with advocacy was not only a reflection of her character but also a response to the injustices she observed in her community.

1.1.4 Discovering Her Own Identity

As Paula navigated her formative years, she began to grapple with her own identity. Growing up in a society that often imposed rigid norms regarding gender and sexuality, Paula found herself questioning these expectations. The process of self-discovery was fraught with challenges, as she struggled to reconcile her burgeoning identity with the traditional values she encountered. This internal conflict was exacerbated by societal pressures that dictated how individuals should behave based on their gender and sexual orientation.

1.1.5 Navigating Societal Expectations and Challenges

Lisbon, while a city of opportunities, was not immune to the societal norms and prejudices that permeated Portuguese culture. Paula faced the daunting task of navigating these expectations while remaining true to herself. The pressure to conform to traditional gender roles was palpable, and the fear of rejection loomed large. However, these challenges only served to strengthen her resolve, as she recognized the importance of advocating for authenticity and acceptance.

1.1.6 Finding Solace in Music and Art

In the midst of these challenges, Paula found solace in music and art. The rich cultural heritage of Lisbon provided her with a canvas to express her emotions and experiences. Music became a refuge, allowing her to channel her feelings of joy, pain, and confusion into something beautiful. The rhythms of Fado resonated deeply with her, reflecting the struggles and triumphs of her own journey. This artistic outlet not only provided comfort but also served as a means of connecting with others who shared similar experiences.

1.1.7 The Influence of Her Diverse Friendships

Paula's friendships played a pivotal role in her development. Growing up in a multicultural city, she was exposed to a variety of perspectives and experiences. Her diverse group of friends helped her understand the complexities of identity and the intersectionality of various social issues. These relationships fostered a sense of belonging and community, allowing Paula to explore her own identity in a supportive environment. It was through these friendships that she began to recognize the power of solidarity in the face of adversity.

1.1.8 Starting to Question Norms and Prejudices

As she matured, Paula's questioning of societal norms intensified. She became increasingly aware of the prejudices that existed within her community and the impact they had on individuals who were different. This awareness ignited a fire within her, compelling her to challenge these norms and advocate for change. The seeds of activism were sown during this period, as Paula began to envision a world where acceptance and equality were the norms rather than the exceptions.

1.1.9 Developing a Strong Sense of Justice and Equality

The culmination of her experiences in Lisbon led Paula to develop a robust sense of justice and equality. She recognized that her identity as a queer disabled woman was intertwined with broader social issues, and she felt a profound responsibility to advocate for those who were marginalized. This sense of purpose became a guiding force in her life, shaping her aspirations and motivating her to pursue a path of activism.

1.1.10 Laying the Foundations for a Lifetime of Activism

Ultimately, Paula's childhood in Lisbon laid the foundation for a lifetime of activism. The challenges she faced, the support she received, and the lessons she learned all contributed to her development as a passionate advocate for LGBTQ and disability rights. Lisbon, with its rich cultural tapestry and vibrant community, provided her with the tools and inspiration necessary to challenge societal norms and fight for a more inclusive world. As she embarked on her journey, Paula carried with her the lessons of her childhood, ready to make her mark on the world.
ERROR. thisXsection() returned an empty string with textbook depth = 3.
ERROR. thisXsection() returned an empty string with textbook depth = 3.
ERROR. thisXsection() returned an empty string with textbook depth = 3.

Paula's supportive and loving family

Paula Lupi's journey towards becoming a prominent LGBTQ activist was profoundly shaped by her family environment. Growing up in Lisbon, Paula was surrounded by a family that not only provided her with unconditional love but also instilled in her the values of empathy, compassion, and social justice. This nurturing atmosphere laid the groundwork for her future endeavors in activism.

From an early age, Paula's parents recognized her unique qualities and encouraged her to embrace her individuality. They fostered an open dialogue about identity, acceptance, and diversity, which was crucial during her formative years. This kind of family support is essential in shaping an individual's self-esteem and self-worth, especially for those who may feel marginalized due to their sexual orientation or disability. Research indicates that supportive family dynamics can significantly reduce the risk of mental health issues among LGBTQ youth [?].

$$\text{Mental Health Outcomes} \propto \text{Family Support} \tag{1}$$

Paula's mother, a schoolteacher, often shared stories of historical figures who fought for justice and equality. These narratives inspired Paula and helped her understand the importance of advocacy. Her father, an artist, encouraged her to express herself creatively, allowing Paula to explore her identity through various forms of art and music. This artistic expression became a vital outlet for her emotions and experiences, further solidifying her sense of self.

Moreover, Paula's siblings played a crucial role in her development. They were her first allies, standing by her side as she navigated the complexities of growing up in a society that often held rigid views on gender and sexuality. The bond they shared was one of mutual respect and understanding, which is critical in a supportive family structure. According to studies, having siblings who are accepting can buffer against the negative effects of societal discrimination [?].

$$\text{Resilience} = \text{Support from Siblings} + \text{Family Acceptance} \qquad (2)$$

Paula's family also engaged in community activities that emphasized inclusivity and compassion. They volunteered at local shelters and participated in events that promoted social justice. This active involvement not only strengthened their family bond but also exposed Paula to the realities of social inequities. Witnessing her parents advocate for marginalized communities instilled in her a strong sense of justice and the belief that everyone deserves equal rights.

As Paula began to discover her own identity, her family's unwavering support became even more critical. They provided a safe space for her to express her feelings and explore her sexuality without fear of judgment. This acceptance was vital, as research shows that LGBTQ individuals who experience familial rejection are at a higher risk for mental health issues, substance abuse, and suicidal ideation [?].

$$\text{Risk Factors} \propto \text{Familial Rejection} \qquad (3)$$

In contrast, Paula's family exemplified what it means to be a pillar of support. They celebrated her victories and stood by her during her struggles, reinforcing her belief in the power of love and acceptance. Their encouragement helped her develop a resilient spirit, which would later fuel her activism.

In summary, Paula Lupi's supportive and loving family played an instrumental role in shaping her identity and commitment to social justice. Their acceptance and encouragement allowed her to thrive, paving the way for her to become a fierce advocate for LGBTQ and disability rights. The lessons she learned from her family about empathy, justice, and the importance of community would resonate throughout her life and activism, ultimately inspiring countless others to join the fight for equality.

Early signs of activism and advocacy

From a young age, Paula Lupi exhibited an innate sense of justice that would later define her life as an activist. Growing up in Lisbon, a city rich in culture and diversity, she was surrounded by contrasting narratives of acceptance and prejudice. This environment became the backdrop for her formative years, where early signs of activism began to emerge.

Paula's family was instrumental in nurturing her budding advocacy spirit. Her parents, both educators, instilled in her the values of empathy and critical thinking. They encouraged her to question societal norms and to stand up against injustices she witnessed in her community. This familial support created a safe space for Paula to express her thoughts and feelings about the world around her.

One of the earliest instances of Paula's activism occurred during her elementary school years. Witnessing a classmate being bullied for their appearance, Paula felt a surge of anger and sadness. Instead of remaining a passive observer, she decided to take action. Paula rallied her classmates to create an anti-bullying campaign, which included posters, discussions, and a school assembly aimed at promoting kindness and acceptance. This initiative not only highlighted her leadership qualities but also marked her first foray into advocacy, demonstrating her commitment to creating a supportive environment for all students.

As she progressed through school, Paula began to engage with broader social issues. She was particularly drawn to discussions about LGBTQ rights, sparked by her own experiences of feeling different. In her teenage years, she discovered a passion for human rights and began to educate herself about the systemic inequalities faced by marginalized groups. This self-directed learning was crucial in shaping her understanding of intersectionality—the concept that various forms of discrimination (such as those based on gender, sexuality, and disability) are interconnected and cannot be examined separately.

Paula's early activism was not without challenges. She faced societal expectations that often discouraged outspoken behavior, especially for young women. Many in her community held traditional views that limited discussions about gender and sexuality. Despite these pressures, Paula found solace in the support of her diverse friendships. Many of her peers shared similar experiences of feeling marginalized, and together they formed a tight-knit group that fostered open dialogue about their identities and the injustices they faced.

In high school, Paula took her advocacy to the next level by joining the student council. Here, she worked on initiatives that aimed to promote inclusivity within the school. One significant project involved organizing a cultural awareness week, where students could share their backgrounds and experiences. This event not only educated her peers about diversity but also highlighted the importance of representation in educational settings. It was during this time that Paula began to understand the power of collective action and the impact of grassroots organizing.

Moreover, Paula's involvement in local community groups further solidified her commitment to activism. She volunteered at organizations that supported LGBTQ youth and individuals with disabilities. This hands-on experience exposed her to the real struggles faced by these communities, deepening her understanding of the systemic barriers they encountered. It was here that she learned about the importance of advocacy beyond just raising awareness; it was about creating tangible change in policies and practices that affect people's lives.

In conclusion, the early signs of activism and advocacy in Paula Lupi were marked by her innate sense of justice, supported by a nurturing family environment, and fueled by her experiences of marginalization. Through her initiatives in school and community involvement, Paula laid the groundwork for her future as a prominent advocate for LGBTQ and disability rights. Her journey reflects the idea that activism often begins in small, personal acts of courage and compassion, which can eventually lead to significant societal change.

Discovering her own identity

In the vibrant heart of Lisbon, amidst the cobblestone streets and sun-drenched plazas, Paula Lupi embarked on a profound journey of self-discovery. This journey was not merely about understanding her personal preferences or inclinations; it was a deep exploration into the very essence of who she was, shaped by a complex interplay of societal norms, familial expectations, and her own burgeoning sense of identity.

The process of discovering one's identity can be understood through various theoretical frameworks, one of which is Erik Erikson's psychosocial development theory. Erikson posits that identity formation is a crucial stage in adolescence, where individuals grapple with their sense of self in relation to the social world. For Paula, this meant navigating the intricate dynamics of being a queer disabled woman in a society that often marginalizes such identities.

$$\text{Identity} = \text{Personal Self} + \text{Social Context} \qquad (4)$$

This equation illustrates that identity is not formed in isolation but is influenced by the broader societal context. For Paula, the bustling city of Lisbon provided both a backdrop and a catalyst for her exploration. Surrounded by a diverse community, she found herself questioning the traditional norms that dictated how individuals were expected to behave, love, and express themselves.

Paula's supportive family played a pivotal role in her journey. While many young people might face rejection or misunderstanding at home, Paula was fortunate to have a family that embraced her uniqueness. This familial acceptance allowed her to explore her identity without the fear of alienation, fostering an environment where she could express her true self.

However, the journey was not without its challenges. As Paula began to embrace her queer identity, she encountered societal prejudices that sought to impose rigid definitions of gender and sexuality. The internal conflict between her emerging identity and the expectations of society often left her feeling isolated. This struggle can be likened to the concept of cognitive dissonance, where an individual experiences discomfort due to conflicting beliefs or values.

$$\text{Cognitive Dissonance} = \text{Belief A} \neq \text{Belief B} \tag{5}$$

For Paula, Belief A might have been the societal expectation of heterosexuality, while Belief B was her own realization of her queer identity. The dissonance created by these conflicting beliefs propelled her towards a deeper understanding of herself and the world around her.

Music and art became vital outlets for Paula during this tumultuous period. They served as both a refuge and a means of expression, allowing her to articulate feelings that words alone could not capture. Through her engagement with the arts, Paula discovered a community of like-minded individuals who shared similar struggles and aspirations. This connection provided her with a sense of belonging, further solidifying her identity as part of the LGBTQ community.

Moreover, the influence of diverse friendships played a crucial role in Paula's identity formation. Each relationship brought new perspectives, challenging her to reconsider her assumptions and biases. As she interacted with peers from various backgrounds, Paula began to understand the intersectionality of her identity—how her experiences as a queer disabled woman were shaped by multiple layers of social identity, including race, class, and culture.

The concept of intersectionality, coined by Kimberlé Crenshaw, emphasizes that individuals experience overlapping systems of discrimination and privilege. For Paula, this meant acknowledging that her struggles were not solely about being queer or disabled but also about how these identities interacted with other aspects of her life.

$$\text{Intersectionality} = \text{Identity A} + \text{Identity B} + \text{Context} \tag{6}$$

In Paula's case, her queer identity combined with her experience of disability created a unique perspective that informed her activism and advocacy work. This realization empowered her to embrace her multifaceted identity, recognizing that it was not a limitation but a source of strength.

As Paula navigated the complexities of her identity, she began to question societal norms and prejudices more critically. She developed a strong sense of justice and equality, fueled by her personal experiences of marginalization. This awakening laid the groundwork for her future activism, as she sought to challenge the very structures that sought to confine her identity.

In conclusion, the journey of discovering her own identity was a transformative experience for Paula Lupi. It was a process marked by introspection, resilience, and the courage to defy societal expectations. Through her exploration, she not only found her place within the LGBTQ community but also forged a path towards becoming a powerful advocate for change. This journey of self-discovery was not just about understanding who she was; it was about embracing every facet of her identity and using it as a catalyst for social justice and equality.

Navigating societal expectations and challenges

Growing up in Lisbon, Paula Lupi was not immune to the weight of societal expectations that often dictate the lives of young individuals, especially those who identify as part of the LGBTQ community or have disabilities. The cultural landscape of Portugal, while rich in history and diversity, was also marred by traditional values and norms that often clashed with the ideals of acceptance and inclusion. Navigating these societal expectations was both a challenge and a catalyst for Paula's early activism.

The Pressure of Conformity

From a young age, Paula faced the pressure to conform to societal norms regarding gender roles and sexuality. The Portuguese society of the late 20th and early 21st centuries was still grappling with the remnants of conservative ideologies, which often stigmatized those who deviated from the heterosexual and able-bodied norms. This societal pressure can be understood through the lens of *social conformity theory*, which posits that individuals often change their beliefs or behaviors to align with group norms to gain acceptance or avoid rejection [1].

For Paula, the internal conflict between her burgeoning identity and societal expectations was palpable. She often found herself at a crossroads, torn between the desire to express her true self and the fear of ostracization. This struggle is emblematic of the challenges faced by many LGBTQ individuals, particularly in environments where traditional values are deeply entrenched.

Facing Discrimination and Prejudice

As Paula began to openly question her identity, she encountered various forms of discrimination and prejudice. The societal challenges were not limited to mere expectations; they manifested in tangible forms of bias and exclusion. Research indicates that LGBTQ individuals often experience higher rates of bullying, harassment, and discrimination, which can lead to significant mental health issues, including anxiety and depression [1].

Paula's experiences in school were marked by instances of bullying and isolation from peers who could not understand or accept her differences. This isolation was compounded by her disability, which further marginalized her within an already vulnerable community. The intersectionality of her identity—being both queer and disabled—meant that Paula faced compounded challenges, a phenomenon described by *intersectionality theory* [3]. This theory highlights how overlapping identities can create unique modes of discrimination and disadvantage.

Finding Community and Support

Despite the challenges, Paula's journey was not one of solitude. She found solace and strength in the diverse friendships she cultivated during her formative years. These relationships became a critical support system, providing her with the encouragement needed to embrace her identity. The importance of community in navigating societal expectations cannot be overstated; it is often within these supportive networks that individuals find the courage to advocate for themselves and others.

Paula's involvement with local LGBTQ organizations provided her with a platform to voice her concerns and connect with like-minded individuals. This engagement was crucial in developing her understanding of the broader LGBTQ rights movement, which was gaining momentum in Portugal at the time. By participating in advocacy efforts, she began to challenge societal norms and push back against the prejudices she had faced.

The Role of Art and Expression

Art and music also played a significant role in Paula's journey of self-discovery and empowerment. Engaging with creative outlets allowed her to express her feelings and experiences in ways that transcended the limitations imposed by societal expectations. The therapeutic nature of art is well-documented; it serves as a means of processing emotions and experiences, particularly those related to trauma and discrimination [4].

Through her artistic endeavors, Paula discovered a powerful avenue for activism. She began to use her art as a form of protest, challenging societal norms and advocating for acceptance and inclusion. This form of expression not only helped her navigate her own challenges but also resonated with others who faced similar struggles, amplifying her voice within the community.

Challenging Norms and Advocating for Change

As Paula matured, she became increasingly aware of the need to challenge the societal norms that sought to confine her. The journey of navigating societal expectations transformed into a mission to advocate for change. Paula's activism was rooted in a profound understanding of the injustices faced by marginalized communities, and she recognized that her voice could be a catalyst for change.

This realization aligns with the principles of *social justice theory*, which emphasizes the importance of equity and fairness in society. Paula's commitment to advocating for LGBTQ and disability rights became a driving force in her life, as she sought to dismantle the barriers that perpetuated discrimination and exclusion.

In conclusion, navigating societal expectations and challenges was a complex and multifaceted journey for Paula Lupi. Through her experiences of discrimination, the support of her community, and the power of artistic expression, she laid the groundwork for a lifetime of activism. Her early struggles not only shaped her identity but also fueled her passion for advocating for a more inclusive and equitable society. The lessons learned during this formative period would serve as the foundation for her future endeavors, as she emerged as a prominent voice for LGBTQ and disability rights in Portugal and beyond.

Bibliography

[1] Asch, S. E. (1951). *Effects of group pressure upon the modification and distortion of judgments*. In *Groups, Leadership, and Men* (pp. 177-190). Pittsburgh: Carnegie Press.

[2] Meyer, I. H. (2003). *Prejudice, social stress, and mental health in gay men*. American Psychologist, 58(5), 123-134.

[3] Crenshaw, K. (1989). *Demarginalizing the intersection of race and sex: A black feminist critique of antidiscrimination doctrine, feminist theory and antiracist politics*. University of Chicago Legal Forum, 1989(1), 139-167.

[4] Malchiodi, C. A. (2003). *Art therapy: Using art to cope with trauma*. Trauma, Violence, & Abuse, 4(1), 1-11.

Finding solace in music and art

In the vibrant tapestry of Lisbon, where the streets resonate with the soulful sounds of Fado and the colors of street art breathe life into the city's architecture, Paula Lupi found her refuge in music and art. For many individuals, especially those navigating the complexities of identity, the arts serve as a powerful medium of expression and healing. This section delves into how Paula utilized music and art as a sanctuary, a means of self-discovery, and a platform for activism.

The Therapeutic Power of Music

Music has long been recognized for its therapeutic benefits, providing an emotional outlet and a means of connection. According to the *Journal of Music Therapy*, engaging with music can lead to significant improvements in emotional well-being and self-identity (Bradt & Dileo, 2014). For Paula, the melodies of Fado, which often explore themes of longing and love, resonated deeply with her experiences as a queer disabled woman. The raw emotion conveyed through the music allowed her to process her feelings of isolation and desire for acceptance.

$$E = mc^2 \tag{7}$$

While this equation by Einstein is not directly related to music, it serves as a metaphor for the energy exchange that occurs when one engages with art. The energy invested in creating or experiencing music can lead to profound emotional transformations, akin to the mass-energy equivalence in physics.

Paula often attended local Fado performances, where she found solace not only in the music but also in the community that surrounded it. The shared experience of listening to poignant lyrics and heartfelt melodies fostered a sense of belonging, allowing her to connect with others who shared similar struggles and joys. This communal aspect of music became a cornerstone of her identity as she navigated her own journey of self-acceptance.

Art as a Form of Expression

Art, in its myriad forms, offers another avenue for self-exploration and expression. The *American Journal of Public Health* highlights the role of art in fostering social change and personal empowerment (Sullivan, 2015). For Paula, painting and creating visual art became a means to articulate her experiences and advocate for LGBTQ and disability rights.

Through her artwork, Paula challenged societal norms and prejudices, often depicting themes of resilience and empowerment. Her pieces served as a visual representation of her inner struggles and triumphs, allowing her to communicate her identity in ways that words sometimes could not. For instance, one of her notable pieces, titled *"Breaking Chains"*, illustrated the liberation from societal expectations through vibrant colors and dynamic forms.

$$A = \frac{1}{2}bh \tag{8}$$

This formula for the area of a triangle symbolizes the foundational role that art played in Paula's life. Just as the area represents the space contained within the triangle, Paula's artwork encapsulated the complexities of her identity and experiences, providing a safe space for her emotions and thoughts.

The Intersection of Music, Art, and Activism

The intersection of music, art, and activism is a powerful conduit for social change. Scholars like Susan Sontag have argued that art can provoke thought and inspire action, making it an essential tool for advocates (Sontag, 1977). Paula recognized this potential early in her journey, using her artistic talents to raise awareness about LGBTQ and disability issues.

By organizing community art shows and music events, Paula created platforms for marginalized voices to be heard. These events not only showcased local talent but also served as fundraisers for LGBTQ and disability rights organizations. For example, her initiative, *"Art for Equality"*, brought together artists from diverse backgrounds to create pieces that highlighted the struggles and triumphs of the LGBTQ community. The proceeds went directly to advocacy groups, further amplifying the impact of her artistic endeavors.

Challenges and Triumphs

Despite the therapeutic benefits of music and art, Paula faced challenges in her pursuit of creative expression. The societal stigma surrounding LGBTQ identities often permeated the art world, leading to a lack of representation and support for queer artists. Paula encountered instances where her work was dismissed or marginalized due to her identity, which fueled her determination to create space for others like herself.

In response to these challenges, Paula became an advocate for inclusivity in the arts. She collaborated with local art institutions to develop programs that supported LGBTQ artists and provided resources for those with disabilities. Her efforts not only enriched the cultural landscape of Lisbon but also empowered countless individuals to embrace their identities through artistic expression.

Conclusion

Finding solace in music and art became a transformative aspect of Paula Lupi's life. These creative outlets not only provided her with emotional refuge but also served as platforms for activism and community building. By harnessing the power of music and art, Paula laid the groundwork for a lifetime of advocacy, inspiring others to find their voices and express their identities. As she navigated the complexities of her existence, the rhythms and colors of her experiences intertwined, creating a vibrant narrative of resilience, empowerment, and love.

Bibliography

[1] Bradt, J., & Dileo, C. (2014). Music interventions for mechanically ventilated patients. *Journal of Music Therapy*, 51(3), 290-303.

[2] Sontag, S. (1977). On Photography. New York: Delta.

[3] Sullivan, M. (2015). The role of the arts in public health. *American Journal of Public Health*, 105(8), 1552-1555.

The influence of her diverse friendships

In the vibrant tapestry of Lisbon, Paula Lupi's friendships were not merely connections; they were the lifeblood of her identity and activism. Growing up in a city that thrived on cultural diversity, Paula found herself surrounded by individuals from various backgrounds, each bringing their unique perspectives and experiences to the table. This rich social environment played a pivotal role in shaping her understanding of intersectionality—a concept that recognizes the interconnected nature of social categorizations such as race, class, and gender, which can create overlapping systems of discrimination or disadvantage.

Paula's friendships transcended the boundaries of traditional social groups. She formed bonds with fellow LGBTQ individuals, disabled activists, artists, and allies from different ethnic and socioeconomic backgrounds. This diversity not only broadened her horizons but also deepened her empathy and understanding of the multifaceted challenges faced by marginalized communities. As she navigated her own identity as a queer disabled woman, the support and solidarity she found in her friendships became a source of strength and resilience.

One significant relationship was with Sofia, a fellow activist who identified as a transgender woman. Their friendship blossomed in the early days of Paula's activism, and Sofia's experiences with discrimination and violence opened Paula's eyes to the harsh realities faced by transgender individuals. This connection propelled Paula to advocate more fiercely for transgender rights, ensuring that her activism was inclusive and representative of the diverse spectrum of the LGBTQ community.

Moreover, Paula's friendship with Miguel, a disabled artist, demonstrated the power of art in activism. Miguel's ability to articulate his struggles through his artwork inspired Paula to harness her creative talents in her advocacy efforts. They collaborated on projects that highlighted the intersection of disability and LGBTQ rights, using art as a medium to raise awareness and challenge societal norms. Their joint exhibitions not only showcased their talents but also served as platforms for dialogue, fostering understanding and acceptance among viewers from various walks of life.

However, the influence of diverse friendships was not without its challenges. Paula often encountered tensions when navigating the complexities of identity politics. For instance, her friendship with a well-meaning ally who belonged to a privileged background sometimes led to misunderstandings about the nuances of oppression. This friction prompted Paula to engage in difficult conversations about privilege and representation, emphasizing the importance of listening to and uplifting marginalized voices within their activist circles. These discussions, while uncomfortable, ultimately strengthened their bond and fostered a deeper commitment to inclusive activism.

The theoretical framework of social capital, as articulated by Pierre Bourdieu, provides insight into the significance of Paula's diverse friendships. Bourdieu posited that social capital encompasses the networks of relationships among people who live and work in a particular society, enabling that society to function effectively. Paula's diverse friendships exemplified this concept, as they not only enriched her personal life but also enhanced her activist efforts. By drawing on the social capital embedded in her relationships, Paula was able to mobilize resources, share knowledge, and amplify the voices of those who were often silenced.

In her journey, Paula also encountered the challenge of maintaining authenticity in her friendships. As she gained prominence in the activist community, some individuals sought to align themselves with her for personal gain rather than genuine solidarity. This experience taught Paula the importance of discerning true allies from opportunists. She became more intentional in nurturing relationships that were rooted in mutual respect and shared values, reinforcing her commitment to authenticity in both her personal and activist life.

Ultimately, the influence of her diverse friendships laid a solid foundation for Paula Lupi's lifelong commitment to activism. These relationships enriched her understanding of the complexities of identity and oppression, enabling her to advocate for a more inclusive and equitable society. They served as a reminder that the fight for LGBTQ and disability rights is not a solitary journey but a collective effort that thrives on collaboration, empathy, and shared experiences.

In summary, Paula's friendships were a microcosm of the broader social movements she would later champion. They provided her with the tools to navigate the intricacies of activism, instilling in her the belief that true change comes from embracing diversity and fostering solidarity across different identities. As she continued to grow and evolve, the lessons learned from her diverse friendships remained at the forefront of her advocacy, guiding her towards a more inclusive future for all.

Starting to question norms and prejudices

As Paula Lupi navigated the vibrant streets of Lisbon, she began to encounter the complex tapestry of societal norms and prejudices that shaped her world. Growing up in a bustling city filled with opportunities, Paula was not immune to the expectations that society placed upon her. However, her inquisitive nature and the diverse friendships she cultivated allowed her to challenge these norms and develop a critical perspective on the world around her.

The process of questioning societal norms can be understood through the lens of social constructivism, which posits that our understanding of reality is constructed through social interactions and cultural contexts. This theory suggests that norms are not inherent truths but rather agreements among members of society. Paula's early experiences in Lisbon exposed her to a variety of cultural influences, prompting her to reflect on the validity of these norms.

One significant moment in Paula's life occurred during a school project where she was tasked with researching the history of LGBTQ rights in Portugal. As she delved into the subject, she discovered a rich legacy of resistance and resilience among queer individuals who had fought against systemic oppression. This exploration ignited a fire within her, compelling her to question why certain identities were marginalized and why societal acceptance seemed to hinge on conformity to heteronormative standards.

Paula's questioning was not merely academic; it was deeply personal. She began to recognize the prejudices that permeated her own life and the lives of those around her. For example, she witnessed the struggles of a close friend who faced discrimination due to their gender identity. This experience was a turning point for Paula, as it highlighted the tangible consequences of societal norms on individual lives.

Furthermore, the intersectionality of identity played a crucial role in Paula's journey of questioning. Kimberlé Crenshaw's theory of intersectionality elucidates how various forms of discrimination (such as racism, sexism, and homophobia) interconnect, creating unique experiences of oppression. Paula began to understand that her own identity as a queer disabled woman placed her at the intersection of multiple marginalized identities, intensifying her resolve to challenge societal prejudices.

The influence of her diverse friendships also cannot be overstated. Paula surrounded herself with individuals from various backgrounds, each bringing their own perspectives and experiences. Conversations with friends who identified as LGBTQ, disabled, or from different cultural backgrounds opened her eyes to the nuances of prejudice and the importance of empathy in activism. These friendships served as a support network, allowing her to explore her own identity while questioning the norms that sought to constrain it.

One poignant example of this questioning came during a community event where Paula was invited to speak about her experiences. As she stood before a diverse audience, she realized that the stories she shared resonated with many who had faced similar struggles. This moment crystallized her belief that questioning norms was not only necessary but also empowering. It was a reminder that by sharing her truth, she could inspire others to do the same, fostering a sense of solidarity and collective resistance against prejudice.

In summary, Paula Lupi's journey of questioning norms and prejudices was marked by a deep engagement with social constructivism, personal experiences, and the influence of intersectionality. Through her exploration of LGBTQ history, the impact of friendships, and her growing awareness of systemic discrimination, Paula laid the groundwork for a lifetime of activism. This critical questioning not only shaped her identity but also ignited her passion for advocating for justice and equality, ultimately leading her to become a formidable voice for LGBTQ and disability rights in Portugal.

Developing a strong sense of justice and equality

From an early age, Paula Lupi began to cultivate a deep-rooted sense of justice and equality, one that would later define her activism and advocacy work. This development was not merely a personal journey; it was influenced by her environment, her experiences, and the complexities of societal structures that often marginalized voices like hers. The concept of justice, particularly in the context of social movements, can be understood through various theoretical frameworks, including John Rawls's theory of justice, which emphasizes fairness and equality as fundamental principles.

Theoretical Foundations

John Rawls's *Theory of Justice* (1971) posits that a just society is one where individuals are given equal rights and opportunities, and where inequalities are arranged to benefit the least advantaged members of society. This idea resonated with Paula as she navigated her identity as a queer disabled woman in a society that often failed to recognize her rights. Rawls's principles of justice, particularly the *difference principle*, became a guiding framework for her understanding of social justice. The equation for Rawls's difference principle can be expressed as:

$$\text{Justice} = \text{Fairness} + \text{Equality} + \text{Equity} \qquad (9)$$

This equation illustrates that for justice to be achieved, fairness must be coupled with equality and equity, which are crucial for addressing the disparities faced by marginalized communities.

Personal Experiences and Societal Challenges

Paula's formative years in Lisbon were marked by moments that challenged her understanding of justice. As she observed the struggles of her peers—many of whom faced discrimination based on their sexual orientation or disabilities—she began to question the status quo. The societal expectations placed upon her, as both a woman and a member of the LGBTQ community, often felt suffocating. This led her to confront the injustices that permeated her surroundings.

One significant incident that shaped her perspective occurred during a school event where a fellow student faced bullying due to their sexual orientation. Witnessing this act of cruelty was a turning point for Paula. It ignited a fire within her, compelling her to speak out against the injustices she saw. This moment crystallized her understanding that justice was not merely an abstract concept but a lived reality that required active engagement and advocacy.

Influence of Diverse Friendships

The friendships Paula formed with individuals from various backgrounds further enriched her understanding of justice and equality. These relationships exposed her to different perspectives and experiences, highlighting the intersectionality of identity. Scholars like Kimberlé Crenshaw have emphasized the importance of intersectionality in understanding how overlapping identities can compound discrimination. Crenshaw's framework can be summarized as follows:

$$\text{Intersectionality} = \text{Identity}_1 + \text{Identity}_2 + \ldots + \text{Identity}_n \qquad (10)$$

This equation signifies that each identity contributes to a unique experience of oppression or privilege. Paula's diverse friendships allowed her to recognize that justice must encompass a broad spectrum of identities and experiences, thus deepening her commitment to advocating for all marginalized groups.

Developing Advocacy Skills

As Paula's sense of justice evolved, so did her skills in advocacy. She began to engage in community discussions and workshops focused on LGBTQ rights and disability advocacy. These experiences equipped her with the tools necessary to articulate her beliefs and challenge injustices effectively. The concept of *advocacy* can be broken down into several key components:

$$\text{Advocacy} = \text{Awareness} + \text{Action} + \text{Allyship} \tag{11}$$

This equation illustrates that advocacy involves raising awareness about injustices, taking action to address them, and forming alliances with others who share similar goals. Paula embraced these components, recognizing that her voice could amplify the struggles of others and foster a sense of solidarity within the community.

The Road Ahead

Developing a strong sense of justice and equality was not a linear journey for Paula. It was fraught with challenges, setbacks, and moments of doubt. However, each experience contributed to her resilience and determination. Her commitment to social justice became a guiding principle, one that would inform her future endeavors as an activist and advocate.

In conclusion, Paula Lupi's journey toward developing a strong sense of justice and equality was shaped by her personal experiences, theoretical influences, and the diverse relationships she cultivated. This foundation would ultimately empower her to confront societal injustices head-on and advocate for the rights of LGBTQ individuals and those with disabilities. As she continued to grow and evolve, Paula would become not just a voice for herself, but for countless others who sought justice in an often unjust world.

Laying the foundations for a lifetime of activism

From the cobbled streets of Lisbon, where the sun paints the buildings in hues of gold, Paula Lupi's journey towards activism began to take shape. The vibrant culture of her childhood was not just a backdrop; it was the fertile ground where her seeds of advocacy were sown. Paula's early experiences, infused with the colors of diversity and the sound of dissent, laid the groundwork for a lifelong commitment to social justice.

Paula's family was a microcosm of support and love, a sanctuary where she could explore her identity without fear of judgment. This nurturing environment was crucial, as studies in developmental psychology suggest that supportive familial relationships significantly enhance a child's self-esteem and resilience (Rosenberg, 1989). It was here that Paula learned the values of empathy and compassion, not just as abstract concepts but as actionable principles.

The bustling city of Lisbon, with its rich history of resistance and revolution, served as an inspiration. The echoes of past movements, like the Carnation Revolution of 1974, resonated in her heart, teaching her that change is possible through collective action. This historical context is vital; as noted by social theorists such as Charles Tilly, social movements often draw upon historical precedents to galvanize support and frame their narratives (Tilly, 2004). Paula internalized this lesson, understanding that her activism was part of a larger continuum of struggle.

As she navigated the complexities of her identity, Paula began to question the societal norms that dictated her existence. The process of questioning is a hallmark of critical consciousness, a theory developed by Paulo Freire, which posits that awareness of social injustices is the first step towards transformative action (Freire, 1970). Paula's realization that she was not alone in her struggles—encountering friends and peers who faced similar challenges—further fueled her desire to advocate for change. The power of community became evident, as she witnessed firsthand how collective voices could challenge the status quo.

In her formative years, Paula found solace in music and art, mediums that provided both an escape and a platform for expression. The arts have long been recognized as powerful tools for social change, capable of conveying complex messages and evoking empathy (Baker, 2011). Paula's involvement in local art initiatives and music groups allowed her to connect with others who shared her passion for justice, fostering a sense of belonging and purpose. This engagement not only honed her skills as a communicator but also reinforced her commitment to using her voice for those who felt voiceless.

The early signs of activism manifested as Paula began to engage with local LGBTQ groups, participating in discussions and events that addressed issues of representation and rights. This involvement was not without challenges; she faced skepticism from some who questioned her commitment due to her youth and inexperience. However, these obstacles only served to strengthen her resolve. The theory of resilience, articulated by researchers like Ann Masten, highlights the importance of overcoming adversity as a catalyst for growth (Masten, 2001). Paula embraced this concept, recognizing that her struggles were integral to her development as an activist.

Through her diverse friendships, Paula was exposed to a myriad of perspectives, enriching her understanding of intersectionality. The concept, popularized by Kimberlé Crenshaw, emphasizes the interconnected nature of social categorizations and their compounded effects on individuals (Crenshaw, 1989). Paula's interactions with friends from various backgrounds illuminated the complexities of identity, prompting her to consider how race, gender, and disability intersected with LGBTQ issues. This awareness became a cornerstone of her advocacy, as she sought to uplift marginalized voices within the community.

As Paula began to question societal norms and prejudices, she found herself drawn to the principles of social justice, which advocate for equity and the dismantling of systemic barriers. Theories of justice, such as those proposed by John Rawls, emphasize the importance of fairness in societal structures (Rawls, 1971). Paula's burgeoning sense of justice aligned with these ideals, igniting her passion for activism. She understood that her journey was not just about her own rights but about creating a more equitable society for all.

In laying the foundations for her activism, Paula developed a strong sense of justice and equality, principles that would guide her throughout her life. Her early experiences cultivated a deep-seated belief that everyone deserves dignity and respect, regardless of their identity. This belief was further reinforced by her academic pursuits, where she encountered theories of human rights that emphasized the universality of rights for all individuals (Donelly, 2013).

Ultimately, Paula's childhood in Lisbon was not merely a backdrop; it was a crucible where her identity as an activist was forged. The combination of supportive relationships, exposure to diverse perspectives, and a deep understanding of justice laid the groundwork for her future endeavors. As she embarked on her journey, Paula carried with her the lessons learned during these formative years—a commitment to advocacy that would resonate throughout her life and inspire countless others to join the fight for equality.

In conclusion, the foundations of Paula Lupi's activism were built on a rich tapestry of experiences that shaped her worldview. From her supportive family and the vibrant culture of Lisbon to her encounters with diverse communities and the principles of social justice, each element played a crucial role in her development. As she moved forward, these early influences would serve as both a compass and a source of strength, guiding her in the pursuit of a more inclusive and equitable world.

Educational Journey

The struggle for acceptance at school

Paula Lupi's early educational experiences were marked by a profound struggle for acceptance, one that would shape her identity and activism in the years to come. The school environment, often seen as a microcosm of society, was fraught with challenges for Paula, particularly as she began to understand her place within the LGBTQ community and as a person with disabilities.

From a young age, Paula exhibited a deep curiosity about the world around her, a trait that often set her apart from her peers. In a bustling city like Lisbon, where cultural diversity thrived, the school system was a complex tapestry of varying beliefs, attitudes, and social norms. Unfortunately, this diversity did not always translate into acceptance.

Social Dynamics and Bullying

The social dynamics in Paula's school were typical of many educational settings, where conformity often overshadowed individuality. As Paula began to express her unique identity, she faced bullying and ostracism from her classmates. This bullying wasn't just a simple matter of teasing; it was a systemic issue that reflected broader societal prejudices. Research indicates that LGBTQ youth are significantly more likely to experience bullying in schools, leading to detrimental effects on their mental health and academic performance [?].

Paula's experience was no exception. She often found herself the target of derogatory remarks and exclusion from social groups. The psychological impact of this bullying manifested in feelings of isolation and self-doubt, as she grappled with the harsh reality that her true self was not accepted by those around her.

The Role of Educators

While some educators were supportive, others perpetuated the cycle of discrimination by failing to address bullying or by fostering an environment that did not encourage diversity. A study by the Gay, Lesbian & Straight Education Network (GLSEN) highlights that schools with supportive staff are crucial in creating a safe environment for LGBTQ students [?]. However, Paula often encountered teachers who either turned a blind eye to the bullying or, worse, contributed to it through their own biases.

This lack of support from authority figures compounded her struggles, reinforcing the idea that acceptance was not something she could expect from her school environment. Paula's experiences reflect the findings of the National School Climate Survey, which reported that 60% of LGBTQ students felt unsafe at school because of their sexual orientation [?].

Coping Mechanisms and Resilience

In the face of such adversity, Paula developed several coping mechanisms that would serve her well throughout her life. She found solace in artistic expression, using music and art as outlets for her emotions. These creative pursuits not only provided an escape but also allowed her to connect with like-minded individuals who shared her experiences and struggles.

Additionally, Paula began to seek out supportive friendships, gravitating toward peers who were also marginalized. These relationships became a source of strength and resilience, enabling her to navigate the tumultuous waters of adolescence with a sense of community. The importance of peer support is well-documented; according to research, students with supportive friends are less likely to experience negative mental health outcomes related to bullying [?].

The Impact of Intersectionality

Paula's struggle for acceptance was further complicated by the intersectionality of her identity. As a queer disabled woman, she faced unique challenges that her peers could not fully understand. The concept of intersectionality, introduced by Kimberlé Crenshaw, emphasizes how overlapping social identities can create distinct experiences of discrimination and privilege [3].

In Paula's case, her disability added another layer to her struggle for acceptance, as societal norms often marginalized those who did not fit the traditional mold of able-bodiedness. This intersection of identities made it imperative for Paula to advocate not only for LGBTQ rights but also for disability rights, recognizing that the two were inextricably linked.

Laying the Groundwork for Activism

Ultimately, the struggles Paula faced at school were foundational in shaping her future as an activist. The pain of exclusion and the desire for acceptance ignited a fire within her, compelling her to fight for a more inclusive society. Her experiences underscored the necessity of advocacy, not just for herself but for all those who felt marginalized.

As she navigated her school years, Paula began to lay the groundwork for her activism, developing a keen awareness of the systemic issues that perpetuated discrimination. Her journey through the struggles of acceptance at school would serve as a catalyst for her lifelong commitment to fighting for equality and justice for LGBTQ individuals and those with disabilities.

In conclusion, Paula Lupi's struggle for acceptance at school was not merely a personal battle; it was a reflection of broader societal issues that persist today. Her resilience in the face of adversity, combined with her commitment to advocacy, would ultimately position her as a formidable voice for change in Portugal and beyond.

Meeting influential mentors and allies

In the journey of activism, the presence of influential mentors and allies can serve as a guiding light, illuminating paths that may otherwise remain obscured. For Paula Lupi, the formative years of her educational journey were marked by encounters with individuals who not only recognized her potential but also encouraged her to embrace her identity and advocate for her community. This section explores the pivotal role these mentors played in shaping Paula's activism, highlighting the theories surrounding mentorship, the challenges faced in these relationships, and notable examples of her allies.

Theoretical Framework of Mentorship

Mentorship is a multifaceted relationship that transcends mere guidance; it embodies a dynamic exchange of knowledge, support, and inspiration. According to Kram's (1985) developmental model of mentoring, the mentor-mentee relationship can be segmented into two primary functions: career development and psychosocial support. Career development encompasses the mentor's role in providing opportunities, exposure, and feedback that enhances the mentee's professional growth. Psychosocial support, on the other hand, focuses on the emotional and psychological dimensions, fostering self-esteem, identity, and resilience.

In the context of Paula's life, her mentors provided both career-oriented guidance and the emotional support necessary to navigate the complexities of her identity as a queer disabled woman. This duality is essential, as it aligns with the intersectional framework proposed by Crenshaw (1989), which emphasizes the importance of considering overlapping social identities and the unique challenges they present.

Challenges in Mentorship Relationships

While mentorship can be profoundly beneficial, it is not without its challenges. Paula faced several obstacles in her relationships with mentors and allies, particularly concerning the intersectionality of her identity. One significant issue was the lack of representation within the mentoring community. Many mentors were well-meaning individuals who lacked an understanding of the specific challenges faced by LGBTQ and disabled individuals. This gap often led to miscommunication and a lack of tailored support.

Moreover, the power dynamics inherent in mentorship can sometimes create barriers. Mentors may unintentionally perpetuate systemic biases or overlook the unique struggles of their mentees. For Paula, navigating these complexities required her to assert her identity and advocate for her needs within the mentorship dynamic. This aligns with the concept of "critical consciousness" articulated by Freire (1970), which emphasizes the importance of awareness and reflection in addressing societal inequities.

Notable Mentors and Allies

Throughout her educational journey, Paula encountered several influential figures who played a crucial role in her development as an activist. One such mentor was Dr. Ana Ribeiro, a prominent advocate for disability rights in Portugal. Dr. Ribeiro's commitment to intersectionality resonated deeply with Paula, as she often emphasized the importance of addressing the unique challenges faced by disabled individuals within the LGBTQ community. Under Dr. Ribeiro's guidance, Paula learned to articulate her experiences and advocate for inclusive policies that addressed the needs of both communities.

Another significant ally was Marco Silva, a fellow student and LGBTQ activist. Marco's fearless approach to activism inspired Paula to embrace her voice and engage in grassroots organizing. Together, they participated in local demonstrations, raising awareness about the intersection of disability and LGBTQ rights. Marco's unwavering support provided Paula with the confidence to challenge societal norms and advocate for change.

The Impact of Mentorship on Paula's Activism

The relationships Paula cultivated with her mentors and allies were instrumental in shaping her activism. Through their guidance, she developed a nuanced understanding of the intersectionality of her identity, which became a cornerstone of her advocacy work. Paula learned to navigate the complexities of her dual identity, recognizing that her experiences as a queer disabled woman were not merely additive but rather constituted a unique perspective that informed her activism.

Furthermore, the support she received from her mentors instilled in her a sense of responsibility to uplift others within her community. Inspired by Dr. Ribeiro and Marco, Paula began to mentor younger activists, fostering a culture of support and collaboration. This cycle of mentorship reflects the principles of social capital theory, which posits that social networks and relationships can enhance individual and collective action (Putnam, 2000).

Conclusion

In conclusion, the meeting of influential mentors and allies was a transformative aspect of Paula Lupi's educational journey. These relationships not only provided her with the guidance and support necessary to navigate her identity but also empowered her to become a formidable advocate for LGBTQ and disability rights. By understanding the theoretical frameworks surrounding mentorship, recognizing the challenges inherent in these relationships, and acknowledging the impact of notable mentors, we can appreciate the critical role that mentorship plays in the development of future activists. As Paula continues her journey, she remains committed to fostering mentorship relationships that uplift and empower the next generation of advocates, ensuring that the voices of marginalized communities are heard and celebrated.

The power of education in shaping perspectives

Education is often heralded as a transformative force, one that can profoundly shape individual perspectives and societal norms. In the case of Paula Lupi, her educational journey was not merely about acquiring knowledge; it was a crucible that forged her identity as an activist and advocate for LGBTQ and disability rights.

At its core, education serves multiple functions: it imparts knowledge, cultivates critical thinking, and fosters empathy. These elements are crucial in shaping perspectives, particularly in a world rife with biases and prejudices. Theoretical frameworks, such as Paulo Freire's concept of critical pedagogy, underscore the importance of education as a means of liberation. Freire posited that education should not be a one-way transmission of knowledge but rather a dialogical process that encourages learners to question the status quo and engage with their world critically [?].

Critical Consciousness = Awareness of Oppression + Action Against Oppression (12)

This equation illustrates that the awareness gained through education can lead to action, a principle that resonates with Paula's experiences. As she navigated the complexities of her identity and the societal expectations surrounding her, education became a powerful tool for self-discovery and advocacy.

However, the struggle for acceptance within educational institutions is a reality faced by many marginalized individuals. Paula's early experiences in school were fraught with challenges, as she encountered both overt discrimination and subtle biases that sought to undermine her identity. The educational system often reflects broader societal prejudices, making it imperative to advocate for inclusive curricula and policies that recognize and celebrate diversity.

Research has shown that inclusive education not only benefits marginalized students but also enriches the learning experience for all. According to a study by the National Center for Learning Disabilities, inclusive classrooms foster empathy and understanding among peers, breaking down stereotypes and fostering a sense of belonging [?]. This aligns with Paula's advocacy for inclusive education policies, as she recognized the profound impact that a supportive educational environment can have on shaping perspectives.

Paula's passion for human rights was ignited during her time in academia, where she encountered mentors who encouraged her to explore the intersectionality of LGBTQ and disability rights. This intersectional approach, rooted in Kimberlé Crenshaw's theory, emphasizes that individuals experience multiple, overlapping forms of discrimination that cannot be understood in isolation [?]. By embracing this framework, Paula was able to articulate the unique challenges faced by queer disabled individuals, thus broadening the discourse around both LGBTQ and disability rights.

The importance of education in shaping perspectives also extends beyond formal academic settings. For Paula, informal learning through community engagement and activism played a pivotal role in her development. Participating in workshops, attending lectures, and engaging in discussions with fellow activists expanded her understanding of the issues at hand and reinforced her commitment to advocacy.

Moreover, the role of storytelling in education cannot be overstated. Narratives have the power to humanize issues, making them relatable and accessible. Paula's journey of self-acceptance and her advocacy work were deeply informed by the stories of others within the LGBTQ community. By sharing her own experiences and amplifying the voices of marginalized individuals, she fostered a culture of empathy and understanding that transcended traditional educational boundaries.

In conclusion, the power of education in shaping perspectives is multifaceted and profound. For Paula Lupi, education was not just a means to an end; it was a transformative journey that equipped her with the tools to challenge societal norms and advocate for justice. By fostering critical consciousness, embracing intersectionality, and leveraging the power of storytelling, education became a catalyst for change in both her life and the lives of countless others. As we reflect on the role of education in advocacy, it is essential to recognize its potential to inspire future generations to continue the fight for equality and inclusion.

Discovering her passion for human rights

Paula Lupi's journey towards discovering her passion for human rights began in the vibrant streets of Lisbon, where the echoes of history and the whispers of change coalesced into a symphony of possibilities. Growing up in a city that had seen both oppression and liberation, Paula was acutely aware of the struggles faced by marginalized communities. This awareness was not merely an abstract concept; it was woven into the fabric of her daily life.

From a young age, Paula exhibited a keen sense of justice. She often found herself questioning the status quo, challenging the norms that dictated how individuals should behave based on their gender, sexual orientation, or ability. This questioning was not without its challenges; societal expectations loomed large, often casting shadows over her budding sense of identity. Yet, it was within these very shadows that her passion for human rights began to take root.

Theoretical Foundations

The foundations of Paula's activism can be traced back to several key theories in human rights discourse. One such theory is the *Universal Declaration of Human Rights* (UDHR), adopted by the United Nations General Assembly in 1948. The UDHR outlines fundamental human rights that are to be universally protected, emphasizing the inherent dignity and equal rights of all individuals. Paula resonated with Article 1, which states, "All human beings are born free and equal in dignity and rights." This principle became a guiding light in her advocacy work.

Moreover, the concept of *intersectionality*, coined by scholar Kimberlé Crenshaw, played a pivotal role in shaping Paula's understanding of human rights. Intersectionality posits that individuals experience multiple, overlapping identities that can compound discrimination and oppression. For Paula, being a queer disabled woman meant navigating a complex landscape of societal biases, and she recognized that human rights advocacy must address these intersecting identities to be truly effective.

Personal Experiences

Paula's passion for human rights was further ignited through her personal experiences. During her teenage years, she volunteered at local shelters for LGBTQ youth and disabled individuals, witnessing firsthand the struggles they faced. One poignant moment occurred during a community event where she met a young transgender girl who had been ostracized by her family. The girl's story of resilience and courage resonated deeply with Paula, solidifying her resolve to fight for those whose voices were silenced.

In addition to her volunteer work, Paula was also influenced by the writings of prominent human rights activists. She devoured books by figures such as Audre Lorde and Nelson Mandela, whose words inspired her to envision a world where justice and equality were not just ideals but attainable realities. These literary influences provided her with a framework to articulate her own experiences and aspirations, further fueling her passion for activism.

Challenges and Revelations

However, the path to discovering her passion for human rights was not without obstacles. Paula faced significant challenges, including internalized prejudice and societal backlash. As she began to advocate for LGBTQ and disability rights, she encountered resistance not only from those outside her community but also from individuals within it. This backlash often took the form of criticisms questioning her credibility as a queer disabled woman in the activist space. Such challenges forced Paula to confront her insecurities and develop a resilient sense of self.

A pivotal revelation came during a workshop on advocacy strategies, where Paula learned about the importance of storytelling in human rights activism. She realized that sharing her personal narrative could empower others and foster a sense of community among marginalized individuals. This realization marked a turning point in her journey, as she began to embrace her identity and use it as a tool for advocacy.

Community Engagement

Engaging with her community became a cornerstone of Paula's activism. She joined local organizations dedicated to LGBTQ and disability rights, collaborating with like-minded individuals who shared her vision for a more inclusive society. Through these engagements, she honed her skills in organizing events, facilitating discussions, and mobilizing support for various causes. One notable initiative was the "Lisbon Pride and Disability Awareness" campaign, which aimed to raise awareness about the intersection of LGBTQ and disability rights. The campaign not only garnered significant media attention but also highlighted the importance of inclusivity within the broader human rights movement.

Paula's passion for human rights continued to evolve as she recognized the interconnectedness of various social justice issues. She began to advocate for policies that addressed systemic inequalities, understanding that the fight for LGBTQ rights could not be separated from the fight for disability rights, racial justice, and economic equality. This holistic approach to activism became a hallmark of her work, as she sought to build coalitions across different movements to amplify the voices of the most marginalized.

Conclusion

In conclusion, Paula Lupi's discovery of her passion for human rights was a multifaceted journey shaped by personal experiences, theoretical foundations, and community engagement. Her commitment to advocating for marginalized communities stemmed from a deep-seated belief in the inherent dignity and worth of all individuals. As she navigated the complexities of her identity and the challenges of activism, Paula emerged as a powerful voice for change, laying the groundwork for a lifetime of advocacy that would inspire countless others to join the fight for equality and justice.

Through her journey, Paula exemplified the notion that passion for human rights is not merely a personal endeavor; it is a collective movement that thrives on solidarity, resilience, and the unwavering belief that a better world is possible.

Advocating for inclusive education policies

Inclusive education is a fundamental right that ensures all students, regardless of their backgrounds or abilities, have access to quality education in an environment that respects and values diversity. For Paula Lupi, advocating for inclusive education policies became a cornerstone of her activism, driven by her personal experiences and the pressing need for systemic change within the educational framework of Portugal.

The concept of inclusive education is rooted in the principles of equity and social justice. According to the *UNESCO Salamanca Statement* (1994), inclusive education means that "schools should accommodate all children regardless of their physical, intellectual, social, emotional, linguistic or other conditions." This framework highlights the necessity of adapting educational systems to meet the diverse needs of all students, rather than forcing students to conform to a one-size-fits-all model.

$$\text{Inclusive Education} = \text{Equity} + \text{Diversity} + \text{Quality} \qquad (13)$$

Despite the clear benefits of inclusive education, numerous barriers persist. These include societal stigma, inadequate training for educators, and a lack of resources to support diverse learners. Paula recognized these challenges early in her educational journey. She experienced firsthand the marginalization faced by students with disabilities and those from LGBTQ backgrounds, often finding herself in environments that were not equipped to support her identity or her learning needs.

One of the primary issues in advocating for inclusive education policies is the pervasive stigma surrounding disabilities and LGBTQ identities. Many educators and administrators hold unconscious biases that can affect their attitudes toward inclusion. Studies have shown that teachers who lack training in inclusive practices are less likely to implement effective strategies in their classrooms, which can lead to further marginalization of already vulnerable students (Avramidis & Norwich, 2002).

Paula's advocacy work focused on several key strategies to promote inclusive education policies:

1. **Training and Professional Development**: Recognizing the need for educators to be equipped with the skills necessary to support diverse learners, Paula campaigned for comprehensive training programs. These programs emphasized the importance of understanding intersectionality—the interconnected nature of social categorizations such as race, class, and gender—so that teachers could better support students from various backgrounds.

2. **Policy Reform**: Paula worked closely with policymakers to advocate for reforms that would mandate inclusive practices in schools. This included lobbying for legislation that required schools to develop individualized education plans (IEPs) for students with disabilities and to implement anti-discrimination policies that protect LGBTQ students.

3. **Community Engagement**: Understanding that change must come from within the community, Paula organized workshops and forums that brought together parents, educators, and students. These events aimed to raise awareness about the importance of inclusive education and to foster collaboration among stakeholders. For instance, she initiated a campaign called "Voices for Inclusion,"

which highlighted success stories from schools that had successfully integrated inclusive practices.

4. **Resource Allocation**: Paula also emphasized the need for adequate funding and resources to support inclusive education. She argued that schools should receive financial assistance to provide necessary accommodations, such as assistive technologies and mental health support services, ensuring that all students have equal opportunities to succeed.

5. **Research and Data Collection**: To advocate effectively, Paula understood the importance of data in demonstrating the need for inclusive education policies. She collaborated with researchers to gather data on the academic and social outcomes of students in inclusive settings versus segregated environments. The findings consistently showed that inclusive education not only benefits students with disabilities and LGBTQ identities but also enriches the learning environment for all students (Hehir, 2005).

In her quest for inclusive education, Paula faced significant opposition. Critics often argued that inclusive practices could dilute educational standards or overwhelm teachers. However, Paula countered these arguments by presenting evidence that inclusive education leads to improved academic performance and social skills among all students.

For example, a study conducted by the *National Center for Learning Disabilities* (2017) found that students in inclusive classrooms demonstrated higher levels of engagement and collaboration, which are essential skills in today's workforce. Paula utilized such data to advocate for a shift in perception regarding inclusive education, framing it not as a burden but as an opportunity for growth and innovation within the educational system.

Ultimately, Paula Lupi's advocacy for inclusive education policies was not just about changing laws and practices; it was about transforming lives. By championing the rights of marginalized students, she laid the groundwork for a more equitable educational landscape in Portugal, one where every student could thrive regardless of their identity or abilities. Her work continues to inspire educators and activists alike, reminding us that inclusive education is not merely an aspiration but a necessity for a just society.

Bibliography

[1] Avramidis, E., & Norwich, B. (2002). Teachers' attitudes towards integration/inclusion: A review of the literature. *European Journal of Special Needs Education*, 17(2), 129-147.

[2] Hehir, T. (2005). New Directions in Special Education: Eliminating the Disproportionate Representation of Culturally and Linguistically Diverse Students in Special Education. *Harvard Education Press*.

[3] UNESCO. (1994). Salamanca Statement and Framework for Action on Special Needs Education. *UNESCO*.

[4] National Center for Learning Disabilities. (2017). The State of Learning Disabilities: Understanding the 1 in 5. *NCLD*.

Uncovering the intersectionality of LGBTQ and disability rights

The concept of intersectionality, first coined by legal scholar Kimberlé Crenshaw in the late 1980s, serves as a vital framework for understanding how various social identities overlap and interact, particularly regarding systems of oppression and privilege. This framework is essential in analyzing the intersectionality of LGBTQ and disability rights, as individuals often navigate multiple marginalized identities simultaneously. For Paula Lupi, her journey as a queer disabled woman exemplifies the complexities and nuances of this intersectionality, highlighting both the unique challenges faced and the strengths derived from her multifaceted identity.

Theoretical Framework

Intersectionality posits that individuals do not experience discrimination or privilege in isolation; rather, their experiences are shaped by the interplay of various social categories, including race, gender, sexual orientation, and disability. The following equation illustrates this concept:

$$E = f(I_1, I_2, I_3, \ldots, I_n) \qquad (14)$$

where E represents an individual's experience, and $I_1, I_2, I_3, \ldots, I_n$ represent various intersecting identities. In the context of LGBTQ and disability rights, this equation signifies that the experiences of individuals like Paula cannot be understood solely through the lens of their LGBTQ identity or their disability; rather, it is the interaction of both identities that shapes their lived experiences.

Unique Challenges

Individuals at the intersection of LGBTQ and disability identities face unique challenges that can exacerbate their marginalization. For instance, societal stigma surrounding both sexual orientation and disability can lead to compounded discrimination. Research indicates that LGBTQ individuals with disabilities often encounter barriers in accessing healthcare services, which are crucial for both their physical and mental well-being. According to a study by the National LGBTQ Task Force, nearly 30% of LGBTQ individuals with disabilities reported experiencing discrimination in healthcare settings, a statistic that underscores the urgent need for inclusive healthcare policies.

Moreover, the lack of representation within both the LGBTQ community and disability advocacy groups can lead to feelings of isolation and invisibility. Paula's advocacy work sought to bridge this gap by amplifying the voices of those who exist at this intersection, fostering a sense of community and belonging. She often stated, "We cannot fight for one identity without acknowledging the struggles of another. Our liberation is intertwined."

Examples of Intersectional Advocacy

One poignant example of intersectional advocacy is the work of organizations like *Sins Invalid*, a performance project that celebrates and elevates the voices of disabled and LGBTQ artists. By centering the experiences of queer disabled individuals, *Sins Invalid* challenges dominant narratives that often marginalize these identities. Their performances not only showcase the talents of disabled artists but also serve as a platform for critical discussions around the intersections of sexuality, disability, and social justice.

Another notable instance is the advocacy surrounding the Americans with Disabilities Act (ADA) and its implications for LGBTQ individuals. While the

ADA was a monumental step forward for disability rights, its implementation often overlooked the specific needs of LGBTQ individuals with disabilities. Paula's work involved lobbying for amendments that would explicitly include protections for LGBTQ individuals under the ADA, thereby ensuring that their rights were not only recognized but actively upheld.

The Importance of Inclusive Policies

To address the intersectionality of LGBTQ and disability rights, it is imperative to develop inclusive policies that recognize and accommodate the unique needs of individuals at this intersection. For example, educational institutions must implement comprehensive anti-discrimination policies that explicitly protect LGBTQ students with disabilities. This includes ensuring access to resources such as counseling services, support groups, and inclusive curricula that reflect diverse identities.

Furthermore, healthcare providers must be trained to understand the specific challenges faced by LGBTQ individuals with disabilities, including the need for culturally competent care that respects and affirms their identities. By fostering an environment that prioritizes inclusivity, we can begin to dismantle the barriers that perpetuate discrimination and inequality.

Conclusion

In conclusion, uncovering the intersectionality of LGBTQ and disability rights is crucial for creating a more equitable society. Paula Lupi's journey serves as a powerful reminder that advocacy must be inclusive and intersectional, addressing the unique challenges faced by individuals who navigate multiple marginalized identities. By embracing intersectionality, we can build a stronger, more united movement that champions the rights of all individuals, regardless of their sexual orientation or ability. As Paula often emphasized, "Our fight for justice is not just for ourselves but for everyone who has been silenced. Together, we rise."

Overcoming obstacles and discrimination in academia

Navigating the academic landscape can be a formidable challenge for anyone, but for Paula Lupi, as a queer disabled woman, the obstacles were particularly daunting. The academic environment, often touted as a bastion of enlightenment and progress, can paradoxically perpetuate systemic discrimination and biases that marginalize individuals based on their identity. This section delves into Paula's experiences and the broader implications of overcoming such barriers.

Understanding Systemic Barriers

Systemic barriers in academia can manifest in various forms, including implicit biases, institutional discrimination, and a lack of representation. These barriers often create a hostile environment for marginalized groups. According to the *Social Model of Disability*, which posits that disability is not merely a physical limitation but a result of societal structures that fail to accommodate diverse needs, Paula encountered numerous challenges that were not inherently due to her disability but rather the inflexibility of academic institutions.

$$D = S - A \tag{15}$$

Where D represents the degree of disability experienced, S signifies the societal structures in place, and A denotes the accommodations provided. This equation illustrates that the experience of disability is exacerbated by the absence of adequate support systems within educational frameworks.

Experiences of Discrimination

Paula's journey through academia was marked by instances of overt and covert discrimination. For example, during her undergraduate studies, she faced skepticism from peers and faculty regarding her capabilities. In one notable incident, a professor dismissed her contributions in class discussions, attributing them to her disability rather than her intellect. This aligns with the findings of a study conducted by [?], which highlights that disabled students often encounter lower expectations from educators, leading to a self-fulfilling prophecy of underachievement.

Moreover, Paula's identity as a queer woman added another layer of complexity. The intersectionality of her identities meant that she often felt invisible in discussions surrounding LGBTQ rights within academia, which predominantly centered on able-bodied narratives. This lack of representation can be explained through the framework of *Intersectionality*, coined by [3], which emphasizes the interconnected nature of social categorizations and their compounded impact on individuals.

Strategies for Overcoming Obstacles

Despite these challenges, Paula developed a toolkit of strategies to navigate and eventually thrive in the academic realm. One of her key strategies was to seek out mentors who understood and championed diversity. By aligning herself with progressive faculty members who recognized the importance of inclusivity, she was able to find support and validation for her experiences.

Additionally, Paula became actively involved in student organizations focused on LGBTQ and disability rights. These organizations provided a sense of community and empowerment, allowing her to advocate for change within the institution. For instance, she played a pivotal role in establishing a task force aimed at improving accessibility on campus, which included advocating for physical accommodations as well as mental health resources.

The Role of Allyship

Allyship played a crucial role in Paula's academic journey. Allies within the faculty and student body not only amplified her voice but also helped to dismantle the barriers she faced. For example, a supportive professor collaborated with Paula to develop a curriculum that included diverse perspectives, ensuring that the contributions of disabled and LGBTQ scholars were recognized and valued.

Moreover, the concept of *Critical Disability Theory* informed Paula's approach to advocacy. This theory critiques the traditional narratives surrounding disability and emphasizes the importance of lived experiences. By sharing her story and those of her peers, Paula contributed to a more nuanced understanding of disability within academic discourse, challenging the prevailing stereotypes and assumptions.

Impact and Legacy

Paula's resilience in overcoming obstacles in academia not only paved the way for her personal success but also created ripple effects that benefitted future generations of students. Her advocacy for inclusive policies and practices led to tangible changes in her institution, such as the implementation of training programs for faculty on disability awareness and LGBTQ inclusivity.

Ultimately, Paula's journey illustrates the power of perseverance and the importance of community in overcoming discrimination in academia. Her experiences serve as a testament to the potential for change within educational institutions when individuals from marginalized backgrounds assert their voices and advocate for their rights.

In conclusion, the journey of overcoming obstacles and discrimination in academia is fraught with challenges, but it is also filled with opportunities for growth and transformation. Paula Lupi's story exemplifies how one can navigate these complexities and emerge as a leader in the fight for equality, leaving a lasting impact on the academic landscape for LGBTQ and disabled individuals.

Graduating with honors and a sense of purpose

As Paula Lupi approached the culmination of her academic journey, she found herself at a pivotal intersection of knowledge, identity, and activism. Graduating with honors was not merely a personal achievement; it was a testament to her resilience and unwavering commitment to advocating for LGBTQ and disability rights. This milestone was steeped in significance, reflecting years of hard work, late nights spent poring over texts, and a relentless pursuit of justice.

The rigorous academic environment at her university provided Paula with the tools to articulate her beliefs and understand the complexities of social justice. Through her studies, she encountered various theories that informed her activism. One such theory was the **Social Model of Disability**, which posits that disability is not an inherent trait of an individual but rather a result of the interaction between individuals and their environments. This perspective resonated deeply with Paula, as it aligned with her experiences navigating both her disability and her identity as a queer woman in a society that often marginalized both aspects of her being.

In her final year, Paula undertook a thesis project that explored the intersectionality of LGBTQ and disability rights. This project was groundbreaking, as it challenged the prevailing narratives that often separated these movements. She argued that the struggles faced by individuals at this intersection were compounded by societal prejudices, and she sought to highlight the voices that were frequently silenced. Her thesis drew upon a range of qualitative data, including interviews with activists and community members, illustrating the real-world implications of theoretical frameworks.

The challenges she faced during her studies were not insignificant. Paula encountered skepticism from peers and faculty who were not familiar with the intersectional approach she championed. Some viewed her focus on both LGBTQ and disability rights as overly ambitious, while others dismissed it as irrelevant. However, Paula's determination only grew stronger in the face of adversity. She formed study groups with like-minded individuals, fostering an environment of support and collaboration. This sense of community not only bolstered her academic performance but also reinforced her belief in the power of collective action.

In her graduation ceremony, Paula's name was called, and she walked across the stage with a sense of pride and purpose. The honors she received were not just accolades; they were a recognition of her commitment to creating a more equitable society. As she accepted her diploma, she reflected on the journey that had brought her to this moment. The struggles, the late-night debates, the laughter shared with friends—all of these experiences had shaped her into the activist she was destined to become.

Moreover, Paula's graduation was a pivotal moment not just for her, but for the communities she represented. It symbolized hope and progress, serving as an inspiration for others who faced similar challenges. She envisioned a future where education would serve as a catalyst for change, empowering individuals to challenge societal norms and advocate for their rights.

With her diploma in hand, Paula was ready to embark on the next chapter of her life. The sense of purpose she felt was palpable; she knew that her education was not an endpoint but rather a launching pad for her activism. Graduating with honors was a profound achievement, but it also marked the beginning of a lifelong commitment to fighting for justice. Paula was determined to influence policy, educate others, and amplify the voices of those who had been historically marginalized.

In conclusion, Paula Lupi's graduation was a defining moment that encapsulated her journey of self-discovery and empowerment. It was a celebration of her academic achievements and a reaffirmation of her commitment to advocacy. As she stepped into the world beyond academia, she carried with her not only a sense of accomplishment but also a profound sense of responsibility to continue the fight for LGBTQ and disability rights, inspiring future generations to do the same.

The beginning of a lifelong commitment to education

In the vibrant streets of Lisbon, where the echoes of fado intertwine with the laughter of children playing in sunlit squares, Paula Lupi's educational journey began to take shape. It was here, amidst the rich tapestry of culture and diversity, that she first encountered the transformative power of education. This section explores the pivotal moments that ignited her lifelong commitment to learning and advocacy, setting the stage for her future endeavors in human rights.

Education, often described as the great equalizer, played a crucial role in Paula's development. According to Paulo Freire's critical pedagogy, education is not merely a transfer of knowledge; it is a practice of freedom. Freire posits that education should empower individuals to question and challenge the status quo, fostering critical consciousness. For Paula, this philosophy resonated deeply as she navigated the complexities of her identity and the societal norms that sought to confine her.

$$C = \frac{1}{N} \sum_{i=1}^{N} (x_i - \bar{x})^2 \qquad (16)$$

Where C represents the critical consciousness, N is the number of experiences, x_i are the individual experiences, and $\bar{x}$ is the average experience. This equation metaphorically illustrates how each moment of learning contributes to a broader understanding of justice and equality.

Paula's commitment to education was not without its challenges. The struggle for acceptance in her academic environment often mirrored the societal prejudices she faced outside the classroom. Discrimination based on her identity as a queer disabled woman was a constant reminder of the barriers that existed within educational institutions. The lack of inclusive policies and representation in academia highlighted the urgent need for change. Paula's experiences were emblematic of a broader issue; many students from marginalized backgrounds faced similar obstacles, often feeling alienated and unsupported in their pursuit of knowledge.

The turning point in Paula's educational journey came when she encountered mentors who recognized her potential and encouraged her activism. One such mentor was Professor Maria Santos, a renowned advocate for inclusive education. Professor Santos introduced Paula to the concept of intersectionality, a term coined by Kimberlé Crenshaw, which emphasizes the interconnected nature of social categorizations such as race, class, and gender. This framework allowed Paula to understand her experiences not as isolated incidents but as part of a larger systemic issue.

$$I = \sum_{j=1}^{M}(w_j \cdot x_j) \qquad (17)$$

Where I represents the intersectionality of experiences, M is the number of social categories, w_j are the weights of each category, and x_j represents the experiences associated with each category. This equation illustrates how various identities can compound the challenges faced by individuals, reinforcing Paula's resolve to advocate for inclusive policies in education.

As Paula progressed through her studies, she became increasingly aware of the power of education to effect change. She began to actively participate in student organizations focused on promoting diversity and inclusion. These groups provided a platform for students to share their stories and advocate for policies that addressed the needs of marginalized communities. Paula's involvement in these organizations was not just about personal growth; it was about creating a ripple effect that would inspire others to join the fight for equality.

One notable example of her activism occurred during a university-wide forum on disability rights. Paula organized a panel discussion featuring students with disabilities who shared their experiences navigating the educational system. The event was a resounding success, drawing attention to the urgent need for accessibility in academic institutions. This experience solidified Paula's belief that education was not merely a personal journey but a collective endeavor that required solidarity and collaboration.

In her quest for knowledge, Paula also recognized the importance of educating others. She began to mentor younger students, providing guidance and support as they navigated their own paths. This commitment to mentorship was rooted in her understanding of the challenges faced by those who lacked representation in academia. By empowering others, Paula aimed to create a more inclusive educational environment that would foster the next generation of activists.

As she graduated with honors, Paula's sense of purpose was palpable. She understood that her educational journey was just the beginning of a lifelong commitment to advocacy. With each lesson learned and each barrier overcome, she laid the groundwork for a future dedicated to promoting social justice and equality. Paula's resolve to influence educational policies and practices would become a cornerstone of her activism, as she sought to ensure that all individuals, regardless of their identity, had access to quality education.

In conclusion, the beginning of Paula Lupi's lifelong commitment to education was marked by a series of transformative experiences that shaped her understanding of justice and equality. Through the lens of critical pedagogy and intersectionality, she recognized the need for inclusive educational practices that addressed the diverse needs of all students. Her journey reflects the profound impact that education can have on individuals and communities, inspiring a generation of activists to continue the fight for equality and justice in all spheres of life.

Influencing the next generation of activists through teaching

Paula Lupi understood that education is not merely a pathway to knowledge; it is a powerful tool for social change. By stepping into the role of an educator, she aimed to inspire and empower the next generation of activists, equipping them with the skills, knowledge, and passion necessary to continue the fight for LGBTQ and disability rights. Her teaching philosophy was rooted in the belief that education should be inclusive, intersectional, and transformative.

Theoretical Foundations

Paula's approach to teaching was influenced by several key educational theories:

- **Critical Pedagogy:** Drawing on the work of Paulo Freire, Paula emphasized the importance of dialogue and critical thinking in education. She believed that students should not be passive recipients of knowledge but active participants in their learning process. By fostering an environment where students could question societal norms and engage in critical discussions, she aimed to cultivate a sense of agency and responsibility.
- **Constructivism:** Embracing the principles of constructivist theory, Paula understood that knowledge is constructed through experiences and interactions. She encouraged her students to share their personal stories and perspectives, recognizing that their lived experiences were valuable contributions to the classroom discourse.
- **Intersectionality:** Inspired by Kimberlé Crenshaw's concept of intersectionality, Paula integrated discussions of race, gender, sexuality, and disability into her curriculum. She highlighted how these identities intersect and shape individuals' experiences, emphasizing the need for a multifaceted approach to activism.

Challenges in Teaching Activism

Teaching activism is not without its challenges. Paula encountered various obstacles that tested her resolve and commitment to her students:

- **Resistance from Traditional Educational Structures:** Many institutions were hesitant to embrace her progressive teaching methods. Paula often faced pushback from administrators who preferred a more traditional, lecture-based approach. She navigated these challenges by demonstrating the effectiveness of her methods through student engagement and success.
- **Addressing Diverse Needs:** Her classroom was a microcosm of society, filled with students from varied backgrounds and experiences. Paula worked diligently to create an inclusive environment, tailoring her teaching to accommodate different learning styles and needs. This required continuous reflection and adaptation on her part.
- **Emotional Labor:** Discussing topics related to LGBTQ and disability rights often brought up painful histories and traumas. Paula recognized the emotional toll this could take on her students and herself. She implemented self-care practices and encouraged open dialogue about mental health, fostering a supportive community within her classroom.

Practical Examples of Her Influence

Paula's influence on the next generation of activists was profound and far-reaching. Here are some practical examples of how she shaped her students' journeys:

- **Empowerment through Storytelling:** Paula encouraged her students to share their personal narratives as a means of empowerment. One student, who identified as a queer disabled woman, shared her experiences of discrimination in both the LGBTQ and disability communities. This act of vulnerability not only fostered solidarity among peers but also inspired others to advocate for their rights.

- **Community Engagement Projects:** Paula initiated community-based projects that allowed her students to apply their learning in real-world contexts. One such project involved collaborating with a local LGBTQ organization to develop workshops focused on mental health resources for queer youth. Through this initiative, students gained hands-on experience in activism while making a tangible impact in their community.

- **Mentorship and Networking:** Recognizing the importance of mentorship, Paula connected her students with established activists and organizations. This networking facilitated internships and volunteer opportunities, allowing students to gain practical experience and build relationships within the activist community.

Legacy of Activism Through Education

Paula's commitment to teaching went beyond the classroom; it was a lifelong dedication to nurturing future leaders in the fight for equality. Her students emerged as passionate advocates, equipped with the knowledge and skills to challenge injustice. Many went on to pursue careers in activism, education, and public policy, carrying forward the torch of change that Paula had ignited.

In conclusion, Paula Lupi's influence on the next generation of activists through teaching exemplified the transformative power of education. By fostering critical thinking, promoting intersectionality, and encouraging community engagement, she laid the groundwork for a new wave of advocates dedicated to creating a more inclusive and equitable world. Her legacy endures in the hearts and minds of those she taught, inspiring them to continue the fight for LGBTQ and disability rights with passion and purpose.

The Personal Journey

Navigating relationships and intimacy

Navigating relationships and intimacy can be a complex journey, particularly for individuals who identify as LGBTQ and disabled. Paula Lupi's experiences in this realm reflect the myriad challenges and triumphs that come with forging meaningful connections in a society that often marginalizes both her identities.

Intimacy, defined as the close familiarity or friendship that involves emotional connection, is a fundamental human need. However, for queer disabled individuals, societal norms and expectations can create barriers to forming intimate relationships. The intersection of disability and LGBTQ identities often leads to unique challenges, including societal stigma, internalized prejudice, and accessibility issues.

Theoretical Framework

To understand the dynamics of intimacy in Paula's life, we can draw upon several theoretical frameworks. One relevant theory is **Attachment Theory**, which posits that early relationships with caregivers shape an individual's ability to form healthy relationships in adulthood. According to Bowlby (1969), secure attachment leads to positive relationship outcomes, while insecure attachment can result in anxiety and avoidance in intimacy.

For Paula, her supportive and loving family provided a foundation for secure attachment, which would later influence her ability to navigate relationships as an adult. However, societal attitudes toward LGBTQ individuals often complicate this attachment, leading to fears of rejection and abandonment.

Another important framework is **Intersectionality**, introduced by Crenshaw (1989). This concept emphasizes that individuals experience overlapping systems of oppression, which can affect their social interactions and relationships. For Paula, being both queer and disabled meant that she faced discrimination on multiple fronts, complicating her journey toward intimacy.

Challenges in Relationships

Paula faced several challenges in her romantic relationships, stemming from both societal perceptions and personal insecurities. One significant issue was the fear of rejection based on her identities. Research indicates that LGBTQ individuals often experience higher rates of rejection in romantic contexts, which can lead to anxiety and reluctance to pursue relationships (Meyer, 2003).

Additionally, the stigma surrounding disability can create barriers to intimacy. Many disabled individuals report feelings of being seen as less desirable or unworthy of love, which can lead to internalized stigma. Paula struggled with these feelings, often questioning whether her disability would deter potential partners. This internal conflict is supported by studies showing that disabled individuals frequently face societal stereotypes that paint them as asexual or dependent (Shakespeare, 2000).

Examples of Navigating Intimacy

Despite these challenges, Paula's journey toward intimacy was marked by resilience and growth. Early in her life, she discovered the LGBTQ community in Lisbon, where she found a supportive network of friends who shared similar experiences. These friendships laid the groundwork for her understanding of intimacy, as they provided a safe space to explore her identity and desires.

One poignant example of Paula's navigation of intimacy occurred during her university years. She met a fellow activist, Sofia, who shared her passion for social justice. Their relationship blossomed, but it was not without its hurdles. Paula often felt insecure about her disability, fearing that Sofia might view her as a burden. However, through open communication and mutual support, they were able to cultivate a deep emotional connection. This relationship illustrated the importance of vulnerability and honesty in overcoming barriers to intimacy.

Moreover, Paula's experiences reflect the concept of **Social Capital**, which refers to the resources available to individuals through their social networks. By engaging with the LGBTQ community, Paula built a support system that enhanced her ability to navigate romantic relationships. This network not only provided emotional support but also practical resources, such as access to LGBTQ-friendly spaces and events where she could meet potential partners.

Empowerment Through Intimacy

Ultimately, Paula's journey through relationships and intimacy became a source of empowerment. By embracing her identity as a queer disabled woman, she learned to advocate for her needs and desires in romantic contexts. This self-advocacy is crucial, as studies show that individuals who assert their needs in relationships report higher satisfaction and fulfillment (Reis & Shaver, 1988).

Paula also recognized the importance of self-love and acceptance in fostering healthy relationships. By embracing her uniqueness and rejecting societal stereotypes, she was able to approach intimacy with confidence. This shift in perspective allowed her to engage in relationships that were not only fulfilling but also aligned with her values of justice and equality.

In conclusion, navigating relationships and intimacy as a queer disabled woman involves a complex interplay of societal expectations, personal insecurities, and the pursuit of authentic connections. Paula Lupi's experiences highlight the resilience required to overcome these challenges and the transformative power of intimacy in fostering self-acceptance and empowerment. Through her journey, Paula not only navigated her own relationships but also paved the way for others to embrace their identities and seek meaningful connections.

Embracing self-acceptance and self-love

In the journey of personal growth, particularly for individuals navigating the complexities of identity within the LGBTQ community, embracing self-acceptance and self-love is fundamental. For Paula Lupi, this journey was not merely a personal endeavor but a crucial aspect of her activism. Self-acceptance refers to recognizing and embracing one's true self, including all aspects of identity, while self-love involves nurturing oneself with kindness and compassion.

Theoretical Framework

The concept of self-acceptance can be understood through the lens of *Humanistic Psychology*, particularly the works of Carl Rogers. Rogers emphasized the importance of unconditional positive regard, which is the acceptance and support of a person regardless of what they say or do. This theory posits that self-acceptance is essential for personal growth and well-being.

In mathematical terms, we can represent self-acceptance (SA) as a function of various factors:

$$SA = f(A, C, R)$$

where: - A = Awareness of one's identity - C = Compassion towards oneself - R = Recognition of personal worth

This equation suggests that a higher level of self-acceptance is achieved through increased awareness, compassion, and recognition of one's inherent value.

Problems Encountered

For many individuals, including Paula, the path to self-acceptance is fraught with challenges. Societal norms often dictate narrow definitions of identity and success, leading to internalized stigma and self-doubt. This can result in a phenomenon known as *internalized homophobia*, where individuals harbor negative feelings towards their own sexual orientation, significantly impacting their self-esteem and mental health.

Moreover, the intersectionality of being both LGBTQ and disabled can compound these challenges. As Paula navigated her identity, she faced societal expectations that often marginalized her existence, leading to feelings of isolation and inadequacy.

Examples of Self-Acceptance in Action

Paula's journey towards self-acceptance was marked by pivotal moments that shaped her understanding of self-love. One significant example occurred during her teenage years when she discovered the vibrant LGBTQ community in Lisbon. Engaging with diverse individuals who shared similar experiences allowed her to see reflections of herself in others, fostering a sense of belonging.

Through participation in local LGBTQ events and gatherings, Paula began to embrace her identity openly. This process was not instantaneous; it involved confronting her fears and insecurities. She often recalled moments of vulnerability where she shared her story with others, which in turn empowered her to accept herself fully. The act of sharing became a therapeutic outlet, reinforcing her belief in the importance of authenticity.

Additionally, the influence of supportive friendships played a critical role in her journey. Paula surrounded herself with individuals who celebrated her for who she was, providing a safe space for exploration and self-discovery. These relationships were foundational in cultivating her self-love, as they taught her the value of mutual support and acceptance.

The Role of Self-Love in Activism

Self-love is not merely a personal benefit; it is a powerful tool in activism. For Paula, embracing self-love allowed her to advocate for others more effectively. When individuals cultivate a positive relationship with themselves, they are better equipped to stand against societal injustices. The confidence gained through self-acceptance fueled Paula's passion for activism, enabling her to confront discrimination and fight for equality.

Moreover, self-love acts as a protective factor against burnout, a common issue among activists. By prioritizing her well-being, Paula was able to sustain her efforts in advocating for LGBTQ and disability rights, ensuring that her voice remained strong and impactful.

Conclusion

In conclusion, the journey of embracing self-acceptance and self-love is a transformative process that lays the groundwork for personal empowerment and effective activism. For Paula Lupi, this journey was marked by theoretical insights, personal challenges, and supportive relationships that collectively shaped her identity. Through her experiences, she not only found peace within herself but also became a beacon of hope for others, inspiring them to embark on their own journeys of self-acceptance and love. The legacy of her self-acceptance continues to resonate within the LGBTQ community, reminding individuals that true strength lies in embracing one's authentic self.

Discovering the LGBTQ community in Lisbon

As Paula Lupi navigated her formative years in the vibrant streets of Lisbon, she began to uncover a rich tapestry of identities and experiences that would shape her understanding of herself and her activism. Lisbon, known for its historical charm and picturesque landscapes, was also a city pulsating with a dynamic LGBTQ community that was both visible and vibrant. This discovery marked a pivotal moment in Paula's life, as she began to engage with a world that resonated with her own struggles and aspirations.

The LGBTQ community in Lisbon was characterized by its diversity, encompassing a wide range of identities, including gay, lesbian, bisexual, transgender, and non-binary individuals. Each subgroup brought its own unique narratives and challenges, contributing to a broader dialogue about acceptance, representation, and rights. Paula's initial exposure to this community came through local youth organizations and cultural events that celebrated queer identities.

One of the key venues for LGBTQ expression in Lisbon was the Bairro Alto district, a lively neighborhood known for its nightlife and open-minded atmosphere. Here, Paula found herself drawn to the pulsating energy of bars and clubs that welcomed LGBTQ patrons. The atmosphere was electric, filled with laughter, music, and an undeniable sense of belonging. It was within these spaces that Paula began to forge connections with individuals who shared her experiences and aspirations.

$$\text{Sense of Belonging} = \frac{\text{Community Support}}{\text{Isolation}} \tag{18}$$

This equation encapsulates the essence of Paula's experience as she transitioned from feelings of isolation to a profound sense of belonging. The support she received from the community not only validated her identity but also empowered her to embrace her queerness openly. This newfound acceptance was crucial in a society that often imposed strict norms and expectations regarding gender and sexuality.

As she delved deeper into the LGBTQ scene, Paula encountered various activist groups that were at the forefront of advocating for rights and recognition. Organizations such as ILGA Portugal (International Lesbian, Gay, Bisexual, Trans and Intersex Association) played a significant role in shaping the landscape of LGBTQ activism in the country. Through workshops, discussions, and protests, Paula learned about the historical struggles faced by the LGBTQ community, including the fight against discrimination, violence, and the ongoing battle for legal rights.

Paula's involvement with these organizations provided her with a platform to voice her concerns and aspirations. She participated in campaigns aimed at raising awareness about issues affecting LGBTQ individuals, such as mental health, access to healthcare, and the importance of inclusive education. The intersectionality of her identity as a queer disabled woman became increasingly apparent, as she recognized the unique challenges faced by individuals who navigated multiple marginalized identities.

$$\text{Intersectional Advocacy} = \text{LGBTQ Rights} + \text{Disability Rights} \quad (19)$$

This equation illustrates Paula's understanding that advocacy must address the interconnected nature of various forms of discrimination. By recognizing the overlap between LGBTQ rights and disability rights, she positioned herself as a holistic advocate, striving to ensure that no one was left behind in the fight for equality.

The journey of discovering the LGBTQ community in Lisbon also involved confronting societal prejudices and stereotypes. Paula witnessed firsthand the challenges that many individuals faced, including bullying, harassment, and systemic discrimination. These experiences fueled her passion for activism and reinforced her commitment to creating safe spaces for marginalized voices.

Through her connections within the community, Paula learned about the power of storytelling as a tool for change. She was inspired by the narratives of resilience and courage shared by others, which highlighted the importance of visibility in combating stigma. This realization motivated her to share her own story, embracing vulnerability as a means of empowering others to do the same.

In her exploration of the LGBTQ community, Paula also became aware of the cultural nuances that shaped the experiences of its members. The intersection of Portuguese culture and LGBTQ identity created a unique landscape that influenced how individuals expressed their identities. Traditional values often clashed with the desire for self-expression, leading to complex dynamics within families and communities.

To navigate these challenges, Paula engaged in dialogue with her peers, fostering understanding and empathy. She organized workshops that encouraged open discussions about sexuality, gender identity, and the importance of acceptance within families. These initiatives aimed to bridge the gap between traditional values and modern understandings of identity, creating a more inclusive environment for future generations.

As Paula continued to immerse herself in the LGBTQ community, she recognized the importance of allyship. She sought to educate those outside the community about the struggles faced by LGBTQ individuals, advocating for a more inclusive society. This commitment to allyship extended beyond her immediate circle, as she actively participated in campaigns that aimed to raise awareness about LGBTQ issues on a national level.

In conclusion, Paula Lupi's discovery of the LGBTQ community in Lisbon was a transformative experience that shaped her identity and fueled her activism. Through her engagement with this vibrant community, she found a sense of belonging, developed a deeper understanding of intersectionality, and committed herself to advocating for the rights of marginalized individuals. This chapter of her life laid the groundwork for her future endeavors, as she emerged as a powerful voice for LGBTQ and disability rights in Portugal and beyond.

The impact of LGBTQ activism on personal relationships

LGBTQ activism has a profound influence on personal relationships, shaping the dynamics of connections, intimacy, and community among individuals. As Paula Lupi navigated her journey through activism, she discovered that her commitment to advocacy not only transformed her own identity but also redefined her interactions with friends, family, and romantic partners.

At the core of LGBTQ activism lies the pursuit of authenticity and acceptance. Activists often find themselves in a continuous struggle to assert their identities in spaces that may not always be welcoming. This quest for self-acceptance can significantly impact personal relationships. For many, coming out is a pivotal moment that alters the nature of their connections. Research indicates that the process of coming out can lead to both positive and negative outcomes in relationships. According to [1], the minority stress model suggests that LGBTQ individuals often face unique stressors that can strain interpersonal relationships.

For example, Paula's coming out journey was met with mixed reactions from her family and friends. While some embraced her identity, others struggled to understand it, leading to moments of tension and conflict. This dichotomy illustrates the challenges many LGBTQ individuals face when seeking acceptance from loved ones. The fear of rejection can deter individuals from being open about their identities, which may lead to feelings of isolation or resentment.

Moreover, LGBTQ activism fosters a sense of community that can enrich personal relationships. Engaging with like-minded individuals often leads to the formation of deep, supportive bonds. Paula found solace and strength in the friendships she cultivated within LGBTQ circles. These relationships provided a safe space where she could express her true self without fear of judgment. The solidarity experienced in activist communities can create a powerful support network, allowing individuals to navigate the complexities of their identities together.

However, the intersection of activism and personal relationships can also introduce complications. The time and energy devoted to advocacy can strain romantic partnerships, particularly when one partner is more involved than the other. For instance, Paula's dedication to her activism sometimes meant late nights at protests or meetings, which could lead to feelings of neglect in her relationships. The balance between personal commitments and activism is a common struggle faced by many activists. According to [2], maintaining a healthy relationship while being deeply involved in activism requires open communication and mutual understanding.

Additionally, the impact of activism on romantic relationships can be profound. As individuals become more engaged in advocacy, they may seek partners who share their values and commitment to social justice. Paula's experiences highlight the importance of alignment in values; she found that her most fulfilling relationships were with individuals who understood and supported her activism. This alignment can foster deeper intimacy and connection, as partners work together towards common goals.

However, relationships can also be tested when partners have differing views on activism. For example, Paula encountered challenges in a previous relationship where her partner did not prioritize LGBTQ rights. This disparity in values led to significant friction, ultimately resulting in the dissolution of the relationship. This scenario underscores the critical role that shared values play in sustaining personal connections within the context of activism.

In conclusion, LGBTQ activism profoundly impacts personal relationships, shaping the dynamics of connection, intimacy, and community. While it can lead to enriching experiences and deep bonds, it also introduces challenges that require careful navigation. Paula Lupi's journey illustrates the complexities of balancing activism with personal relationships, emphasizing the importance of open communication, shared values, and mutual support. As LGBTQ individuals continue to advocate for their rights, the interplay between activism and personal relationships remains a vital aspect of their experiences.

Bibliography

[1] Meyer, I. H. (2003). Prejudice, social stress, and mental health in gay men. *American Psychologist*, 58(5), 400-410.

[2] Kollman, K. (2013). The relationship between activism and personal life: A study of LGBTQ activists. *Journal of Social Issues*, 69(2), 284-301.

Breaking free from societal expectations

Paula Lupi's journey of self-discovery was not merely a personal endeavor; it was a profound act of defiance against the societal norms that sought to confine her identity. Growing up in Lisbon, a city rich in culture yet often steeped in traditional values, Paula faced immense pressure to conform to conventional expectations of gender, sexuality, and ability. This section delves into the multifaceted challenges she encountered and the theoretical frameworks that illuminate her struggle for liberation.

Theoretical Frameworks

To understand Paula's resistance to societal expectations, we can draw upon Judith Butler's theory of gender performativity, which posits that gender is not an innate quality but rather a series of acts and performances shaped by societal norms. Butler argues that these performances create the illusion of a stable gender identity, which can be subverted through non-conformity. Paula's rejection of traditional gender roles exemplifies this theory; by embracing her identity as a queer disabled woman, she dismantled the performative aspects of gender that sought to define her.

$$G = P_1 + P_2 + P_3 + \ldots + P_n \qquad (20)$$

Where G represents gender, and P_i represents the various performances that contribute to one's gender identity. Paula's journey illustrates how the sum of her unique performances led to a redefined sense of self, one that was authentic and liberated from societal constraints.

Societal Pressures and Challenges

The societal expectations placed upon Paula were manifold, manifesting as familial pressures, peer influences, and cultural norms that dictated how she should behave, who she should love, and how she should present herself. The stigma surrounding disability compounded these pressures, often relegating disabled individuals to the margins of society. Paula encountered prejudice not only for her sexual orientation but also for her disability, which forced her to navigate a complex landscape of discrimination.

For instance, when Paula began to express her interest in the LGBTQ community, she faced backlash from peers who adhered to traditional norms. This backlash was not merely social; it often seeped into institutional settings, where educators and administrators failed to provide an inclusive environment. Paula's experience reflects the broader societal tendency to enforce conformity, which can be detrimental to individual identity formation.

Personal Stories of Resistance

Paula's path to breaking free from societal expectations was paved with personal stories of resistance. One significant moment occurred during her teenage years when she attended a local LGBTQ event. Surrounded by individuals who shared her struggles, she felt a sense of belonging that had eluded her in mainstream society. This event was transformative, igniting a fire within her to advocate for herself and others.

In a poignant reflection, Paula recounted, "For the first time, I saw people like me—people who were proud of who they were. I realized that I didn't have to hide; I could be loud and unapologetic about my identity." This moment of realization was a catalyst for her activism, propelling her to challenge the norms that sought to silence her.

The Role of Community

Community played an essential role in Paula's journey of breaking free from societal expectations. The support and solidarity she found within the LGBTQ community provided her with the strength to defy the limitations imposed upon her. This sense of belonging fostered resilience, allowing her to confront the challenges of being both queer and disabled.

The concept of intersectionality, introduced by Kimberlé Crenshaw, further elucidates Paula's experience. Intersectionality recognizes that individuals have multiple, overlapping identities that influence their experiences of oppression and privilege. Paula's identity as a queer disabled woman positioned her at the intersection of various forms of discrimination, but it also provided her with a unique perspective on the need for inclusive advocacy.

$$I = \sum_{j=1}^{m}(O_j + P_j) \qquad (21)$$

Where I represents individual identity, O_j represents oppression faced due to each identity facet, and P_j represents the privileges that may arise from other facets. For Paula, the combination of her identities meant that she had to navigate a complex web of societal expectations that often failed to recognize her multifaceted self.

Empowerment Through Defiance

Breaking free from societal expectations was not merely about rejecting norms; it was also about empowerment. Paula learned to embrace her differences as strengths rather than weaknesses. By challenging the stereotypes associated with her identity, she became a beacon of hope for others who felt trapped by societal constraints.

One powerful instance of her defiance occurred when she organized a protest against the exclusion of disabled individuals from LGBTQ spaces. This act of courage not only highlighted the need for intersectionality within activism but also inspired others to stand up against discrimination. Paula's leadership in this movement showcased the importance of advocating for oneself and others, emphasizing that breaking free from societal expectations is a collective endeavor.

Conclusion

In conclusion, Paula Lupi's journey of breaking free from societal expectations is a testament to the power of self-acceptance and activism. Through her defiance, she not only carved out a space for herself but also paved the way for future generations to challenge the norms that seek to limit their identities. By embracing her queer disabled identity, Paula exemplified the principles of gender performativity and intersectionality, demonstrating that true liberation lies in the courage to be unapologetically oneself. Her story serves as an inspiration for all those striving to break free from the chains of societal expectations, reminding us that our identities are not defined by others, but by our own choices and actions.

Developing a strong support network

In the journey of advocacy and personal growth, the importance of a strong support network cannot be overstated. For Paula Lupi, this network became a lifeline, providing emotional, social, and practical support as she navigated the complexities of her identity and activism. This section explores the theoretical underpinnings of support networks, the challenges faced in developing them, and the powerful examples of how Paula cultivated her own network.

Theoretical Framework

Support networks are often discussed in the context of social capital, which refers to the resources available to individuals through their social connections. According to Bourdieu (1986), social capital is a fundamental aspect of one's identity and can significantly influence an individual's capacity to mobilize resources for personal and collective goals. In the context of LGBTQ and disability rights, a strong support network can serve as a critical buffer against discrimination and marginalization.

The social support theory (Cohen & Wills, 1985) also provides insight into how emotional and instrumental support can mitigate stress and enhance well-being. This theory posits that social support can be categorized into three types: emotional support, informational support, and tangible support. Each type plays a crucial role in fostering resilience and empowerment among individuals facing societal challenges.

Challenges in Developing a Support Network

While the benefits of a support network are clear, developing one can be fraught with challenges, particularly for individuals from marginalized communities. Paula faced several obstacles in her quest to build a robust network:

- **Isolation and Alienation:** Many LGBTQ individuals experience feelings of isolation, especially in environments that are not accepting. Paula often felt alienated during her formative years, which made it difficult to connect with like-minded individuals.

- **Discrimination:** The intersectionality of Paula's identity as a queer disabled woman meant that she faced unique forms of discrimination that could hinder her ability to form connections. This discrimination often manifested in both overt and subtle ways, leading to mistrust and hesitance in reaching out to others.

- **Lack of Representation:** In many spaces, there was a notable absence of representation for individuals with both LGBTQ and disability identities. This lack of visibility made it challenging for Paula to find peers who could truly understand her experiences.

Building the Network: Strategies and Examples

Despite these challenges, Paula took proactive steps to cultivate a support network that would empower her both personally and in her activism. Her journey exemplifies several effective strategies:

- **Joining LGBTQ Organizations:** Paula began her journey by joining local LGBTQ organizations, where she met individuals who shared her passion for advocacy. These organizations provided a platform for her to connect with others and share experiences, laying the groundwork for lasting friendships.
- **Engaging in Intersectional Activism:** By participating in intersectional activism, Paula found allies who understood the complexities of her identity. Collaborating with disability rights groups allowed her to forge connections with individuals who faced similar challenges, thereby expanding her support network.
- **Utilizing Social Media:** In an age where digital connectivity is paramount, Paula harnessed the power of social media to reach out to others. Online platforms provided her with the opportunity to engage with activists globally, share her story, and find solidarity in shared experiences.
- **Creating Safe Spaces:** Paula took the initiative to create safe spaces for discussions about LGBTQ and disability issues. These gatherings not only fostered community but also allowed individuals to express their concerns and support one another in a nurturing environment.
- **Mentorship and Peer Support:** Recognizing the value of mentorship, Paula sought out mentors who could guide her through the complexities of activism. In turn, she also became a mentor to younger activists, creating a reciprocal support system that enriched her network.

The Impact of a Strong Support Network

The development of a strong support network had profound implications for Paula's personal and professional life. Research indicates that individuals with robust support systems experience lower levels of stress and greater overall well-being (Taylor, 2011). For Paula, her network became a source of strength and resilience, allowing her to:

- **Enhance Advocacy Efforts:** With the backing of her network, Paula was able to amplify her voice and engage more effectively in advocacy efforts. The collective power of her support network meant that her initiatives gained traction and visibility.
- **Foster Personal Growth:** The emotional support she received from her network encouraged Paula to embrace her identity fully. This acceptance was crucial in her journey towards self-love and empowerment.
- **Overcome Adversity:** Facing backlash and discrimination is an inevitable part of activism. However, Paula's support network provided her with the encouragement and resources needed to persevere through challenging times, reinforcing her commitment to her cause.
- **Inspire Others:** As Paula shared her journey and the importance of community, she inspired others to seek out and build their own support networks. Her story became a testament to the transformative power of connection and solidarity.

Conclusion

In conclusion, developing a strong support network was a pivotal aspect of Paula Lupi's journey as an LGBTQ activist. Through the lens of social capital and social support theory, we can understand the profound impact that such networks have on personal well-being and collective advocacy. Despite the challenges she faced, Paula's determination to build connections and foster community not only enriched her life but also strengthened the broader movement for LGBTQ and disability rights. Her legacy serves as a reminder of the power of solidarity and the vital role that support networks play in the fight for equality and justice.

Empowering others through personal storytelling

In the realm of activism, personal storytelling emerges as a powerful tool for empowerment, particularly within marginalized communities such as LGBTQ individuals and those with disabilities. Paula Lupi recognized early on that sharing her own experiences could resonate with others facing similar struggles, fostering a sense of connection and solidarity. This section delves into the significance of personal narratives in activism, the challenges they address, and real-world examples that illustrate their impact.

Theoretical Framework

The theoretical underpinnings of personal storytelling in activism can be traced to narrative theory, which posits that stories shape our understanding of the world and ourselves. According to Bruner (1991), narratives are fundamental to human cognition and communication, allowing individuals to make sense of their experiences. In the context of LGBTQ and disability rights, storytelling serves several functions:

- **Identity Formation:** Sharing personal stories helps individuals articulate their identities, fostering a sense of belonging and community.
- **Awareness Raising:** Personal narratives can illuminate the unique challenges faced by marginalized groups, challenging societal norms and prejudices.
- **Empathy Building:** Hearing the lived experiences of others cultivates empathy, bridging gaps between different communities and fostering understanding.

Challenges Addressed

Despite its power, personal storytelling in activism is not without challenges. Activists like Paula often grapple with:

- **Vulnerability:** Sharing personal stories requires a level of vulnerability that can be daunting, especially when recounting painful experiences.
- **Misinterpretation:** There is a risk that personal narratives may be misinterpreted or co-opted by those outside the community, diluting their original message.
- **Emotional Labor:** The act of recounting traumatic experiences can be emotionally taxing, necessitating self-care and support systems.

Examples of Empowerment through Storytelling

Paula's journey exemplifies how personal storytelling can empower others. Her involvement in local LGBTQ organizations allowed her to share her narrative, which often included themes of resilience, identity, and the fight against discrimination. This not only validated her experiences but also inspired others to share their stories, creating a ripple effect within the community.

One notable example is the "StoryCorps" project, which encourages individuals to share their personal stories in a safe environment. Through this initiative, LGBTQ individuals have voiced their experiences with coming out, navigating relationships, and confronting societal barriers. The impact of these shared narratives is profound; they not only foster a sense of community but also serve as educational tools for allies and advocates.

The Role of Digital Platforms

In the digital age, platforms such as social media have revolutionized personal storytelling, allowing activists like Paula to reach broader audiences. The hashtag movement, particularly on platforms like Twitter and Instagram, has enabled individuals to share their stories in concise yet impactful ways. For instance, the hashtag #ThisIsMe has been instrumental in encouraging LGBTQ individuals and disabled persons to share their narratives, showcasing the diversity of experiences within these communities.

Conclusion

Empowering others through personal storytelling is a cornerstone of Paula Lupi's activism. By sharing her own journey, she not only validated her experiences but also created a space for others to do the same. This practice fosters community, builds empathy, and challenges societal norms, ultimately contributing to the broader fight for LGBTQ and disability rights. As we continue to navigate the complexities of identity and activism, the importance of personal narratives remains clear: they are not just stories; they are powerful catalysts for change.

Bibliography

[1] Bruner, J. (1991). *The narrative construction of reality*. Critical Inquiry, 18(1), 1-21.

Overcoming internalized prejudice and self-doubt

Internalized prejudice and self-doubt can be significant barriers for individuals within marginalized communities, including LGBTQ individuals and those with disabilities. Paula Lupi's journey illustrates the complex interplay between societal expectations, personal identity, and the struggle for self-acceptance. This section explores the theory behind internalized prejudice, its manifestations, and the strategies Paula employed to overcome these challenges.

Understanding Internalized Prejudice

Internalized prejudice refers to the process by which individuals adopt the negative beliefs and stereotypes that society holds about their own group. According to [?], this phenomenon can lead to a diminished sense of self-worth and a disconnection from one's identity. The psychological implications of internalized prejudice often manifest as self-doubt, anxiety, and depression.

The theory of *internalized oppression* posits that marginalized groups may internalize the negative messages about their identities, resulting in feelings of shame and inferiority. This theory is particularly relevant for Paula as she navigated her identity as a queer disabled woman in a society that often marginalizes both aspects of her identity.

Manifestations of Self-Doubt

For Paula, self-doubt took many forms. She often grappled with feelings of inadequacy, questioning whether she was deserving of love and acceptance. These feelings were compounded by societal messages that marginalized her identity, leading her to doubt her capabilities as an activist and leader.

The impact of these feelings can be understood through the lens of *Cognitive Dissonance Theory*, which suggests that individuals experience discomfort when their beliefs and actions are inconsistent. Paula's activism required her to advocate for rights she sometimes felt unworthy to claim, creating a cycle of self-doubt that threatened to undermine her efforts.

Strategies for Overcoming Challenges

Paula employed several strategies to combat internalized prejudice and self-doubt:

1. **Building a Support Network:** Paula recognized the importance of surrounding herself with supportive friends and allies who validated her experiences and identity. This network provided emotional support and encouragement, helping her to challenge negative self-perceptions.

2. **Engaging in Activism:** By actively participating in LGBTQ and disability rights movements, Paula found empowerment in her advocacy. Engaging with others who shared similar experiences allowed her to reframe her identity from one of shame to one of pride.

3. **Personal Storytelling:** Sharing her experiences through storytelling became a vital tool for Paula. By articulating her journey, she not only reclaimed her narrative but also inspired others to confront their own internalized prejudices. This practice aligns with the concept of *narrative therapy*, which posits that storytelling can help individuals reshape their identities and experiences.

4. **Therapeutic Interventions:** Paula sought therapy to address her feelings of self-doubt. Cognitive Behavioral Therapy (CBT) was particularly effective in helping her identify and challenge negative thought patterns. The formula for cognitive restructuring in CBT can be expressed as:

$$\text{Cognitive Restructuring} = \text{Identifying Negative Thoughts} + \text{Challenging Beliefs} +$$

This systematic approach allowed Paula to transform her internal dialogue and foster self-acceptance.

5. **Education and Awareness:** Paula dedicated herself to educating herself about LGBTQ and disability rights. Understanding the historical context of oppression and the resilience of activists before her helped her to contextualize her own struggles within a larger narrative of resistance and empowerment.

Examples of Transformation

Paula's journey is marked by several pivotal moments that exemplify her growth in overcoming internalized prejudice. One such moment occurred during a community organizing event, where she shared her story of navigating both her queer identity and disability. The overwhelmingly positive response from attendees reinforced her belief in the power of her voice and the importance of her experiences.

Additionally, Paula's involvement in mentorship programs allowed her to guide younger activists who faced similar struggles. By empowering others, she not only fostered a sense of community but also solidified her own self-worth.

Conclusion

Overcoming internalized prejudice and self-doubt is a multifaceted process that requires resilience, support, and self-reflection. Paula Lupi's journey exemplifies the power of community, activism, and personal growth in dismantling the barriers imposed by societal expectations. Her story serves as an inspiration for others who may be grappling with similar challenges, highlighting the importance of self-acceptance and the transformative potential of advocacy.

[?] emphasizes that "the journey to self-acceptance is often nonlinear, marked by setbacks and triumphs." Paula's experiences reflect this truth, demonstrating that while the path may be fraught with challenges, it is ultimately one of empowerment and liberation.

Embracing her identity as a queer disabled woman

In a world that often seeks to categorize individuals into neat boxes, Paula Lupi's journey towards embracing her identity as a queer disabled woman is a testament to the complexity of intersectionality. This section delves into the multifaceted layers of her identity and how they shaped her activism, self-perception, and relationships.

From an early age, Paula faced the dual challenges of navigating a society that often marginalized both her sexual orientation and her disability. The intersectionality theory, as proposed by Kimberlé Crenshaw, posits that individuals with overlapping identities experience unique forms of discrimination and privilege. For Paula, this meant that her experiences as a queer person were compounded by societal perceptions of disability, leading to a complex interplay of acceptance and rejection.

$$D = \frac{P_Q + P_D}{2} \qquad (22)$$

Where: - D represents the overall discrimination faced. - P_Q is the level of prejudice against queer individuals. - P_D is the level of prejudice against disabled individuals.

As Paula began to explore her queer identity, she found herself grappling with societal expectations that often dictated how disabled individuals should behave and present themselves. The stereotypes surrounding disability frequently portrayed disabled people as asexual or incapable of romantic relationships, which starkly contrasted with her burgeoning self-awareness as a sexual being. This dissonance fueled her determination to challenge these misconceptions.

Paula's journey of self-acceptance was not without its struggles. Internalized ableism and homophobia often surfaced, leading her to question her worth and place within both the LGBTQ community and the disabled community. She encountered narratives that suggested her disability was a hindrance to her identity as a queer woman, which made her feel like an outsider in both spaces.

To combat these feelings, Paula sought solace in supportive communities that celebrated diversity and inclusivity. Through participation in LGBTQ and disability advocacy groups, she found allies who understood her struggles and validated her experiences. These safe spaces allowed her to share her story, fostering a sense of belonging and empowerment.

An example of this empowerment can be seen in the creation of workshops and support groups aimed at queer disabled individuals. Paula actively participated in and later organized these gatherings, which provided a platform for individuals to express their identities without fear of judgment. The workshops emphasized the importance of self-love, encouraging attendees to embrace their multifaceted identities and challenge societal norms.

In her personal relationships, Paula learned to navigate the complexities of intimacy as a queer disabled woman. She faced unique challenges in dating, often confronting biases from potential partners who were uneducated about disability or uncomfortable with her identity. However, she also experienced profound moments of connection with those who celebrated her whole self. These relationships reinforced her belief that love and acceptance are not bound by societal standards.

Furthermore, Paula's advocacy work was deeply informed by her identity. She often highlighted the importance of inclusive representation in LGBTQ and disability activism, arguing that the voices of queer disabled individuals must be amplified. This perspective was not merely theoretical; it was grounded in her lived experiences. She fought against the marginalization of voices within her community, striving to ensure that queer disabled individuals were not only included in discussions but were also at the forefront of advocacy efforts.

$$A = \sum_{i=1}^{n} R_i \qquad (23)$$

Where: - A represents the total impact of advocacy efforts. - R_i is the representation of each individual voice in the community.

Through her activism, Paula aimed to dismantle the barriers faced by queer disabled individuals, advocating for policies that recognized the intersectionality of identity. She worked tirelessly to ensure that healthcare, education, and social services were accessible and inclusive, addressing the unique challenges faced by those at the intersection of queerness and disability.

Ultimately, Paula's journey towards embracing her identity as a queer disabled woman was one of resilience and empowerment. By confronting societal norms and advocating for inclusivity, she not only forged a path for herself but also paved the way for future generations. Her story serves as a powerful reminder of the importance of embracing all facets of one's identity and the strength that comes from community and solidarity.

In conclusion, Paula Lupi's experience as a queer disabled woman highlights the necessity of intersectional approaches in activism. By recognizing and celebrating the complexity of identities, advocates can create more inclusive spaces that honor the diverse experiences of individuals. Paula's legacy is one of empowerment, reminding us that embracing our identities is a vital step towards achieving equality and justice for all.

The journey towards self-empowerment and self-advocacy

The journey towards self-empowerment and self-advocacy is a transformative process, particularly for individuals like Paula Lupi, who navigate the complexities of identity as a queer disabled woman. This journey is not merely about personal growth but also about reclaiming one's voice in a society that often marginalizes and silences underrepresented communities.

Self-empowerment can be defined as the process of gaining the confidence and strength to make choices and decisions that affect one's life. According to [?], self-empowerment involves three key components: the development of personal skills, the establishment of supportive relationships, and the engagement in advocacy efforts. These components are essential for individuals to assert their rights and advocate for themselves and others.

Paula's path to self-advocacy began in her formative years, where she faced societal expectations that often contradicted her identity. The challenges she encountered, such as navigating a school environment that was not always inclusive, served as catalysts for her self-discovery. This environment was rife with biases and stereotypes, which, while disheartening, ignited a fire within her to challenge the status quo.

One significant theoretical framework that can be applied to Paula's journey is the **Empowerment Theory**, which posits that empowerment occurs when individuals gain control over their lives through knowledge, skills, and support. This theory emphasizes the importance of understanding the systemic barriers that contribute to oppression. For Paula, recognizing these barriers was crucial; it allowed her to identify the areas where she could effect change, both personally and within her community.

The process of self-advocacy requires individuals to articulate their needs and rights clearly. In Paula's case, she began by sharing her experiences and challenges with her peers, which helped her to build a network of support. For example, during her high school years, she initiated discussions about the lack of resources for LGBTQ and disabled students, which not only raised awareness but also fostered a sense of solidarity among her classmates. This early activism was pivotal in shaping her identity as a self-advocate.

Moreover, Paula's journey was marked by the adoption of various strategies to empower herself and others. One such strategy involved engaging in community organizing, where she collaborated with local LGBTQ groups to create safe spaces for dialogue and support. This grassroots approach not only amplified her voice but also provided her with the tools to advocate effectively for systemic changes.

A poignant example of her advocacy work is her involvement in the campaign for inclusive education policies in Portugal. Paula recognized that many disabled LGBTQ students faced unique challenges that were often overlooked in mainstream discussions about education. By sharing her story and the stories of her peers, she was able to highlight the need for tailored support systems that acknowledged the intersectionality of their identities.

In addition to community organizing, Paula also embraced the power of storytelling as a means of self-advocacy. Research by [?] indicates that personal narratives can significantly influence public perception and foster empathy. Paula's willingness to share her journey not only empowered her but also inspired others to embrace their identities and advocate for their rights. Her story became a beacon of hope for many who felt isolated and unheard.

However, the journey towards self-empowerment is not without its challenges. Paula faced significant backlash from those who disagreed with her activism, which tested her resilience and commitment to her cause. The psychological impact of such opposition can be profound, often leading to feelings of self-doubt and questioning one's worth. To combat this, Paula relied on the support of her community, which provided her with a sense of belonging and validation.

The concept of **intersectionality**, as introduced by [3], plays a crucial role in understanding Paula's advocacy. Intersectionality acknowledges that individuals experience multiple, overlapping identities that shape their experiences of oppression and privilege. For Paula, this meant recognizing the unique challenges faced by queer disabled individuals, which informed her approach to activism. By advocating for intersectional policies, she aimed to ensure that the voices of those at the margins were included in the broader discourse on rights and representation.

Ultimately, Paula's journey towards self-empowerment and self-advocacy is a testament to the power of resilience and community. By embracing her identity and advocating for herself and others, she not only transformed her own life but also inspired countless others to do the same. As she often reminds her peers, "Your voice is your power; use it to create change." This mantra encapsulates the essence of her journey, emphasizing the importance of self-advocacy in the ongoing fight for equality and justice.

In conclusion, the journey towards self-empowerment and self-advocacy is a multifaceted process that requires individuals to confront societal barriers, build supportive networks, and engage in advocacy efforts. For Paula Lupi, this journey has been marked by personal growth, resilience, and a commitment to amplifying the voices of marginalized communities. Through her activism, she has laid the groundwork for future generations to continue the fight for LGBTQ and disability rights, ensuring that no one is left behind in the quest for equality.

The Activist Emerges

Witnessing the struggles of the LGBTQ community

Growing up in the vibrant streets of Lisbon, Paula Lupi was not just a passive observer of the world around her; she was an astute witness to the myriad struggles faced by the LGBTQ community. The colorful facades of her city, often draped in the hues of pride flags, masked the underlying currents of discrimination, prejudice, and systemic inequality that many individuals faced daily. This juxtaposition of beauty and hardship ignited a fire within Paula, urging her to delve deeper into the challenges that plagued her community.

The struggles of the LGBTQ community can be understood through various theoretical frameworks, including the Social Model of Disability and Queer Theory. The Social Model of Disability posits that it is society's failure to accommodate individuals with disabilities that creates barriers, rather than the disabilities themselves. Similarly, Queer Theory challenges the heteronormative assumptions that dominate societal structures, advocating for a more inclusive understanding of gender and sexuality. These frameworks helped Paula contextualize the challenges she observed, allowing her to see the intersections of disability and LGBTQ rights as not merely separate issues but as intertwined struggles for dignity and respect.

One of the most poignant experiences that Paula witnessed was the impact of societal stigma on LGBTQ youth. Reports indicate that LGBTQ youth are significantly more likely to experience bullying, harassment, and mental health issues compared to their heterosexual peers. According to a study conducted by the Williams Institute, LGBTQ youth are nearly three times more likely to attempt suicide than their heterosexual counterparts. Paula saw firsthand the toll that such discrimination took on her friends and peers, who often found themselves grappling with feelings of isolation and despair.

For example, she recalls her friend Miguel, who, despite his vibrant personality, faced relentless bullying at school for being openly gay. The emotional scars from these experiences manifested in Miguel's declining mental health, which culminated in a suicide attempt during their final year of high school. This tragedy propelled Paula into action, as she realized that the silence surrounding such issues only compounded the pain. She began to organize support groups, aiming to provide safe spaces for LGBTQ youth to share their experiences, find solidarity, and foster resilience against societal pressures.

Furthermore, Paula recognized the systemic barriers that perpetuated discrimination against LGBTQ individuals. The legal landscape in Portugal, while progressive in some aspects, still harbored gaps that left many vulnerable. For instance, while same-sex marriage was legalized in 2010, adoption rights for same-sex couples remained a contentious issue. In 2019, a report by ILGA-Europe highlighted that despite legislative advancements, LGBTQ individuals in Portugal still faced discrimination in areas such as housing, employment, and healthcare. Paula's observations of these inequalities motivated her to engage with local advocacy groups, where she began to learn about the legal intricacies that hindered progress and the importance of intersectional advocacy.

The concept of intersectionality, introduced by Kimberlé Crenshaw, became a crucial lens through which Paula viewed the struggles of her community. Intersectionality emphasizes that individuals can experience multiple forms of discrimination simultaneously, and it is essential to consider how these intersecting identities shape one's experiences. Paula's own identity as a queer disabled woman placed her at the crossroads of various struggles, allowing her to empathize with those who faced compounded challenges. She understood that the fight for LGBTQ rights could not be divorced from the fight for disability rights, as both groups often found themselves marginalized within broader societal narratives.

In her quest for justice, Paula also sought to amplify the voices of those who were often silenced. She participated in community forums, where she listened to the stories of LGBTQ individuals from diverse backgrounds, each with unique experiences shaped by their race, gender, and socioeconomic status. One such forum featured a panel of speakers from the Black LGBTQ community, who shared their experiences of discrimination not only based on their sexual orientation but also their race. These narratives underscored the importance of inclusive activism, as Paula realized that the struggles of LGBTQ individuals could not be generalized; they were nuanced and deeply rooted in individual contexts.

As Paula continued to witness the struggles of the LGBTQ community, she became acutely aware of the role that visibility played in advocacy. The power of representation cannot be overstated; seeing individuals who share similar identities in positions of influence can inspire hope and encourage others to embrace their true selves. Paula recognized that her own journey, marked by challenges and triumphs, could serve as a beacon for others navigating their paths. She began to share her story publicly, using her platform to raise awareness about the issues faced by LGBTQ individuals, especially those with disabilities.

Through her advocacy, Paula sought to challenge the narratives that perpetuated stigma and discrimination. She collaborated with local artists and activists to create multimedia projects that highlighted the experiences of LGBTQ individuals, showcasing their resilience and creativity. One project, titled "Voices of Pride," featured a series of short films depicting the lives of LGBTQ individuals in Lisbon, emphasizing their struggles, dreams, and triumphs. This project not only provided a platform for marginalized voices but also fostered dialogue within the community, encouraging empathy and understanding.

In conclusion, witnessing the struggles of the LGBTQ community profoundly shaped Paula Lupi's journey as an activist. Her experiences, grounded in the realities of discrimination and systemic inequality, fueled her passion for advocacy.

By employing theoretical frameworks such as the Social Model of Disability and Queer Theory, Paula was able to contextualize the challenges faced by her community, while also embracing the principles of intersectionality to advocate for inclusive change. Through her work, she aimed to create a world where every individual, regardless of their identity, could live authentically and without fear of discrimination. Paula's commitment to amplifying marginalized voices and fostering solidarity within the LGBTQ community laid the groundwork for her lifelong dedication to activism, setting the stage for her emergence as a prominent advocate for LGBTQ and disability rights.

Joining local LGBTQ organizations and collectives

The journey of activism for Paula Lupi began in earnest when she decided to join local LGBTQ organizations and collectives in Lisbon. This pivotal step not only marked her entry into a vibrant community but also laid the groundwork for her future endeavors in advocacy. In this section, we explore the significance of collective action, the challenges faced by LGBTQ organizations, and the transformative power of community involvement.

The Importance of Collective Action

Collective action is a cornerstone of social movements, particularly within marginalized communities. According to social movement theory, collective action occurs when individuals come together to achieve a common goal that they cannot accomplish alone. This theory is encapsulated in the following equation:

$$A = f(N, R, E) \qquad (24)$$

Where:

- A represents the level of activism,
- N denotes the number of participants,
- R is the resources available (financial, human, etc.),
- E signifies the external environment (political climate, societal attitudes).

In Paula's case, joining local LGBTQ organizations provided her with a network of support, resources, and a platform to amplify her voice. The collective nature of these organizations fostered a sense of belonging and solidarity, enabling Paula to connect with others who shared her experiences and struggles.

Challenges Faced by LGBTQ Organizations

Despite the empowering nature of LGBTQ organizations, they often grapple with significant challenges. One major issue is the internal conflict regarding representation and inclusivity. Many organizations face criticism for not adequately representing the diverse spectrum of identities within the LGBTQ community, particularly those at the intersections of race, disability, and socioeconomic status.

For instance, Paula observed that some organizations prioritized mainstream LGBTQ issues while sidelining the unique challenges faced by queer disabled individuals. This lack of intersectionality can lead to feelings of alienation among marginalized members, as noted by Crenshaw's intersectionality theory, which emphasizes that individuals experience overlapping systems of discrimination.

$$D = f(I_1, I_2, I_3, \ldots, I_n) \tag{25}$$

Where:

- D is the level of discrimination experienced,
- I_n represents various identities (e.g., race, gender, disability).

Paula's commitment to advocating for intersectionality within these organizations became a driving force in her activism. She aimed to address the gaps in representation and ensure that the voices of the most marginalized were heard.

Transformative Power of Community Involvement

Joining local LGBTQ organizations was not merely a step in Paula's activism; it was a transformative experience that shaped her identity and purpose. Engaging with these collectives allowed her to participate in grassroots organizing, where she learned the importance of mobilization and advocacy.

One notable example was her involvement in organizing a pride event that aimed to celebrate diversity within the LGBTQ community while also raising awareness about disability rights. This event highlighted the intersectional nature of identity and the necessity for inclusivity in pride celebrations. Paula's leadership in this initiative demonstrated her ability to galvanize support and foster collaboration among diverse groups.

Moreover, the collective efforts of these organizations often resulted in tangible outcomes, such as policy changes and increased visibility for LGBTQ issues. For instance, a campaign initiated by Paula and her peers successfully lobbied for more inclusive policies in local schools, ensuring that LGBTQ youth received the support and representation they deserved.

Conclusion

Joining local LGBTQ organizations and collectives was a defining moment in Paula Lupi's journey as an activist. It provided her with the tools, support, and community necessary to navigate the complexities of advocacy. Through collective action, Paula not only found her voice but also became a catalyst for change, advocating for a more inclusive and equitable society for all. Her experiences within these organizations shaped her understanding of intersectionality and the importance of amplifying marginalized voices, setting the stage for her future endeavors in the fight for LGBTQ and disability rights.

Participating in protests and demonstrations

Paula Lupi's journey into activism was marked by her passionate participation in protests and demonstrations, pivotal moments that shaped her identity and commitment to LGBTQ and disability rights. These events were not merely gatherings; they were powerful expressions of solidarity, resistance, and the demand for justice.

The Significance of Protests

Protests serve as a crucial mechanism for marginalized communities to voice their grievances and demand change. According to the *Social Movement Theory*, collective action is essential for social change, as it mobilizes individuals around shared interests and grievances. This theory posits that protests can catalyze awareness, influence public opinion, and ultimately lead to policy changes.

$$P = f(A, C, O) \tag{26}$$

Where P represents the level of protest participation, A is the awareness of issues, C is the collective identity of the group, and O is the organizational capacity of the movement.

In Portugal, the LGBTQ community faced significant challenges, including discrimination, violence, and lack of legal recognition. Paula recognized that participating in protests was not just an act of defiance but a necessary step toward dismantling these systemic barriers.

Early Experiences in Protests

Paula's first protest experience occurred during a vibrant Pride parade in Lisbon, where she felt the electric energy of thousands marching for equality. This event was a vivid illustration of intersectionality, showcasing not only LGBTQ rights but also the voices of disabled individuals advocating for their rights. The sense of community and shared purpose ignited a fire within her, compelling her to take a more active role in advocacy.

Organizing and Mobilizing

As Paula became more entrenched in activism, she transitioned from participant to organizer. She began to understand the complexities of mobilizing individuals for a common cause. This involved strategizing, building coalitions, and fostering a sense of urgency among community members. For instance, during the annual International Day Against Homophobia, Transphobia, and Biphobia, Paula played a crucial role in organizing a demonstration that highlighted the intersections of LGBTQ and disability rights.

In her organizing efforts, Paula often employed techniques derived from *Grassroots Mobilization Theory*, which emphasizes the importance of local engagement and personal connections in building a movement. She utilized social media platforms to spread awareness, share stories, and rally support. This approach not only increased participation but also fostered a sense of ownership among community members.

Facing Challenges

Participating in protests was not without its challenges. Paula faced hostility from counter-protesters and systemic barriers that sought to undermine the movement. The backlash often manifested in the form of aggressive rhetoric, physical threats, and attempts to delegitimize the cause.

In one notable instance, during a protest advocating for inclusive healthcare policies, Paula and her allies encountered a group opposing LGBTQ rights. The confrontation escalated, highlighting the stark divisions within society. However, Paula remained resolute, using her platform to emphasize the need for dialogue and understanding, even in the face of adversity.

The Impact of Protests

The impact of Paula's participation in protests extended beyond immediate outcomes. These events served as a catalyst for broader societal change, inspiring others to join the fight for equality. The visibility of protests often attracted media attention, amplifying the message of the LGBTQ and disability rights movements.

For example, after a particularly large demonstration advocating for marriage equality, local news outlets began to cover the stories of LGBTQ individuals and their struggles, shifting public perception and fostering a more inclusive dialogue. Paula understood that media representation was critical in shaping societal attitudes and used her experiences to advocate for better representation of marginalized communities.

Conclusion

In summary, Paula Lupi's participation in protests and demonstrations was a defining aspect of her activism. Through these collective actions, she not only found her voice but also amplified the voices of those who had been silenced. The protests she organized and participated in were not just events; they were transformative experiences that laid the groundwork for a more inclusive society. Paula's unwavering commitment to activism in the face of adversity exemplifies the power of collective action in the ongoing struggle for LGBTQ and disability rights.

As she continued her journey, the lessons learned from these protests would inform her future endeavors, shaping her into a formidable advocate for change. The spirit of resilience and solidarity she experienced would become the cornerstone of her activism, inspiring countless others to join the fight for justice.

Becoming a prominent voice for LGBTQ rights

In the vibrant streets of Lisbon, where the sun casts a golden hue over cobblestone roads, Paula Lupi emerged as a beacon of hope and resilience for the LGBTQ community. Her journey to prominence was not merely a personal triumph; it was a collective struggle against the tides of discrimination and social injustice that had long plagued marginalized communities. Paula's rise as a prominent voice for LGBTQ rights can be understood through a combination of personal experiences, theoretical frameworks, and the pressing need for advocacy in a society grappling with deeply entrenched prejudices.

At the heart of Paula's activism was her understanding of the **social construction of identity**. Theories of identity politics highlight how individuals navigate their identities within the socio-political landscape. Paula recognized that her identity as a queer disabled woman placed her at the intersection of multiple marginalized groups, thus amplifying her commitment to advocacy. This intersectionality, a term coined by Kimberlé Crenshaw, emphasizes the interconnected nature of social categorizations and the unique challenges faced by those who embody multiple identities.

$$I = \{C, S, D\} \tag{27}$$

where I represents identity, C is sexual orientation, S is social status, and D is disability. Paula's activism was driven by the understanding that these elements do not exist in isolation; rather, they interact to create a complex web of experiences that require nuanced approaches to advocacy.

Paula's initial foray into activism was marked by her participation in local LGBTQ organizations. This grassroots involvement provided her with a platform to voice her concerns and connect with others who shared similar struggles. As she became more engaged, she witnessed firsthand the systemic issues that plagued the community, including discrimination in employment, healthcare access, and social services. The lack of representation and visibility for queer disabled individuals in these discussions fueled her determination to become a prominent advocate.

One of the pivotal moments in Paula's journey was her involvement in the **Lisbon Pride Parade**. This annual event, which celebrates LGBTQ identities and rights, became a powerful stage for her to articulate the concerns of the community. Paula seized the opportunity to speak publicly, using her platform to address not only LGBTQ rights but also the pressing need for disability inclusion. Her speeches resonated with the crowd, drawing attention to the often-overlooked intersection of these two identities.

Paula's advocacy was further bolstered by her ability to harness the power of **storytelling**. As she shared her personal narrative, she illuminated the challenges faced by LGBTQ individuals, particularly those with disabilities. This narrative approach aligned with the **narrative theory**, which posits that storytelling is a fundamental way through which individuals make sense of their experiences and communicate their identities. Paula's story was not just her own; it reflected the collective struggles of many, creating a sense of solidarity and urgency within the community.

Theoretical frameworks such as **Framing Theory** also played a significant role in Paula's rise as an advocate. This theory suggests that the way issues are presented influences public perception and discourse. Paula adeptly framed LGBTQ rights as human rights, emphasizing the universal need for dignity and respect. By shifting the narrative from one of stigma to one of equality, she was able to engage a broader audience, including allies who may not have previously considered the implications of LGBTQ advocacy.

$$F = \{R, P, A\} \qquad (28)$$

where F represents framing, R is rights, P is public perception, and A is activism. Paula's effective framing of LGBTQ issues facilitated a shift in public perception, allowing her to garner support from diverse sectors of society.

Despite her growing prominence, Paula faced significant challenges. The backlash from conservative factions within society often manifested in hostility and discrimination, both online and offline. This opposition served as a constant reminder of the work that lay ahead. However, Paula's resilience shone through; she utilized these challenges as fuel for her advocacy, transforming adversity into a rallying cry for change.

In her quest to become a prominent voice for LGBTQ rights, Paula understood the importance of building alliances. She actively sought collaborations with other social movements, recognizing that the fight for justice is interconnected. By forging partnerships with disability rights organizations, feminist groups, and other marginalized communities, Paula expanded her reach and influence. This approach not only amplified her voice but also fostered a sense of unity among diverse groups advocating for social change.

As Paula continued to rise in prominence, she became increasingly aware of the power of **media representation**. The media plays a crucial role in shaping public discourse, and Paula leveraged this to her advantage. She engaged with journalists and media outlets to ensure that LGBTQ issues were covered accurately and sensitively. This engagement not only raised awareness but also humanized the struggles faced by the community.

The culmination of Paula's efforts was evident when she was invited to speak at international conferences, representing Portugal on the global stage. Her eloquence and passion resonated with audiences far and wide, solidifying her status as a prominent advocate. Paula's journey illustrates the profound impact that one individual's voice can have in challenging societal norms and advocating for change.

In conclusion, Paula Lupi's emergence as a prominent voice for LGBTQ rights was a multifaceted journey rooted in personal experiences, theoretical frameworks, and a commitment to social justice. Her ability to navigate the complexities of identity, harness the power of storytelling, and build alliances positioned her as a leading advocate in the fight for equality. Through her unwavering dedication, Paula not only amplified her voice but also inspired countless others to join the movement, leaving an indelible mark on the landscape of LGBTQ advocacy in Portugal and beyond.

The importance of intersectionality in activism

Intersectionality is a critical framework in contemporary activism, particularly within the realms of LGBTQ and disability rights. Coined by legal scholar Kimberlé Crenshaw in 1989, intersectionality examines how various social identities—such as race, gender, sexual orientation, disability, and class—interact and contribute to unique experiences of oppression and privilege. Understanding intersectionality is essential for activists like Paula Lupi, who advocate for rights across multiple marginalized identities.

At its core, intersectionality posits that individuals do not experience discrimination or privilege in isolation; rather, they navigate a complex web of social categorizations that can amplify or mitigate their experiences. For example, a queer disabled woman like Paula faces distinct challenges that differ from those encountered by a cisgender, able-bodied individual. This complexity highlights the necessity for an inclusive approach to activism, which recognizes the varied experiences of individuals within the LGBTQ community and beyond.

One of the primary problems that arise in activism without an intersectional lens is the risk of marginalizing voices that are already silenced. For instance, LGBTQ activism has historically centered on the experiences of white, cisgender gay men, often sidelining the voices of queer women, people of color, and those with disabilities. This oversight can lead to policies and advocacy efforts that fail to address the specific needs of these groups, perpetuating cycles of oppression.

Consider the case of healthcare access for LGBTQ individuals. While many activists have fought for rights such as marriage equality, the intersection of LGBTQ and disability rights reveals additional layers of complexity. Queer disabled individuals may face barriers to accessing healthcare that are not merely about sexual orientation or gender identity but also about physical access, affordability, and the intersection of ableism with homophobia or transphobia. Without an intersectional approach, advocacy efforts may overlook the unique healthcare needs of these individuals, leaving them vulnerable and unsupported.

Moreover, intersectionality allows activists to build coalitions across various movements, fostering solidarity and shared goals. For instance, Paula Lupi's work emphasized the importance of collaborating with racial justice movements, recognizing that LGBTQ rights are inextricably linked to broader struggles against systemic racism. By uniting with other marginalized groups, activists can amplify their voices and create a more powerful collective impact. This approach was evident during events like Pride marches, where intersectional activism brought together various communities to advocate for comprehensive rights.

In practice, embracing intersectionality in activism means actively listening to and uplifting marginalized voices within the movement. It requires a commitment to understanding how different identities interact and shape experiences, as well as an awareness of the privileges one may hold. For Paula, this meant engaging with the stories of queer disabled individuals, recognizing their struggles, and advocating for policies that address their unique challenges.

Theoretical frameworks also support the importance of intersectionality in activism. The *matrix of domination*, as articulated by Patricia Hill Collins, illustrates how different forms of oppression are interrelated and how they can create distinct experiences for individuals based on their social identities. This perspective encourages activists to consider not only the individual aspects of identity but also how they intersect to produce complex social realities.

To further illustrate the significance of intersectionality, consider the example of employment discrimination. LGBTQ individuals with disabilities may face barriers in the workplace that are not solely based on their sexual orientation or disability status but are compounded by other factors such as race or gender. Research has shown that employers often hold biases that intersect, leading to higher rates of unemployment and underemployment among these individuals. Addressing these issues requires an intersectional lens that recognizes the multifaceted nature of discrimination.

In conclusion, the importance of intersectionality in activism cannot be overstated. For activists like Paula Lupi, understanding and applying an intersectional framework is crucial for creating inclusive and effective advocacy efforts. By recognizing the interconnectedness of various social identities, activists can work towards dismantling systemic oppression and fostering a more equitable society for all. Intersectionality not only enriches the discourse within movements but also enhances the potential for meaningful change that truly reflects the diverse experiences of those it aims to serve.

$$\text{Intersectionality} = \sum_{i=1}^{n} \text{Identity}_i \times \text{Oppression}_i \tag{29}$$

This equation symbolizes the cumulative effect of multiple identities and oppressions on an individual's experience, emphasizing the need for a holistic approach in activism that accounts for the complexities of each person's reality. By centering intersectionality in their work, activists can ensure that no one is left behind, paving the way for a future where equality and justice are attainable for all.

Advocating for disability rights within the LGBTQ community

Advocating for disability rights within the LGBTQ community is a crucial intersection that requires nuanced understanding and action. The LGBTQ community has made significant strides in gaining visibility and rights, yet the inclusion of disabled individuals within this movement often remains sidelined. This section explores the theoretical underpinnings, challenges, and practical examples of advocacy in this essential area.

Theoretical Framework

The intersectionality theory, coined by Kimberlé Crenshaw, serves as a foundational framework for understanding how various social identities—such as race, gender, sexual orientation, and disability—interact to create unique modes of discrimination and privilege. In the context of the LGBTQ community, the intersection of disability can lead to compounded marginalization.

$$D = f(L, Q, H) \tag{30}$$

Where:

- D = Disability experience
- L = LGBTQ identity
- Q = Quality of life indicators
- H = Historical context of disability rights

This equation illustrates that the experience of disability D is not solely defined by the disability itself but is influenced by one's LGBTQ identity L, quality of life Q, and the historical context H surrounding disability rights.

Challenges Faced

Despite the theoretical recognition of intersectionality, numerous challenges hinder effective advocacy for disability rights within the LGBTQ community:

- **Visibility and Representation:** Disabled LGBTQ individuals often find themselves invisible within both the LGBTQ movement and disability rights advocacy. This lack of representation can lead to policies and programs that do not address their specific needs.

- **Stereotypes and Prejudices:** There are pervasive stereotypes that portray disabled individuals as asexual or incapable of romantic relationships. These biases can lead to exclusion from LGBTQ spaces, which are often centered around sexual expression and identity.

- **Access to Resources:** Disabled LGBTQ individuals frequently face barriers in accessing healthcare, mental health services, and community support. These barriers are compounded by the stigma surrounding both disability and sexual orientation, leading to a lack of tailored resources.

- **Internalized Oppression:** Many disabled LGBTQ individuals may internalize societal prejudices, leading to self-doubt and reluctance to advocate for their rights. This internal conflict can hinder collective action and solidarity within the community.

Examples of Advocacy Efforts

Despite these challenges, several advocacy efforts have emerged to address the intersection of disability and LGBTQ rights:

- **Inclusive Policy Development:** Organizations like the Human Rights Campaign (HRC) have begun to recognize the importance of disability rights in their advocacy work. By developing inclusive policies that explicitly address the needs of disabled LGBTQ individuals, these organizations work towards a more equitable landscape.

- **Community Education:** Grassroots initiatives, such as workshops and seminars, aim to educate LGBTQ communities about the importance of including disability rights in their advocacy efforts. These programs often focus on dismantling stereotypes and fostering empathy through storytelling.

- **Collaborative Movements:** The collaboration between LGBTQ organizations and disability rights groups has led to powerful coalitions that amplify the voices of disabled individuals. An example is the partnership between the National LGBTQ Task Force and the American Association of People with Disabilities (AAPD), which aims to create a more inclusive environment for all.

- **Art and Activism:** Disabled LGBTQ artists have used their platforms to highlight the intersection of their identities through various forms of art.

For example, performance art and visual storytelling have become powerful mediums to express the unique challenges faced by this community, fostering awareness and empathy.

The Path Forward

To effectively advocate for disability rights within the LGBTQ community, a multi-faceted approach is essential. This includes:

- **Promoting Inclusive Spaces:** LGBTQ organizations must actively work to create accessible environments where disabled individuals feel welcome and valued. This may involve physical accessibility measures, as well as ensuring that events are inclusive of various needs.

- **Empowering Disabled Voices:** It is crucial to center the voices of disabled LGBTQ individuals in advocacy efforts. This can be achieved through leadership training, mentorship programs, and platforms that amplify their stories and experiences.

- **Advocating for Policy Changes:** Engaging in political advocacy to push for legislation that protects the rights of disabled LGBTQ individuals is vital. This includes fighting for healthcare access, anti-discrimination laws, and inclusive education policies.

- **Fostering Solidarity:** Building alliances between LGBTQ organizations and disability rights groups can lead to a stronger, united front in the fight for equality. Solidarity can be fostered through joint campaigns, shared resources, and mutual support.

In conclusion, advocating for disability rights within the LGBTQ community is an essential endeavor that requires commitment, understanding, and action. By recognizing the unique challenges faced by disabled LGBTQ individuals and working collaboratively to address these issues, the movement can become more inclusive, equitable, and powerful. Paula Lupi's journey as an activist exemplifies the importance of intersectional advocacy, paving the way for future generations to continue the fight for justice and equality for all.

Facing backlash and hostility

The journey of an activist is often riddled with challenges, and for Paula Lupi, facing backlash and hostility became a significant aspect of her advocacy for LGBTQ and disability rights. As she emerged as a prominent voice in these movements, she found herself at the crossroads of societal resistance and personal conviction.

Activism, by its very nature, disrupts the status quo. When Paula began to advocate for the rights of marginalized communities, she quickly encountered opposition from various sectors of society. This backlash was not merely a matter of differing opinions; it often manifested as personal attacks, threats, and concerted efforts to undermine her credibility.

One of the theoretical frameworks that can help us understand this phenomenon is the *Social Identity Theory*, which posits that individuals derive a sense of identity from the social groups to which they belong. For many who opposed Paula's activism, their identities were intertwined with traditional views on gender, sexuality, and disability. As Paula challenged these views, she inadvertently threatened the social identity of her opponents, leading to defensive reactions characterized by hostility.

For example, during a pivotal protest advocating for inclusive education policies, Paula faced a barrage of negative responses from conservative groups. These groups organized counter-protests, branding her as a "radical" and accusing her of promoting "immorality." Such rhetoric aimed to delegitimize her message and diminish her influence. The emotional toll of such hostility cannot be overstated; activists like Paula often grapple with feelings of isolation and self-doubt, questioning whether their efforts are worth the backlash they endure.

Moreover, the backlash Paula faced was compounded by the intersectionality of her identity as a queer disabled woman. Studies have shown that individuals who occupy multiple marginalized identities often experience compounded discrimination, referred to as *intersectional oppression*. This concept, articulated by Kimberlé Crenshaw, highlights how societal systems of power interact, creating unique challenges for those at the intersections of various identities. Paula's advocacy, which sought to uplift both LGBTQ and disability rights, made her a target for hostility from multiple fronts, including those within her own community who felt that her focus on intersectionality diluted their specific struggles.

In navigating this backlash, Paula employed several strategies to maintain her resilience and continue her work. One effective approach was fostering alliances with other activists and organizations. By building a coalition of diverse voices, she created a united front that could withstand the hostility directed at her. This coalition-building exemplifies the *Collective Action Theory*, which asserts that individuals are more likely to engage in activism when they perceive that they are part of a larger group with shared goals.

Additionally, Paula utilized social media as a platform to counteract negative narratives. By sharing her experiences and the stories of those she advocated for, she reframed the discourse around LGBTQ and disability rights. This tactic aligns with the *Framing Theory*, which posits that the way information is presented can influence public perception. Through her online presence, Paula not only defended her work but also amplified the voices of those who were often silenced, thereby transforming backlash into opportunities for education and awareness.

Despite these efforts, the hostility did not cease. Paula was often met with threats, both online and offline. The psychological impact of such threats can be profound, leading to anxiety and a sense of vulnerability. However, Paula's commitment to her cause provided her with a strong sense of purpose, allowing her to navigate the treacherous waters of activism with courage and determination.

In conclusion, facing backlash and hostility is an inevitable part of Paula Lupi's journey as an activist. By understanding the theoretical underpinnings of this resistance, including Social Identity Theory and Intersectionality, we can appreciate the complexities of her experiences. Through coalition-building and effective communication strategies, Paula not only confronted the hostility but also transformed it into a catalyst for growth and change within the LGBTQ and disability rights movements. Her resilience serves as an inspiring example for future activists who will undoubtedly face similar challenges in their pursuit of justice and equality.

Building bridges and alliances with other movements

In the ever-evolving landscape of social justice, the importance of building bridges and alliances among various movements cannot be overstated. Paula Lupi recognized early in her activism that the struggles for LGBTQ rights and disability rights were not isolated; they were intertwined with broader movements for racial justice, gender equality, and economic rights. This understanding laid the groundwork for her approach to advocacy, which emphasized intersectionality, collaboration, and solidarity.

Theoretical Framework

The concept of intersectionality, as introduced by Kimberlé Crenshaw, posits that individuals experience overlapping systems of oppression based on their multiple identities, including race, gender, sexual orientation, and disability. This framework is crucial for understanding how different movements can align their efforts to create a more inclusive and effective advocacy landscape. According to Crenshaw (1989), "the intersection of race and gender creates a unique set of experiences that cannot be understood by examining either category in isolation."

Thus, Paula's activism was grounded in the belief that to fight for LGBTQ rights effectively, one must also advocate for the rights of disabled individuals, people of color, and other marginalized communities. By recognizing these intersections, Paula aimed to create coalitions that were not only diverse but also representative of the complexities of social justice.

Challenges in Building Alliances

While the theory of intersectionality provides a solid foundation for collaboration, practical challenges often arise in the pursuit of building these alliances. One significant issue is the potential for competition among movements for resources, visibility, and recognition. For instance, LGBTQ organizations may prioritize issues that resonate more with their constituents, sometimes sidelining concerns that disproportionately affect disabled individuals or people of color within the community.

Additionally, historical tensions between movements can create barriers to collaboration. For example, some feminist movements have been critiqued for centering the experiences of cisgender, white women while neglecting the voices of transgender women and women of color. Paula faced the challenge of addressing these disparities head-on, advocating for a more inclusive approach that acknowledged and uplifted the voices of all marginalized groups.

Strategies for Effective Collaboration

To overcome these challenges, Paula employed several strategies that proved effective in building alliances:

- **Creating Inclusive Spaces:** Paula organized events and workshops that brought together activists from various movements. These gatherings focused on shared goals and the importance of mutual support, fostering an environment where participants could learn from one another's experiences and challenges.

- **Promoting Shared Narratives:** By highlighting the stories of individuals who navigated multiple identities, Paula emphasized the interconnectedness of struggles. For instance, she often shared the experiences of LGBTQ individuals with disabilities, showcasing how their unique challenges required a unified approach to advocacy.

- **Engaging in Joint Campaigns:** Paula spearheaded joint campaigns that addressed issues affecting multiple communities simultaneously. For example, she collaborated with racial justice organizations to advocate for healthcare access, recognizing that marginalized communities often face systemic barriers to quality care.

- **Fostering Intermovement Dialogue:** Paula initiated dialogue sessions between different movements, encouraging open discussions about their respective goals, challenges, and strategies. This approach helped to build trust and understanding, paving the way for more effective collaborations.

Examples of Successful Alliances

One notable example of Paula's successful alliance-building occurred during the annual Lisbon Pride Parade, where she worked with disability rights organizations to ensure that the event was accessible to all participants. This collaboration not only raised awareness about the importance of accessibility within the LGBTQ community but also highlighted the shared struggles faced by disabled individuals and LGBTQ activists.

Another significant moment came when Paula joined forces with environmental activists to address the impact of climate change on marginalized communities. Together, they organized a campaign that linked environmental justice with LGBTQ and disability rights, emphasizing that the fight for a sustainable future must include the voices of those who are often left behind.

The Impact of Collaborative Advocacy

The impact of Paula's efforts to build bridges between movements was profound. By fostering collaboration, she not only strengthened the LGBTQ rights movement but also contributed to a broader understanding of social justice that encompasses multiple identities and experiences. This approach has led to a more inclusive advocacy landscape, where diverse voices are heard and valued.

Moreover, the alliances formed under Paula's leadership have inspired a new generation of activists to adopt an intersectional lens in their work. As they engage in advocacy, these individuals carry forward the lessons learned from Paula's example, recognizing that the fight for justice is most effective when it is collective and inclusive.

In conclusion, Paula Lupi's commitment to building bridges and alliances with other movements exemplifies the power of intersectionality in social justice advocacy. By understanding and addressing the interconnectedness of various struggles, she not only advanced the cause of LGBTQ and disability rights but also laid the groundwork for a more unified and effective approach to activism. The legacy of her work continues to inspire activists to collaborate across movements, ensuring that the fight for justice remains inclusive and representative of all marginalized communities.

Amplifying marginalized voices through grassroots organizing

Grassroots organizing serves as a powerful tool for amplifying marginalized voices, particularly within the LGBTQ and disability rights movements. This approach emphasizes the importance of community engagement, collective action, and local empowerment, enabling individuals to advocate for their rights and challenge systemic inequalities.

At its core, grassroots organizing is rooted in the belief that those most affected by issues should lead the charge for change. This aligns with the principles of participatory democracy, where the voices of all community members are valued and heard. One of the key theoretical frameworks underpinning grassroots organizing is Paulo Freire's concept of "critical consciousness," which encourages individuals to reflect on their social conditions and take action against oppression. Freire posits that education is not merely a transfer of knowledge but a means of fostering critical thought and collective action among marginalized groups [?].

The Importance of Representation

In the context of LGBTQ and disability rights, representation matters immensely. Historically, mainstream narratives have often sidelined the experiences of queer disabled individuals, leading to a lack of visibility and understanding of their unique struggles. Grassroots organizing seeks to rectify this by ensuring that marginalized voices are not only heard but also prioritized in advocacy efforts. For example, organizations like *Sins Invalid* focus on the intersection of disability and sexuality, creating spaces where disabled queer individuals can share their stories and experiences [?].

Challenges in Grassroots Organizing

Despite its potential, grassroots organizing is not without challenges. One significant issue is the fragmentation within the LGBTQ and disability communities. Different groups may have varying priorities and agendas, making it difficult to present a unified front. This fragmentation can lead to competition for resources and visibility, ultimately undermining collective efforts.

Additionally, grassroots organizers often face resistance from established institutions and systems that are resistant to change. This can manifest in various forms, including political pushback, lack of funding, and even hostility from those who benefit from the status quo. For instance, when Paula Lupi and her allies organized protests advocating for inclusive healthcare policies, they encountered significant opposition from governmental entities reluctant to change existing frameworks [?].

Strategies for Effective Grassroots Organizing

To overcome these challenges and effectively amplify marginalized voices, grassroots organizers can employ several strategies:

    1. **Building Alliances**: Forming coalitions with other marginalized groups can strengthen advocacy efforts. For example, LGBTQ organizations partnering with disability rights groups can create a more comprehensive approach to addressing shared issues, such as healthcare access and discrimination.

    2. **Utilizing Social Media**: In the digital age, social media has become a vital tool for grassroots organizing. Platforms like Twitter and Instagram allow activists to share their stories, mobilize supporters, and raise awareness about issues affecting marginalized communities. This visibility can lead to increased support and solidarity from broader audiences.

    3. **Community Education**: Educating community members about their rights and the issues they face is crucial. Workshops, seminars, and informational campaigns can empower individuals to advocate for themselves and each other. For instance, Lupi's workshops on intersectionality within LGBTQ and disability rights have provided participants with the knowledge and tools to engage in activism effectively.

    4. **Storytelling**: Personal narratives play a significant role in grassroots organizing. By sharing their stories, individuals can humanize abstract issues and foster empathy among allies. This strategy can be particularly effective in breaking down prejudices and misconceptions about marginalized communities.

    5. **Creating Safe Spaces**: Establishing safe spaces for marginalized individuals to gather, share, and strategize is essential. These spaces allow for open dialogue and foster a sense of community, which is vital for sustaining activism.

Case Studies and Examples

Several successful grassroots organizing efforts illustrate the effectiveness of these strategies. One notable example is the *Black Lives Matter* movement, which has incorporated LGBTQ and disability rights into its broader agenda. By emphasizing intersectionality, the movement has amplified the voices of marginalized individuals who often face compounded discrimination [?].

Another example is the *Disability Justice* movement, which advocates for the rights of disabled individuals while recognizing the intersectionality of race, gender, and sexuality. This movement has successfully mobilized grassroots efforts to address systemic injustices faced by disabled people, particularly those who identify as LGBTQ [?].

Conclusion

In conclusion, grassroots organizing is a vital mechanism for amplifying marginalized voices within the LGBTQ and disability rights movements. By prioritizing representation, building alliances, and employing effective strategies, activists can challenge systemic inequalities and advocate for meaningful change. As Paula Lupi's journey demonstrates, the power of grassroots organizing lies in its ability to uplift individuals and foster collective action, ultimately paving the way for a more inclusive and equitable society.

Establishing herself as a force to be reckoned with

In the vibrant tapestry of activism, Paula Lupi emerged not merely as a participant but as a formidable force, an indomitable spirit whose voice resonated deeply within the LGBTQ and disability rights movements. This section delves into the multifaceted dimensions of Paula's activism, illustrating how she established herself as a force to be reckoned with in a landscape often fraught with challenges and opposition.

The Power of Personal Narrative

At the heart of Paula's advocacy was her personal narrative, a compelling story that intertwined her identity as a queer disabled woman with the broader struggles faced by marginalized communities. Her ability to articulate her experiences forged a deep connection with others, allowing her to speak not only for herself but for countless individuals who felt voiceless. This phenomenon aligns with the theory of *narrative identity*, which posits that individuals construct their identities through the stories they tell about themselves, thereby influencing how they relate to the world around them [?].

Building Coalitions and Alliances

Recognizing the importance of solidarity, Paula actively sought to build coalitions across various movements. She understood that the fight for LGBTQ rights could not be divorced from the struggles for disability rights, racial justice, and gender equality. By establishing alliances with organizations such as the *International Disability Alliance* and local LGBTQ collectives, she demonstrated the power of intersectionality in activism. As Crenshaw (1989) argues, intersectionality is crucial for understanding how different forms of discrimination overlap, and Paula's work exemplified this principle in action.

Grassroots Organizing and Mobilization

Paula's activism was characterized by grassroots organizing, a method that empowered individuals at the community level to take action. She organized rallies, workshops, and community forums that not only raised awareness but also educated participants about their rights. The *community organizing theory* emphasizes the importance of local engagement, asserting that effective change often begins at the grassroots level [?]. Paula's ability to mobilize people around shared goals exemplified this approach, as she inspired others to join the fight for equality.

Facing Adversity with Resilience

Establishing herself as a force to be reckoned with did not come without its challenges. Paula faced backlash from various quarters, including criticism from within her own community. Detractors questioned her methods and motives, challenging her credibility and integrity. However, Paula's resilience shone through in these moments. She employed *strategic reframing*, a technique that involves redefining the narrative around criticism to highlight the underlying issues at stake [?]. By addressing concerns openly and engaging in dialogue, she not only defended her position but also strengthened her resolve.

Leveraging Media and Public Platforms

In the digital age, media representation plays a pivotal role in shaping public perception. Paula adeptly leveraged social media platforms to amplify her message and connect with a broader audience. Her use of platforms like Twitter and Instagram allowed her to share her story, advocate for policy changes, and mobilize support for various initiatives. The *media framing theory* suggests that the way issues are presented in the media influences public understanding and opinion [?]. Paula's strategic use of media helped frame LGBTQ and disability rights as urgent and essential issues, garnering widespread attention and support.

Legislative Advocacy and Policy Change

Paula's activism transcended grassroots efforts; she also made significant strides in legislative advocacy. By engaging with policymakers and participating in discussions about inclusive policies, she positioned herself as a knowledgeable and respected voice in political circles. Her advocacy efforts led to the introduction of several key pieces of legislation aimed at protecting the rights of LGBTQ and disabled individuals. The *policy advocacy theory* highlights the importance of informed and strategic engagement in the policymaking process, and Paula's work exemplified this principle [?].

Creating Lasting Impact

Ultimately, Paula Lupi established herself as a force to be reckoned with by creating a lasting impact on the LGBTQ and disability rights movements. Her efforts not only advanced the cause of equality but also inspired a new generation of activists to continue the fight. The concept of *legacy building* in activism emphasizes the importance of creating structures and movements that endure beyond individual efforts [?]. Paula's commitment to mentorship and education ensured that her influence would resonate for years to come.

In conclusion, Paula Lupi's journey to becoming a force to be reckoned with was marked by her ability to weave together personal narrative, grassroots organizing, coalition-building, and strategic advocacy. Her resilience in the face of adversity, coupled with her adept use of media and commitment to legislative change, solidified her status as a prominent figure in the fight for LGBTQ and disability rights. As we reflect on her legacy, it is clear that Paula's impact will continue to inspire and empower future generations of activists, ensuring that her voice remains a powerful catalyst for change.

The Rise to Prominence

The Rise to Prominence

The Rise to Prominence

As Paula Lupi began to navigate the complex landscape of activism, her journey toward prominence was not merely a personal evolution but also a reflection of the broader socio-political climate in Portugal and beyond. This chapter delves into the multifaceted path that transformed Paula from a passionate advocate into a leading voice for LGBTQ and disability rights.

The Decision to Enter the Political Arena

In the early stages of her activism, Paula recognized that grassroots movements, while powerful, often lacked the institutional leverage necessary to effect systemic change. This realization catalyzed her decision to enter the political arena. The intersection of her identities as a queer disabled woman provided her with a unique perspective on the challenges faced by marginalized communities. She understood that to advocate effectively for these groups, she needed to influence policy directly.

One of the key theories that guided Paula's approach was the *Theory of Intersectionality*, coined by Kimberlé Crenshaw. This theory posits that individuals can experience overlapping forms of discrimination based on their various identities. For Paula, this meant that her activism needed to address not just LGBTQ rights but also the specific challenges faced by disabled individuals within that community.

Running for Office and Facing Opposition

With a clear vision, Paula launched her campaign for local office, a move that was met with both enthusiasm and resistance. The political landscape in Portugal was still grappling with issues of representation and inclusivity. Paula faced opposition not only from conservative factions but also from those within the LGBTQ community who questioned her approach and qualifications.

During her campaign, Paula encountered the pervasive issue of *tokenism*, where individuals from marginalized groups are included in discussions or initiatives but without real power or influence. She was determined to combat this by ensuring that her candidacy was not merely symbolic but a genuine representation of the community's needs.

Prioritizing LGBTQ and Disability Rights in Political Campaigns

Paula's platform was rooted in her lived experiences, which allowed her to prioritize LGBTQ and disability rights authentically. She proposed policies aimed at improving accessibility in public spaces, advocating for inclusive healthcare, and ensuring comprehensive anti-discrimination laws.

One notable example was her push for the *Accessibility for All Act*, which aimed to enhance physical and social accessibility for disabled individuals across Portugal. This legislation sought to address the systemic barriers that disabled people faced in accessing public services, education, and employment. Paula's ability to articulate these issues resonated with constituents, garnering support from a diverse coalition of allies.

Overcoming Stereotypes and Discrimination in Politics

Throughout her campaign, Paula confronted numerous stereotypes, particularly those related to her identity as a queer disabled woman. She faced questions about her capabilities and suitability for office, often being subjected to scrutiny that her male counterparts did not experience.

To combat these biases, Paula employed a strategy rooted in *narrative storytelling*. She shared her personal journey, illustrating how her experiences shaped her understanding of the systemic inequalities faced by marginalized communities. By humanizing the issues, she was able to connect with voters on a deeper level, turning skepticism into support.

Gaining Support from Allies in High Places

As her campaign gained momentum, Paula attracted the attention of influential allies within the political landscape. Support from established politicians and advocacy organizations played a crucial role in amplifying her message. These endorsements not only lent credibility to her campaign but also helped to mobilize resources and volunteers.

One significant ally was a prominent member of the Portuguese Parliament who had a long history of advocating for LGBTQ rights. Their partnership exemplified the power of coalition-building in politics, demonstrating how diverse groups could unite for a common cause.

Achieving Significant Milestones for LGBTQ and Disability Rights

Paula's election marked a pivotal moment in Portuguese politics. Her presence in office enabled her to champion legislation that directly addressed the needs of LGBTQ and disabled individuals. One of her most notable achievements was the successful passage of the *Equality in Employment Act*, which mandated equal opportunities for all individuals, regardless of sexual orientation or disability status.

This legislation not only provided legal protections but also served as a model for other countries grappling with similar issues. Paula's work in this area highlighted the importance of policy advocacy in creating tangible change for marginalized communities.

The Challenges of Being a Queer Disabled Woman in Politics

Despite her successes, Paula faced ongoing challenges as a queer disabled woman in politics. The intersection of her identities often placed her in the crosshairs of discrimination and prejudice. She encountered microaggressions and overt hostility, which could have deterred a less resilient individual.

However, Paula's commitment to her cause fueled her determination. She often reflected on the concept of *resilience theory*, which posits that individuals can thrive despite adversity. This framework guided her through difficult moments, reminding her of the broader mission that extended beyond her personal struggles.

Establishing Herself as a Respected and Influential Politician

As Paula continued to navigate the political landscape, she established herself as a respected and influential figure. Her ability to engage with constituents, coupled with her advocacy for marginalized communities, earned her a reputation as a dedicated public servant.

Her approach to leadership was characterized by inclusivity and transparency, fostering a sense of trust among her constituents. Paula often emphasized the importance of *community engagement*, believing that effective governance should reflect the voices and needs of the people.

Shaping Policy and Legislation for a More Inclusive Portugal

With her growing influence, Paula was able to shape policy and legislation that promoted inclusivity in Portugal. She spearheaded initiatives aimed at increasing representation of LGBTQ individuals in public life, advocating for comprehensive sex education in schools, and enhancing mental health services for disabled individuals.

One of her landmark initiatives was the *Inclusive Education Framework*, which aimed to create safe and supportive learning environments for LGBTQ and disabled students. This framework emphasized the importance of education in fostering understanding and acceptance, ultimately contributing to a more inclusive society.

Inspiring Future Generations of Queer Politicians

Paula's rise to prominence not only transformed her own life but also inspired future generations of queer politicians. Her story resonated with young activists who saw in her a reflection of their own struggles and aspirations.

She often engaged in mentorship programs, sharing her experiences and encouraging young leaders to pursue their passions fearlessly. Paula understood that the fight for equality was ongoing, and she was committed to nurturing the next generation of activists who would carry the torch forward.

In conclusion, Chapter 2 encapsulates the transformative journey of Paula Lupi as she rose to prominence in the political sphere. Through her unwavering commitment to LGBTQ and disability rights, she not only carved a space for herself but also paved the way for others to follow. Her story serves as a testament to the power of activism and the impact one individual can have on the world.

Making Waves in Politics

The decision to enter the political arena

Paula Lupi's journey into the political arena was not a mere whim; it was a calculated decision born out of necessity and a deep-seated desire for change. The political landscape in Portugal, like many parts of the world, was rife with challenges, particularly for marginalized communities. Paula recognized that while grassroots activism was essential, true systemic change often required the power of legislation and policy-making. This understanding led her to the pivotal decision to step into the world of politics.

The decision to enter politics is often influenced by a variety of factors, including personal experiences, societal needs, and the political climate. For Paula, her formative years in Lisbon provided a backdrop of vibrant culture and diversity but also exposed her to the harsh realities of discrimination and inequality. The intersection of her identity as a queer disabled woman meant that she faced unique challenges, which fueled her passion for advocacy. According to social movement theory, individuals are often motivated to engage in political action when they perceive a discrepancy between their lived experiences and the prevailing societal norms [?].

$$\text{Motivation} = f(\text{Perception of Inequality}, \text{Personal Identity}, \text{Societal Norms}) \tag{31}$$

In this equation, motivation is a function of the perception of inequality, personal identity, and societal norms. Paula's acute awareness of her marginalized status galvanized her resolve to seek a platform where she could effectuate change. Her decision was not merely about personal ambition; it was about amplifying the voices of those who had been historically silenced.

Moreover, Paula's early activism had already established her as a community leader, and her involvement in local LGBTQ organizations provided her with a network of allies and mentors who encouraged her to consider a political career. This support system was crucial, as research shows that social networks play a significant role in political engagement [?].

The political climate in Portugal during Paula's formative years was characterized by a growing recognition of LGBTQ rights, yet significant gaps remained, particularly regarding disability rights. This dual focus on intersectionality became a cornerstone of her political philosophy. Paula understood that to advocate effectively, she needed to bring both issues to the forefront of political discourse.

In her decision-making process, Paula also considered the potential obstacles she would face as a queer disabled woman in politics. The literature on political representation highlights that individuals from marginalized backgrounds often encounter systemic barriers, including discrimination and bias [?]. Paula was acutely aware of these challenges but chose to view them as opportunities to challenge the status quo.

She often reflected on the words of Audre Lorde, who said, "I am not free while any woman is unfree, even when her shackles are very different from my own." This sentiment resonated deeply with Paula and became a guiding principle in her political journey. She believed that entering the political arena was not just about her own rights but about the collective liberation of all marginalized groups.

In preparation for her political campaign, Paula undertook a comprehensive analysis of the political landscape. She studied successful campaigns by other LGBTQ and disability rights advocates, identifying strategies that resonated with voters. This strategic approach is supported by the theory of political opportunity structures, which posits that the success of social movements and political campaigns often depends on the external political environment [?].

$$\text{Success} = f(\text{Political Opportunity, Campaign Strategy, Public Support}) \quad (32)$$

In this equation, success is influenced by political opportunity, campaign strategy, and public support. Paula's decision to enter politics was underpinned by her belief that the time was ripe for change, given the increasing visibility of LGBTQ issues and the growing public support for disability rights in Portugal.

Ultimately, Paula's decision to enter the political arena was a culmination of her personal experiences, her commitment to intersectional advocacy, and her strategic understanding of the political landscape. She was driven by a vision of a more inclusive society where the rights of all individuals, regardless of their identity, were recognized and protected. This decision marked the beginning of a new chapter in her life, one where she would leverage her voice and platform to advocate for those who had been historically marginalized.

As she prepared to announce her candidacy, Paula felt a mix of excitement and trepidation. She knew that this path would be fraught with challenges, but her unwavering commitment to justice and equality propelled her forward. Her decision to enter the political arena was not just a personal ambition; it was a call to action for a community yearning for representation and change.

Running for office and facing opposition

The journey of Paula Lupi into the political arena was not merely a step; it was a leap into a world fraught with challenges, expectations, and fierce opposition. As a queer disabled woman, Paula faced a unique set of hurdles that were both personal and systemic. Running for office meant not only advocating for LGBTQ and disability rights but also embodying those struggles and triumphs within a political landscape that was often hostile to her identity.

The Political Landscape

In Portugal, the political environment had historically been dominated by traditional values, often sidelining the voices of marginalized communities. The representation of LGBTQ individuals in politics was minimal, and the intersection of disability rights within this sphere was even less acknowledged. Paula's decision to run for office was driven by her desire to challenge the status quo and bring visibility to issues that were often ignored.

Theories of representation in political science suggest that diverse representation leads to more comprehensive policy-making. According to [?], "descriptive representation" is crucial for ensuring that the interests of underrepresented groups are considered in legislative processes. Paula's candidacy was a manifestation of this theory, as she aimed to bring the voices of LGBTQ and disabled individuals directly into the halls of power.

Facing Opposition

However, the road to candidacy was paved with opposition. Paula encountered skepticism from both political allies and adversaries. Critics questioned her qualifications, often reducing her identity to stereotypes rather than recognizing her capabilities and vision. The backlash was not limited to political rhetoric; it included personal attacks aimed at undermining her credibility.

$$O = \frac{C}{R} \qquad (33)$$

Where O represents the level of opposition faced, C is the criticism received, and R is the resilience demonstrated. In Paula's case, as she increased her visibility, the criticism multiplied. For every supportive voice, there were multiple naysayers, echoing sentiments of doubt and prejudice. This equation illustrates the balance Paula had to maintain: as her campaign gained momentum, so too did the opposition, necessitating a robust and strategic response.

Strategies for Overcoming Opposition

To combat the challenges she faced, Paula employed several strategies:

1. **Building Coalitions**: Recognizing the power of unity, Paula sought alliances with other marginalized groups. By forming coalitions with disability rights organizations and feminist movements, she created a broader base of support that amplified her message.

2. **Engaging in Dialogue**: Paula understood that opposition often stemmed from misunderstanding. She initiated conversations with critics, aiming to educate them about the intersectionality of LGBTQ and disability rights. This approach was rooted in the theory of deliberative democracy, which posits that open dialogue can lead to more informed and empathetic decision-making [?].

3. **Utilizing Social Media**: In an age where information spreads rapidly, Paula harnessed the power of social media to counteract negative narratives. By sharing her story and the stories of those she represented, she humanized the issues at stake, fostering a connection with voters that transcended traditional political discourse.

4. **Policy Focus**: Paula's campaign was anchored in concrete policy proposals that addressed the needs of her constituents. By prioritizing issues such as healthcare access, inclusive education, and anti-discrimination laws, she shifted the conversation from identity politics to substantive policy discussions, thereby appealing to a broader electorate.

Personal Resilience

The emotional toll of facing opposition was significant. Paula often reflected on her mental health, recognizing the importance of self-care amidst the chaos of a political campaign. She sought support from her community, engaging in practices that fostered resilience and empowerment. This notion aligns with the psychological theory of resilience, which emphasizes the ability to bounce back from adversity through social support and coping strategies [1].

Paula's candidacy was not just about winning an election; it was about redefining what it meant to be a representative in a society that often marginalized voices like hers. Her experience highlighted the intricate dance of politics, where personal identity and public service intersected in profound ways.

Through her determination and strategic engagement, Paula not only faced the opposition but transformed it into a catalyst for change, paving the way for future generations of activists and politicians who would follow in her footsteps.

Conclusion

In conclusion, Paula Lupi's journey of running for office amidst fierce opposition serves as a testament to the power of resilience, coalition-building, and strategic advocacy. Her experiences underscore the critical importance of representation in politics, not just for LGBTQ and disabled individuals, but for all marginalized communities. As she navigated the complexities of her campaign, Paula laid the groundwork for a more inclusive political landscape, proving that the fight for equality is not merely a personal battle but a collective endeavor that requires courage, solidarity, and unwavering commitment.

Prioritizing LGBTQ and disability rights in political campaigns

In the landscape of contemporary politics, the prioritization of LGBTQ and disability rights has emerged as a critical focal point for candidates seeking to resonate with diverse voter bases. This section delves into the strategies, challenges, and implications of integrating these rights into political campaigns, emphasizing the necessity for inclusive policies that address the intersectionality of both communities.

Theoretical Framework

The advocacy for LGBTQ and disability rights within political campaigns can be understood through various theoretical lenses, including intersectionality and social justice theories. Intersectionality, a term coined by Kimberlé Crenshaw, posits that individuals experience overlapping social identities, which can lead to compounded discrimination. Thus, political candidates must recognize that LGBTQ individuals with disabilities face unique challenges that require targeted policy responses.

$$\text{Intersectionality} = \sum_{i=1}^{n} \text{Identity}_i \cdot \text{Discrimination}_i \qquad (34)$$

This equation illustrates the cumulative effect of various identities on an individual's experience of discrimination, underscoring the need for nuanced political strategies.

Challenges in Political Campaigns

Despite the growing recognition of LGBTQ and disability rights, numerous challenges persist in their prioritization within political campaigns. These include:

- **Stereotyping and Misrepresentation:** Political candidates often grapple with the challenge of overcoming stereotypes associated with LGBTQ individuals and people with disabilities. Misrepresentation in media and political discourse can lead to a lack of understanding and support for these communities.

- **Voter Apathy and Opposition:** There exists a segment of the electorate that remains apathetic or openly hostile to LGBTQ and disability rights. Candidates must navigate this landscape carefully, balancing the need to advocate for marginalized groups while not alienating potential voters.
- **Resource Allocation:** Campaigns often prioritize issues that resonate broadly with the electorate, leading to the marginalization of LGBTQ and disability rights. Limited resources can hinder the development of comprehensive policy proposals that address the specific needs of these communities.

Strategies for Inclusion

To effectively prioritize LGBTQ and disability rights, political campaigns can implement several strategies:

- **Inclusive Messaging:** Campaigns should adopt inclusive messaging that resonates with both LGBTQ individuals and those with disabilities. This can be achieved through targeted outreach initiatives and the use of language that reflects the diversity of experiences within these communities.
- **Policy Development:** Candidates must develop concrete policies that address the intersection of LGBTQ and disability rights. This includes advocating for accessible healthcare, anti-discrimination legislation, and inclusive education policies that cater to the needs of all constituents.
- **Coalition Building:** Forming coalitions with LGBTQ and disability rights organizations can amplify a candidate's message and enhance credibility. Collaborating with grassroots organizations allows candidates to tap into the knowledge and experiences of activists who are deeply embedded in these communities.

Examples of Successful Campaigns

Several political campaigns have effectively prioritized LGBTQ and disability rights, serving as models for future candidates:

- **The 2020 U.S. Presidential Election:** Candidates like Pete Buttigieg and Kamala Harris prominently featured LGBTQ rights in their platforms, advocating for policies such as the Equality Act, which aims to prohibit discrimination based on sexual orientation and gender identity. Their campaigns highlighted the importance of representation and inclusivity, resonating with a broad spectrum of voters.

- **Local Initiatives:** In Portugal, local candidates have successfully integrated disability rights into their platforms by advocating for accessible public spaces and inclusive employment practices. These initiatives not only address the needs of disabled individuals but also highlight the importance of an inclusive society for all.

Conclusion

In conclusion, prioritizing LGBTQ and disability rights in political campaigns is not merely a moral imperative; it is essential for fostering an inclusive democracy. By understanding the theoretical frameworks, addressing challenges, and implementing effective strategies, political candidates can create a platform that uplifts marginalized voices and promotes equality. As society continues to evolve, the integration of these rights into political discourse will be crucial in shaping a more just and equitable future for all.

$$\text{Inclusive Democracy} = \text{LGBTQ Rights} + \text{Disability Rights} + \text{Intersectionality} \tag{35}$$

This equation emphasizes that true inclusivity in democracy can only be achieved through the concerted efforts of political leaders to advocate for the rights of all individuals, regardless of their sexual orientation or ability.

Overcoming stereotypes and discrimination in politics

In the realm of politics, stereotypes and discrimination can manifest in various forms, often acting as barriers to the participation and success of marginalized individuals, including those who identify as LGBTQ and disabled. Paula Lupi's journey through these treacherous waters serves as a testament to resilience and the power of advocacy.

Stereotypes, defined as oversimplified and generalized beliefs about a group, can significantly hinder the political aspirations of individuals. For example, LGBTQ individuals often face the stereotype that they are less capable of leadership due to perceived emotional instability or a lack of traditional values. Similarly, disabled individuals may be viewed as incapable of handling the rigors of political life, leading to systemic discrimination in candidacy and governance.

To combat these stereotypes, Paula employed a multifaceted approach. First, she focused on education and awareness. By engaging in public speaking and community outreach, she aimed to dismantle misconceptions about both the LGBTQ community and disabled individuals. One of her notable initiatives was the "Voices of Change" campaign, which featured testimonials from LGBTQ and disabled leaders, showcasing their achievements and capabilities. This campaign not only humanized these groups but also highlighted their contributions to society, thereby challenging existing stereotypes.

Moreover, Paula recognized the importance of representation. As she entered the political arena, she made it a priority to amplify the voices of underrepresented communities. By forming coalitions with other marginalized groups, she created a united front that advocated for intersectionality in policy-making. This approach was exemplified during her campaign for local office, where she collaborated with disability rights organizations to address the unique challenges faced by disabled voters. This collaboration resulted in the development of accessible voting initiatives, ensuring that all voices could be heard.

However, overcoming stereotypes and discrimination was not without its challenges. Paula faced significant backlash from both her political opponents and segments of the public who were resistant to change. For instance, during a televised debate, an opponent attempted to undermine her credibility by questioning her ability to lead due to her identity as a queer disabled woman. Paula responded with poise, stating:

> "I am not defined by my identity but by my actions and commitment to serve my community. My experiences give me a unique perspective that is essential in addressing the needs of all constituents."

This powerful retort not only reframed the narrative but also resonated with many viewers, illustrating that authenticity and confidence can dismantle discriminatory narratives.

Additionally, Paula utilized legislative measures to combat discrimination within the political framework. She championed the implementation of anti-discrimination policies that protected candidates from being judged based on their identity. This legislative effort was critical in creating a more inclusive political environment, where individuals could run for office without fear of prejudice.

Despite these efforts, the journey was fraught with obstacles. Paula encountered instances of systemic discrimination, such as being denied access to certain political events due to physical accessibility issues. Rather than succumbing to frustration, she used these experiences to advocate for broader accessibility standards within political institutions. Her advocacy led to the establishment of the "Access for All" initiative, which aimed to ensure that all political events and offices were accessible to individuals with disabilities.

The intersectionality of Paula's identity played a crucial role in her activism. She understood that the fight against stereotypes and discrimination was not just about her own experiences but also about the collective struggles of various marginalized communities. By embracing her identity and using it as a platform for change, she became a symbol of hope and empowerment for many.

In conclusion, overcoming stereotypes and discrimination in politics requires a concerted effort that encompasses education, representation, and legislative advocacy. Paula Lupi's journey exemplifies how one can confront and dismantle these barriers through resilience, collaboration, and a commitment to justice. Her legacy serves as a reminder that the fight for equality is ongoing and that every voice, regardless of identity, deserves to be heard in the political arena.

$$\text{Stereotypes} + \text{Discrimination} \rightarrow \text{Barriers to Participation} \qquad (36)$$

$$\text{Education} + \text{Representation} + \text{Legislative Advocacy} \rightarrow \text{Overcoming Barriers} \quad (37)$$

Gaining support from allies in high places

In the landscape of activism, particularly for marginalized communities such as the LGBTQ and disabled populations, the importance of strategic alliances cannot be overstated. Paula Lupi, with her relentless spirit and unwavering commitment, recognized early on that to effect meaningful change, she needed to build a coalition of support that extended beyond the grassroots movements. This section explores how Paula garnered support from influential allies, the theoretical underpinnings of such alliances, the challenges faced, and examples of successful collaborations.

Theoretical Framework

The concept of allyship is grounded in various sociological and political theories, primarily focusing on the dynamics of power, privilege, and social justice. According to [3], intersectionality plays a crucial role in understanding how different forms of discrimination overlap, necessitating a broader coalition of allies who can address these complexities. Allies from privileged backgrounds can amplify marginalized voices, providing access to resources and platforms that may otherwise be unavailable.

One pivotal theory relevant to Paula's strategy is the *Social Movement Theory*, which posits that the success of social movements often hinges on their ability to mobilize resources, including social capital. As articulated by [?], resource mobilization involves the strategic use of networks and relationships to garner support and influence decision-makers. Paula adeptly navigated this theoretical landscape, using her personal narrative and the collective experiences of the LGBTQ and disabled communities to forge connections with powerful allies.

Challenges in Gaining Support

Despite her determination, Paula faced significant challenges in building these alliances. One primary obstacle was the skepticism that often accompanies activist movements, particularly from those in positions of power. Many decision-makers were hesitant to engage with activists, viewing them as disruptive forces rather than potential partners in policy-making. This skepticism was compounded by the historical marginalization of LGBTQ and disabled individuals, which led to a lack of understanding and empathy among some allies.

Additionally, the issue of *performative allyship* emerged as a concern. Some individuals in high positions may have expressed support for LGBTQ and disability rights without a genuine commitment to the cause. Paula had to be discerning in identifying allies who were not only willing to lend their names but also actively engage in the work required to bring about systemic change.

Examples of Successful Collaborations

Paula's journey to gain support from allies in high places is marked by several notable collaborations. One significant partnership was with local government officials who shared her vision for inclusive policies. By organizing roundtable discussions that included these officials, Paula created a platform for dialogue where she could articulate the specific needs and challenges faced by the LGBTQ and disabled communities.

For instance, during a pivotal meeting with the mayor of Lisbon, Paula presented compelling data illustrating the disparities in healthcare access for disabled LGBTQ individuals. This data was not merely anecdotal; it was rooted in rigorous research, including surveys and case studies that highlighted the intersectional challenges faced by these populations. The mayor, moved by the evidence and Paula's passionate advocacy, became a vocal supporter of initiatives aimed at improving healthcare access and inclusivity in public services.

Furthermore, Paula's ability to engage with corporate leaders also proved beneficial. In one notable instance, she collaborated with a major tech company to develop a training program focused on LGBTQ and disability awareness. This partnership not only provided financial support for her initiatives but also fostered a corporate culture that prioritized inclusivity. The program became a model for other organizations, illustrating how allyship can extend into the corporate sector, thereby influencing broader societal norms.

The Impact of Allyship on Policy Change

The support Paula garnered from allies in high places had a profound impact on policy change. With the backing of influential politicians and corporate leaders, she was able to advocate for legislative reforms that addressed the needs of LGBTQ and disabled individuals. For example, her efforts were instrumental in the passage of the Inclusive Education Act, which mandated that schools implement policies to accommodate students with disabilities and promote LGBTQ inclusivity.

Moreover, the visibility and credibility that came from these alliances allowed Paula to amplify her message on international platforms. By representing Portugal at global conferences, she not only brought attention to the issues faced by her communities but also showcased the collaborative efforts being made at home. This visibility attracted further support from international organizations, creating a ripple effect that extended beyond Portugal's borders.

In conclusion, Paula Lupi's ability to gain support from allies in high places was a critical component of her advocacy strategy. By leveraging theoretical frameworks of allyship and resource mobilization, she navigated the complexities of building coalitions while overcoming significant challenges. Through successful collaborations with local government officials and corporate leaders, Paula was able to effect meaningful policy changes that advanced the rights of LGBTQ and disabled individuals, leaving a lasting impact on both her community and the broader landscape of social justice.

Achieving significant milestones for LGBTQ and disability rights

Paula Lupi's journey in advocating for LGBTQ and disability rights is marked by a series of significant milestones that not only transformed her life but also left an indelible impact on Portuguese society. These milestones are not just personal achievements; they represent critical points in the broader struggle for equality and justice.

Theoretical Framework

To understand the significance of these milestones, it is essential to consider the theoretical frameworks that underpin LGBTQ and disability rights activism. At the core of this advocacy lies the concept of **intersectionality**, coined by Kimberlé Crenshaw in 1989. Intersectionality posits that individuals experience multiple, overlapping identities that can lead to unique forms of discrimination and privilege. In the context of Paula's activism, this framework is crucial for addressing the complexities of being both queer and disabled, as it highlights the need for inclusive policies that cater to the diverse needs of marginalized communities.

Policy Changes and Legislative Achievements

One of Paula's most notable achievements was her instrumental role in the passage of the *Law on Gender Identity and Gender Expression* in Portugal. This legislation, enacted in 2011, allowed individuals to change their legal gender without the requirement of surgery, a significant step towards recognizing and respecting the rights of transgender individuals. Paula's advocacy was pivotal in raising awareness about the challenges faced by transgender people, particularly those with disabilities, who often encounter additional barriers in accessing healthcare and social services.

Another landmark achievement was her involvement in the *Disability Rights Framework* adopted by the Portuguese government in 2016. This framework aimed to enhance accessibility and inclusion for disabled individuals across various sectors, including education, employment, and healthcare. Paula's advocacy emphasized the importance of creating an inclusive society where disabled LGBTQ individuals could thrive, thereby addressing the intersection of disability and sexual orientation in policy discussions.

Community Mobilization and Grassroots Efforts

Beyond legislative achievements, Paula recognized the power of community mobilization in achieving lasting change. She founded the *LGBTQ and Disability Coalition*, a grassroots organization that brought together activists from both communities to advocate for shared goals. This coalition organized awareness campaigns, workshops, and public demonstrations, effectively amplifying the voices of those often marginalized within both the LGBTQ and disability rights movements.

For instance, during the 2018 Pride Parade in Lisbon, Paula led a contingent specifically highlighting the challenges faced by disabled LGBTQ individuals. The theme of the parade, *"Visibility for All"*, resonated deeply within the community, drawing attention to the need for intersectional representation in pride celebrations. This event not only showcased the diversity of the LGBTQ community but also emphasized the importance of accessibility in public spaces.

Challenges and Backlash

Despite these significant milestones, Paula's journey was not without challenges. She faced backlash from both conservative factions and even some within the LGBTQ community who questioned her dual focus on disability rights. Critics argued that addressing disability issues could dilute the urgency of LGBTQ advocacy. However, Paula countered this narrative by emphasizing that true equality cannot be achieved without considering the unique struggles faced by individuals with intersecting identities.

The backlash highlighted a critical problem within social movements: the tendency to prioritize certain identities over others. Paula's approach was rooted in the belief that **"no one is free until we are all free,"** and she continually advocated for a more inclusive movement that recognized the complexities of identity.

International Recognition and Influence

Paula's milestones in LGBTQ and disability rights advocacy did not go unnoticed on the international stage. In 2019, she was invited to speak at the *Global Conference on LGBTQ Rights and Disability*, where she shared her insights on the importance of intersectionality in activism. Her presentation, titled *"Bridging the Gap: The Intersections of Identity and Activism,"* resonated with activists from around the world, inspiring them to adopt a more inclusive approach in their own movements.

This international recognition further solidified Paula's status as a leader in the field, allowing her to influence policy discussions beyond Portugal. She collaborated with international organizations, such as *ILGA World* and *Disabled People International*, to advocate for global standards that respect the rights of LGBTQ individuals with disabilities.

Conclusion

In conclusion, Paula Lupi's achievements in advocating for LGBTQ and disability rights serve as a testament to the power of intersectional activism. By addressing the unique challenges faced by individuals at the intersection of multiple marginalized identities, Paula not only advanced significant legislative changes but also fostered a sense of community and solidarity among diverse groups. Her legacy continues to inspire new generations of activists to embrace the complexities of identity and to fight for a more inclusive world where everyone can thrive.

$$\text{Intersectionality} = \sum_{i=1}^{n} \text{Identity}_i \qquad (38)$$

where Identity_i represents the various dimensions of identity, including but not limited to gender, sexual orientation, and disability.

Advocacy Impact = Legislative Change+Community Mobilization+International Influ
$$(39)$$
This equation illustrates the multifaceted approach Paula took in her advocacy, demonstrating that lasting change requires a combination of legal, social, and global efforts.

The challenges of being a queer disabled woman in politics

The political landscape has long been a battleground for marginalized voices, and for Paula Lupi, being a queer disabled woman in this arena presents a unique set of challenges that intertwine her identity with her activism. The intersection of her sexual orientation, disability, and gender creates a complex framework through which she navigates the often-turbulent waters of politics. This section delves into the multifaceted challenges she faces, supported by relevant theories and real-world examples.

Intersectionality in Politics

At the core of Paula's experience is the theory of intersectionality, coined by Kimberlé Crenshaw in 1989. Intersectionality posits that individuals experience overlapping systems of discrimination and privilege based on their identities. For Paula, this means that her experiences as a queer woman and a person with a disability are not merely additive; rather, they interact in ways that exacerbate the challenges she faces in the political sphere.

$$D = f(Q, D_i, G) \qquad (40)$$

Where:

- D = Discrimination faced
- Q = Queer identity
- D_i = Disability identity
- G = Gender identity

This equation illustrates how the discrimination faced by Paula is a function of her multiple identities, highlighting the compounded nature of her experiences.

Stereotypes and Misconceptions

Paula often encounters stereotypes that undermine her credibility and authority as a politician. The perception that disabled individuals are less capable of fulfilling political roles is a pervasive issue. This stigma is rooted in ableism, which is the discrimination against individuals with disabilities. Such stereotypes can manifest in various ways, from condescending attitudes to outright exclusion from important discussions.

For example, during her campaign for office, Paula faced questions about her ability to handle the demands of political life due to her disability. Comments like, "Are you sure you can manage the stress of being in politics?" reflect the societal bias that equates disability with incapacity. This not only challenges her authority but also reinforces harmful narratives that can deter other disabled individuals from pursuing political careers.

Navigating Political Spaces

The political environment can be particularly hostile for queer disabled women. Paula often finds herself navigating spaces that are predominantly male and heteronormative, where her identity is marginalized. The lack of representation for queer disabled individuals in politics means that Paula frequently has to advocate for her community while simultaneously defending her right to be there.

Moreover, the political discourse often lacks sensitivity to the needs of disabled individuals. For instance, during legislative sessions, accessibility issues such as wheelchair ramps and sign language interpreters are frequently overlooked. Paula's presence in these spaces not only highlights these shortcomings but also positions her as a critical voice advocating for necessary changes.

Backlash and Hostility

Entering the political arena as a queer disabled woman inevitably invites backlash. Paula has faced hostility from both political opponents and segments of the public who resist the changes she advocates. This backlash can take various forms, from derogatory comments on social media to organized campaigns aimed at discrediting her work.

For example, during a public forum on LGBTQ rights, Paula was met with protests from conservative groups who labeled her as "unfit" to represent the community. Such hostility not only affects her personally but also poses a threat to her political career and the broader movement for inclusion.

Building Alliances

Despite these challenges, Paula recognizes the importance of building alliances with other marginalized groups. The solidarity among various movements—such as those advocating for racial justice, gender equality, and disability rights—can amplify her voice and create a more inclusive political landscape. By collaborating with other activists and organizations, Paula can challenge the systemic barriers that affect not only her community but also others facing similar struggles.

For instance, Paula has worked closely with organizations focused on disability rights to create comprehensive policy proposals that address the needs of both LGBTQ individuals and disabled persons. This collaborative approach not only strengthens her advocacy but also fosters a sense of community among diverse groups.

Resilience and Empowerment

Ultimately, Paula's journey in politics is one of resilience and empowerment. While she faces numerous challenges as a queer disabled woman, her experiences fuel her commitment to advocacy. She embodies the spirit of resistance, using her platform to uplift others who share similar identities.

By sharing her story and the stories of those she represents, Paula challenges the narratives that seek to marginalize her and her community. Her activism serves as a powerful reminder that diversity in politics is not just beneficial but essential for a truly representative democracy.

In conclusion, the challenges of being a queer disabled woman in politics are significant and multifaceted. From navigating intersectional discrimination to overcoming stereotypes and building alliances, Paula's journey highlights the need for greater representation and inclusivity in political spaces. As she continues to advocate for LGBTQ and disability rights, Paula Lupi stands as a testament to the power of resilience and the importance of amplifying marginalized voices in the fight for equality.

Establishing herself as a respected and influential politician

As Paula Lupi stepped into the political arena, she faced the dual challenge of being both a queer disabled woman and an advocate for marginalized communities. Her journey to establishing herself as a respected and influential politician was marked by a series of strategic actions, personal convictions, and the ability to navigate a complex political landscape.

Building Credibility

The foundation of Paula's political credibility was her extensive background in activism. She had spent years advocating for LGBTQ and disability rights, participating in protests, and working with local organizations. This grassroots experience allowed her to build a network of supporters who believed in her vision for a more inclusive society. Establishing credibility also involved engaging with constituents, listening to their concerns, and demonstrating her commitment to their needs.

$$\text{Credibility} = \frac{\text{Experience} + \text{Engagement}}{\text{Perception}} \tag{41}$$

Where: - **Experience** refers to Paula's activism history. - **Engagement** represents her interactions with constituents. - **Perception** is how the public views her integrity and intentions.

Overcoming Stereotypes

Paula's identity posed unique challenges in the political realm. Stereotypes about disabled individuals and LGBTQ people often led to skepticism regarding her capabilities. To counter this, she focused on her qualifications and experience, emphasizing her academic achievements and her successful advocacy initiatives. Paula utilized public speaking engagements to articulate her vision, effectively dismantling preconceived notions about her abilities.

$$\text{Stereotype Reduction} = \text{Public Speaking} + \text{Visibility} + \text{Achievements} \tag{42}$$

Through her visibility in the media and her achievements in advocacy, Paula was able to reduce the impact of stereotypes, allowing her to gain respect as a politician.

Strategic Alliances

Understanding the importance of collaboration, Paula actively sought alliances with other politicians and activists. By forming coalitions, she amplified her voice and increased her influence. These alliances were crucial in advancing legislation that supported LGBTQ and disability rights. For example, her partnership with established politicians helped her navigate the complexities of the legislative process, resulting in the successful passage of inclusive policies.

$$\text{Influence} = \text{Alliances} \times \text{Coalition Strength} \tag{43}$$

Where: - **Alliances** indicates the number of partnerships formed. - **Coalition Strength** reflects the collective power of the groups involved.

Public Engagement and Media Presence

Paula recognized that effective communication was vital for her political journey. She harnessed the power of social media to connect with a broader audience, sharing her experiences and advocating for her causes. Her candidness and authenticity resonated with many, turning her into a relatable figure for constituents who felt marginalized. Paula's media presence allowed her to articulate her policies and engage in meaningful dialogues about LGBTQ and disability rights.

$$\text{Engagement} = \text{Social Media} + \text{Public Forums} + \text{Media Appearances} \tag{44}$$

Legislative Achievements

Through her relentless advocacy, Paula made significant strides in the legislative landscape. She championed bills that provided protections for LGBTQ individuals and improved accessibility for disabled citizens. These legislative achievements not only solidified her reputation but also demonstrated her effectiveness as a politician. For instance, her sponsorship of the "Equality in Education" bill showcased her commitment to inclusive policies, garnering widespread support from various sectors of society.

$$\text{Legislative Impact} = \text{Bills Passed} + \text{Public Support} \tag{45}$$

Navigating Political Challenges

Despite her successes, Paula faced numerous political challenges, including opposition from conservative factions. These groups often questioned her motives and sought to undermine her authority. However, Paula's resilience and ability to articulate her vision helped her navigate these obstacles. She remained steadfast in her commitment to justice and equality, continually working to foster dialogue and understanding, even among her critics.

$$\text{Resilience} = \frac{\text{Commitment} + \text{Adaptability}}{\text{Opposition}} \tag{46}$$

Conclusion

In summary, Paula Lupi's establishment as a respected and influential politician was a multifaceted journey characterized by her activism, strategic alliances, public engagement, and legislative achievements. Her ability to overcome stereotypes and navigate political challenges underscored her commitment to advocacy and her vision for a more inclusive society. Paula not only redefined what it meant to be a politician but also inspired a new generation of leaders who would continue the fight for LGBTQ and disability rights.

Shaping policy and legislation for a more inclusive Portugal

Paula Lupi's journey into the political arena marked a pivotal moment for LGBTQ and disability rights in Portugal. With her unique perspective as a queer disabled woman, Paula understood the complexities of intersectionality and the urgent need for comprehensive policy reform. This section explores her strategies for shaping inclusive legislation that addressed the multifaceted challenges faced by marginalized communities.

Understanding Intersectionality

At the heart of Paula's advocacy was the theory of intersectionality, a framework developed by Kimberlé Crenshaw in the late 1980s, which posits that individuals experience overlapping systems of discrimination and privilege based on various social identities, including race, gender, sexuality, and disability. Paula recognized that LGBTQ individuals who also identified as disabled faced compounded discrimination, often overlooked in mainstream discussions about rights and representation.

The equation representing intersectionality can be simplified as follows:

$$D = f(I_1, I_2, I_3, \ldots, I_n) \tag{47}$$

where D is the degree of discrimination experienced, and I_n represents various intersecting identities. This understanding guided Paula's approach to policy-making, ensuring that legislation was inclusive of all marginalized groups.

Identifying Legislative Gaps

Upon entering the political landscape, Paula conducted a thorough analysis of existing laws and policies in Portugal. She identified significant gaps in protections for LGBTQ individuals and those with disabilities. For instance, while Portugal had made strides in legalizing same-sex marriage in 2010, many LGBTQ individuals still faced discrimination in employment, healthcare, and housing.

Paula organized community forums to gather testimonies from individuals directly affected by these legislative shortcomings. These narratives highlighted the urgent need for comprehensive anti-discrimination laws that addressed not only sexual orientation but also disability status.

Advocacy Strategies

1. **Coalition Building**: Paula understood the power of collaboration. She formed coalitions with other advocacy groups focused on disability rights, women's rights, and racial equality. By uniting diverse voices, she amplified the call for inclusive legislation. This coalition-building was instrumental in creating a broad-based support network that could challenge discriminatory policies effectively.

2. **Public Awareness Campaigns**: Recognizing the importance of public opinion, Paula launched campaigns aimed at raising awareness about the challenges faced by LGBTQ individuals with disabilities. These campaigns utilized social media, public speaking engagements, and community events to educate the public and mobilize support for legislative changes.

3. **Policy Proposals**: Armed with data and community input, Paula drafted comprehensive policy proposals that addressed the identified gaps. These proposals included:

 - **Comprehensive Anti-Discrimination Laws**: Legislation that explicitly prohibits discrimination based on sexual orientation, gender identity, and disability in all areas of public life, including employment, housing, and healthcare.

- **Inclusive Healthcare Access**: Policies ensuring that LGBTQ individuals with disabilities receive equitable healthcare services, including mental health support tailored to their unique experiences.
- **Education and Awareness Programs**: Initiatives aimed at educating public servants, educators, and healthcare providers about the intersectionality of LGBTQ and disability rights, fostering a more inclusive environment.

Legislative Successes

Through relentless advocacy, Paula achieved significant milestones in shaping policy for a more inclusive Portugal. One notable success was the passage of the "LGBTQ and Disability Rights Act," which incorporated many of her proposed measures. This landmark legislation not only expanded protections for LGBTQ individuals but also established funding for programs aimed at supporting disabled members of the community.

Furthermore, Paula's efforts led to the establishment of the "Inclusive Portugal Initiative," a government program designed to promote awareness and training around LGBTQ and disability issues within public institutions. This initiative emphasized the importance of intersectionality in policy-making and sought to ensure that all voices were heard in the legislative process.

Challenges and Resistance

Despite these successes, Paula faced significant challenges and resistance. Conservative factions within the government and society often opposed her initiatives, framing them as unnecessary or overly progressive. Misinformation campaigns sought to undermine her credibility, portraying her as an extremist rather than a champion of inclusivity.

To combat this resistance, Paula engaged in strategic communication, emphasizing the economic and social benefits of inclusive policies. Research indicated that inclusive workplaces and communities not only fostered diversity but also enhanced productivity and innovation.

The Path Forward

As Paula continued her work, she remained committed to ensuring that the policies she helped shape would not only benefit the current generation but also lay the groundwork for future progress. She advocated for regular reviews of legislation to adapt to the evolving needs of LGBTQ and disabled communities, emphasizing the importance of ongoing dialogue and engagement.

In conclusion, Paula Lupi's efforts in shaping policy and legislation for a more inclusive Portugal stand as a testament to the power of advocacy rooted in intersectionality. Her work not only transformed the legal landscape but also inspired a new generation of activists to continue the fight for equality and justice. By addressing the complexities of identity and discrimination, Paula paved the way for a more inclusive society where all individuals can thrive, regardless of their sexual orientation or disability status.

Inspiring future generations of queer politicians

The journey of Paula Lupi into the political arena was not merely a personal endeavor; it was a clarion call for the future of queer representation in governance. As a queer disabled woman, Paula understood the profound importance of visibility and representation in politics. Her ascent to prominence served as a beacon of hope, illuminating the path for future generations of queer politicians who might have previously felt marginalized or silenced within the political landscape.

The Importance of Representation

Representation matters. It is a fundamental principle of democracy that all voices should be heard and included in the decision-making processes that affect their lives. According to [?], representation in politics goes beyond mere numbers; it involves ensuring that diverse perspectives are integrated into policy-making. Paula's success demonstrated that queer individuals could not only participate in politics but could also excel and lead. Her presence in the political sphere challenged the traditional narratives that often excluded LGBTQ voices, effectively reshaping the political discourse to be more inclusive.

Mentorship and Support Networks

Paula actively engaged in mentorship, understanding that the challenges faced by queer politicians could be alleviated through guidance and support. She established programs aimed at nurturing young queer activists, providing them with the tools and resources necessary to pursue political careers. This mentorship was crucial, as many aspiring politicians lacked access to networks that could facilitate their entry into political life.

For example, Paula initiated the "Future Leaders" program, which paired young queer activists with seasoned politicians. This program not only provided practical training in political campaigning and public speaking but also fostered a sense of community and solidarity among participants. As [?] notes, mentorship can significantly enhance the confidence and capabilities of emerging leaders, which was evident in the success stories of those who participated in Paula's initiatives.

Creating Safe Spaces

Recognizing the often-hostile environment faced by queer individuals in politics, Paula advocated for the creation of safe spaces within political organizations. These spaces allowed queer politicians to share their experiences, discuss challenges, and strategize on how to navigate the complexities of political life. The establishment of these safe havens was crucial for fostering resilience and solidarity among queer politicians.

Moreover, Paula's commitment to intersectionality ensured that these safe spaces were inclusive of all identities within the LGBTQ spectrum, acknowledging that race, gender, and disability intersect with sexual orientation in complex ways. This approach aligns with the theories of [3], who emphasized the importance of understanding how various social identities intersect to create unique experiences of oppression.

Advocating for Inclusive Policies

In her political campaigns, Paula prioritized the development of policies that directly addressed the needs of LGBTQ individuals, particularly those from marginalized backgrounds. She pushed for comprehensive anti-discrimination laws, healthcare access for queer individuals, and educational reforms that included LGBTQ history and rights in school curricula. By advocating for these policies, Paula not only benefited her constituents but also set a precedent for future queer politicians to follow.

As [?] argues, policy advocacy is a critical aspect of political representation. When queer politicians actively work to create inclusive policies, they pave the way for future leaders to build upon their successes and continue the fight for equality.

Empowering Through Visibility

Paula's visibility as a queer politician was instrumental in inspiring others. Her public speeches, media appearances, and participation in pride events showcased the possibility of queer representation at the highest levels of government. By sharing her story, Paula empowered countless individuals to embrace their identities and consider a future in politics.

In a poignant moment during a national LGBTQ rights rally, Paula stated, "When you see someone who looks like you, who shares your struggles, it ignites a fire within you. It tells you that you too can be a leader." This sentiment resonates with the findings of [?], who noted that representation can inspire individuals to pursue careers in fields where they have been historically underrepresented.

Challenges and Resilience

While Paula's journey was inspiring, it was not without challenges. As a queer disabled woman, she faced unique hurdles, including discrimination and skepticism from both allies and opponents. However, her resilience in the face of adversity served as a powerful lesson for future queer politicians. Paula often spoke about the importance of perseverance and the need to remain steadfast in one's beliefs, even when faced with significant opposition.

For instance, during her campaign for office, Paula encountered organized resistance from conservative groups. Rather than backing down, she used these challenges as opportunities to engage in dialogue, educate the public, and amplify her message. This resilience not only solidified her position but also inspired others to stand firm in their convictions.

The Ripple Effect of Paula's Legacy

The impact of Paula Lupi's advocacy extends far beyond her immediate political achievements. Her legacy is evident in the growing number of queer individuals who are stepping into political roles, emboldened by her example. The rise of openly queer politicians in Portugal and around the world can be traced back to the groundwork laid by Paula and her contemporaries.

As [?] highlights, the visibility of queer politicians can create a ripple effect, encouraging others to engage in politics and advocate for their communities. Paula's legacy is a testament to the power of representation and the importance of fostering an environment where future generations can thrive.

Conclusion

Inspiring future generations of queer politicians is not merely about individual success; it is about creating a movement rooted in solidarity, mentorship, and resilience. Paula Lupi's journey exemplifies the transformative power of representation in politics. By championing inclusive policies, creating safe spaces, and empowering young activists, Paula has set a precedent for the future of queer political representation. Her legacy will continue to inspire and guide those who dare to dream of a more inclusive and equitable political landscape.

International Advocacy

The realization of the global impact of her activism

As Paula Lupi's journey unfolded, she began to recognize that her activism extended far beyond the borders of Portugal. The realization of the global impact of her efforts was a pivotal moment in her life, transforming her perspective on advocacy and the interconnectedness of social justice movements worldwide.

The Ripple Effect of Local Actions

Paula's early activism, rooted in local LGBTQ and disability rights issues, demonstrated a fundamental principle of social movements: local actions can have global ramifications. This phenomenon can be understood through the concept of the *ripple effect*, where individual actions create waves of change that can reach distant shores. For example, her work in advocating for inclusive education policies in Lisbon inspired similar initiatives in other countries, showcasing how localized efforts can catalyze broader movements.

Global Networks and Solidarity

The rise of digital communication platforms provided Paula with unprecedented access to global networks of activists. She began to engage with organizations such as *ILGA World* and *Human Rights Watch*, which emphasized the importance of solidarity among marginalized groups. Paula learned that her struggles were not isolated; they resonated with activists fighting for LGBTQ and disability rights in places like Brazil, South Africa, and the United States. This interconnectedness is encapsulated in the theory of *transnational advocacy networks*, which illustrates how activists across borders collaborate to address shared challenges.

The Power of International Conferences

Paula's first international conference was a transformative experience. At the *International Conference on LGBTQ Rights*, she witnessed firsthand the power of collective voices. Activists from diverse backgrounds shared their stories, highlighting the universal nature of their struggles. This gathering underscored the significance of intersectionality in activism, as it became clear that issues of race, class, and gender identity were intricately linked to the fight for LGBTQ and disability rights. Paula's participation in such events allowed her to amplify her message and learn from others, solidifying her understanding of global activism.

The Role of Media in Shaping Perceptions

Media played a crucial role in elevating Paula's work to an international audience. Through interviews, articles, and social media, she was able to share her advocacy journey and the challenges faced by the LGBTQ and disabled communities in Portugal. The concept of *framing* became apparent as she realized how narratives could shape public perception. By framing her activism within the broader context of human rights, Paula was able to garner support from individuals and organizations around the globe.

Challenges of Global Activism

However, with global recognition came challenges. Paula faced backlash from conservative groups who sought to undermine her credibility. The intersectionality of her identity as a queer disabled woman often made her a target for criticism. This backlash highlighted the complexities of global activism, where cultural differences and varying degrees of acceptance could lead to misunderstandings and conflict. Paula navigated these challenges by emphasizing the importance of dialogue and education, advocating for a nuanced understanding of LGBTQ and disability rights across cultures.

Building Bridges Through Collaboration

Recognizing the importance of collaboration, Paula sought to build bridges between various movements. She understood that the fight for LGBTQ rights was intrinsically linked to other social justice issues, such as racial equality and disability rights. By collaborating with activists from different backgrounds, she was able to create a more inclusive movement that addressed the needs of all marginalized communities. This approach is supported by the theory of *intersectional activism*, which posits that addressing multiple forms of oppression simultaneously can lead to more effective advocacy.

A Legacy of Global Impact

Ultimately, Paula's realization of the global impact of her activism solidified her commitment to creating change on an international scale. She became a mentor to emerging activists, emphasizing the importance of understanding global contexts and the interconnectedness of struggles. Her legacy is one of resilience and collaboration, inspiring future generations to recognize that while local actions matter, the fight for justice is a collective endeavor that transcends borders.

In summary, Paula Lupi's journey illuminated the profound impact of her activism on a global scale. By embracing the principles of solidarity, intersectionality, and collaboration, she not only advanced the cause of LGBTQ and disability rights in Portugal but also contributed to a broader movement for social justice worldwide. The realization that her voice could resonate beyond her immediate community empowered Paula to continue her work with renewed vigor, knowing that her efforts were part of a larger tapestry of change.

Representing Portugal at international conferences and events

As Paula Lupi's activism gained traction within Portugal, her influence began to resonate beyond national borders. Recognizing the potential for international collaboration, Paula stepped onto the global stage, representing Portugal at numerous conferences and events dedicated to LGBTQ and disability rights. This transition marked a significant evolution in her advocacy, where local issues were framed within a broader, global context.

One of the primary challenges Paula faced in representing Portugal internationally was the need to articulate the unique cultural and political landscape of her home country while addressing universal themes of human rights. The intersection of LGBTQ rights and disability advocacy was not only a personal mission for Paula but also a critical issue that required nuanced understanding and representation on the global stage.

In her presentations, Paula often highlighted the progress Portugal had made in recent years, including the legalization of same-sex marriage in 2010 and the introduction of anti-discrimination laws. She used these achievements as a foundation for discussing ongoing challenges, such as the persistent stigma faced by LGBTQ individuals with disabilities. This dual focus allowed her to illustrate the complexities of intersectionality, emphasizing that the fight for rights is not monolithic but rather multifaceted.

For example, at the International LGBTQ Rights Conference in Berlin, Paula delivered a keynote speech that captivated the audience with her passionate call for global solidarity. She stated:

> "The fight for LGBTQ rights cannot be separated from the fight for disability rights. We must unite our voices, for only together can we

dismantle the barriers that keep us marginalized."

This assertion resonated deeply with attendees, many of whom were activists from various backgrounds facing similar issues in their own countries. Paula's ability to weave personal narratives with statistical data showcased the importance of lived experiences in advocacy. She often cited studies indicating that LGBTQ individuals with disabilities experience higher rates of discrimination and violence, a fact that underscored the urgent need for intersectional approaches in policy-making.

In addition to her speeches, Paula engaged in workshops and panel discussions, where she encouraged dialogue on best practices for inclusive activism. For instance, during a panel on "Innovative Strategies for Advocacy," she shared insights from her grassroots organizing experiences in Lisbon. She emphasized the significance of community engagement and the necessity of creating safe spaces for dialogue among marginalized groups.

$$\text{Advocacy Success} = f(\text{Community Engagement, Intersectionality, Global Collaboration}) \tag{48}$$

This equation encapsulates Paula's belief that successful advocacy is a function of these three critical components. She argued that without engaging the community, recognizing intersectional identities, and fostering global collaboration, efforts would be fragmented and less effective.

Moreover, Paula's participation in international events allowed her to forge connections with other activists and organizations, creating a network of support that transcended borders. At the United Nations Human Rights Council, she collaborated with fellow activists to draft a resolution that called for the inclusion of LGBTQ and disability rights in the UN's Sustainable Development Goals. This collaboration was pivotal, as it marked one of the first times that intersectionality was formally recognized in a UN resolution.

Despite these successes, Paula also encountered significant challenges. She faced cultural and political pushback, particularly from conservative factions within the international community who viewed her advocacy as a threat to traditional values. At one conference, a heated debate erupted when a representative from a conservative organization accused Paula of promoting a "Western agenda" that undermined local cultures. Paula responded with poise, emphasizing that human rights are universal and should not be subject to cultural relativism.

> "Human rights are not negotiable. They are the foundation of our shared humanity, transcending borders and cultures. We must not

allow the guise of tradition to perpetuate discrimination and violence."

This confrontation highlighted the ongoing struggle for recognition and respect for LGBTQ and disability rights on a global scale. Paula's steadfast commitment to her principles, even in the face of hostility, earned her respect among her peers and solidified her position as a formidable advocate.

In conclusion, Paula Lupi's representation of Portugal at international conferences and events was a defining aspect of her activism. By articulating the complexities of LGBTQ and disability rights through a lens of intersectionality, she not only elevated the discourse but also inspired a generation of activists worldwide. Her ability to navigate cultural sensitivities while advocating for universal human rights exemplifies the transformative power of inclusive activism. As she continues her journey, Paula remains a beacon of hope and a catalyst for change, proving that when voices unite, the impact can be profound and far-reaching.

Collaborating with international organizations and allies

In the journey of advocacy, collaboration with international organizations and allies is not merely beneficial; it is essential. For Paula Lupi, the act of joining forces with global entities was a strategic maneuver that amplified her voice and the voices of those she represented. This section delves into the theoretical underpinnings, challenges faced, and real-world examples that illustrate the significance of these collaborations.

Theoretical Framework

Collaboration can be understood through the lens of *network theory*, which posits that the connections between individuals and organizations can lead to enhanced resource sharing, knowledge exchange, and collective efficacy. In the context of LGBTQ and disability rights, this theory underscores the importance of building coalitions that transcend geographic and cultural boundaries.

Let C represent the collaborative potential, defined as:

$$C = \sum_{i=1}^{n} R_i \tag{49}$$

where R_i denotes the resources available from each collaborating entity i, and n is the total number of allies involved. The greater the number of allies, the more robust the advocacy efforts can become.

Challenges in Collaboration

Despite the potential benefits, collaboration is fraught with challenges. One significant issue is the *divergence of goals*. Organizations may have overlapping but distinct objectives, leading to conflicts in priorities. For instance, while Paula aimed to advocate for both LGBTQ and disability rights, some international organizations might focus solely on one aspect, creating friction in joint initiatives.

Another challenge is the *cultural differences* that can arise during international collaborations. These differences can affect communication styles, decision-making processes, and even the framing of issues. Understanding and navigating these cultural nuances is critical for successful partnerships.

Examples of Collaboration

Paula's collaboration with international organizations began with her engagement in global forums such as the *International LGBTQI+ Youth and Student Organisation (IGLYO)*. This partnership allowed her to share insights from Portugal's unique socio-political landscape while learning from the experiences of activists worldwide.

Moreover, during the *United Nations Human Rights Council* sessions, Paula represented Portugal, advocating for inclusive policies that addressed both LGBTQ and disability rights. Her presence in these high-stakes environments showcased the importance of intersectionality in advocacy, emphasizing that the fight for rights cannot be compartmentalized.

One notable initiative was the *Global Fund for Women*, which partnered with Paula to develop educational programs aimed at empowering LGBTQ disabled women in developing countries. This collaboration not only provided funding but also facilitated knowledge transfer, allowing grassroots activists to adopt successful strategies employed in Portugal.

Impact of Collaboration

The impact of Paula's collaborations extended beyond immediate outcomes. By working with international organizations, she helped to create a *global narrative* around LGBTQ and disability rights, shifting perceptions and fostering a sense of solidarity among activists.

For example, through her engagement with the *World Health Organization* (WHO), Paula contributed to the development of guidelines that addressed health disparities faced by LGBTQ disabled individuals. These guidelines, adopted by various nations, serve as a testament to the power of collaborative advocacy.

In mathematical terms, the effectiveness of these collaborations can be represented by the equation:

$$E = \frac{C \cdot I}{D} \tag{50}$$

where E is the effectiveness of the collaboration, C is the collaborative potential, I is the impact achieved, and D represents the difficulties encountered. A higher collaborative potential combined with significant impact, when appropriately managed to mitigate difficulties, leads to a more effective advocacy effort.

Conclusion

In conclusion, Paula Lupi's collaborations with international organizations and allies exemplify the power of collective action in the fight for LGBTQ and disability rights. By leveraging network theory, navigating challenges, and drawing on successful examples, Paula not only advanced her cause but also inspired a global movement towards inclusivity. The alliances forged during her advocacy journey continue to resonate, shaping policies and practices that pave the way for future generations of activists. The lessons learned from these collaborations serve as a guiding framework for those who wish to amplify their impact in an increasingly interconnected world.

Speaking truth to power on the global stage

In an era where global interconnectedness has reached unprecedented levels, the ability to speak truth to power has become a critical component of effective activism. For Paula Lupi, this meant not only advocating for LGBTQ and disability rights within Portugal but also extending her voice to international platforms, where the stakes were often higher and the challenges more complex.

The Importance of Global Advocacy

Global advocacy serves as a powerful mechanism for change, allowing activists to highlight injustices that transcend national borders. Paula recognized that many LGBTQ individuals and disabled persons faced systemic discrimination not only in Portugal but worldwide. By addressing these issues on a global stage, she aimed to foster solidarity among marginalized communities and galvanize international support.

One of the core theories underpinning global activism is the *Theory of Global Justice*, which posits that all individuals, regardless of their geographical location, deserve equal rights and opportunities. This theory emphasizes the interconnectedness of human rights, suggesting that injustices in one part of the world can have ripple effects elsewhere. Paula's advocacy was rooted in this theory, as she sought to illuminate the struggles of LGBTQ and disabled individuals globally, thereby building a case for universal human rights.

Navigating Challenges

However, speaking truth to power on the global stage is fraught with challenges. Activists often face backlash from governments, social institutions, and even within their communities. For Paula, these challenges manifested in various forms, including:

- **Cultural Resistance:** Many cultures have deeply entrenched beliefs that oppose LGBTQ rights and disability inclusion. Paula often encountered resistance when attempting to address these issues in countries where traditional values clashed with her advocacy.

- **Political Backlash:** Governments may view outspoken activists as threats to their authority or social order. Paula faced significant political pushback when she criticized policies that marginalized LGBTQ individuals, especially in countries with authoritarian regimes.

- **Resource Limitations:** Effective global advocacy often requires substantial resources—financial, human, and informational. Paula had to navigate the complexities of securing funding and support for her initiatives, particularly when collaborating with organizations in less affluent regions.

Examples of Impactful Advocacy

Despite these challenges, Paula's efforts to speak truth to power yielded significant outcomes. One notable example was her participation in the *International LGBTQ Rights Conference*, where she delivered a keynote address that resonated with activists from diverse backgrounds. In her speech, she emphasized the importance of intersectionality in advocacy, stating:

> "Our struggles are not isolated; they are interconnected. The fight for LGBTQ rights cannot be separated from the fight for disability rights. We must stand together, united in our diversity, to challenge the oppressive systems that seek to silence us."

This address not only garnered international attention but also inspired collaborative initiatives among various human rights organizations, leading to the formation of coalitions that focused on intersectional issues.

Another significant moment came when Paula spearheaded a campaign against the *Global Gag Rule*, which restricted funding for organizations that provide abortion services or referrals. By rallying support from international allies, she was able to bring attention to how such policies disproportionately affect marginalized communities, particularly LGBTQ and disabled individuals. The campaign culminated in a resolution passed at the *United Nations Human Rights Council*, which called for the repeal of the Global Gag Rule, marking a pivotal victory for human rights advocates.

Theoretical Framework: Advocacy as Resistance

To understand the dynamics of Paula's global advocacy, it is essential to consider the *Theory of Advocacy as Resistance*. This framework posits that activism is inherently a form of resistance against oppressive systems. Paula's approach exemplified this theory, as she consistently challenged the status quo, advocating for policy changes that would benefit marginalized communities.

Mathematically, we can represent the effectiveness of advocacy as a function of three variables:

$$E = f(R, A, I) \tag{51}$$

where:

- E = Effectiveness of advocacy
- R = Resources available (financial, human, informational)
- A = Alliances formed (collaborations with other organizations)
- I = Impact of initiatives (measured through policy changes, awareness raised, etc.)

This equation underscores the importance of resource mobilization, strategic alliances, and measurable impact in advocacy efforts. Paula's ability to effectively leverage these variables allowed her to amplify her voice and the voices of those she represented.

Conclusion

In conclusion, speaking truth to power on the global stage is a multifaceted endeavor that requires courage, resilience, and strategic thinking. Paula Lupi's advocacy exemplifies the power of intersectional activism, demonstrating that the fight for LGBTQ and disability rights is not just a local issue but a global imperative. By navigating the complexities of international advocacy, Paula not only raised awareness but also inspired a new generation of activists to continue the fight for equality and justice.

Her legacy serves as a reminder that when marginalized voices unite and speak truth to power, they can effect meaningful change, challenging oppressive systems and paving the way for a more inclusive world.

Advocating for LGBTQ and disability rights on an international scale

In the global landscape of human rights, the intersectionality of LGBTQ and disability rights has emerged as a pivotal area of advocacy. Paula Lupi recognized early on that the struggles faced by LGBTQ individuals with disabilities were often overlooked, both within the LGBTQ rights movement and the disability rights movement. This dual advocacy is crucial as it highlights the unique challenges faced by individuals who exist at this intersection, often resulting in compounded discrimination and marginalization.

Theoretical Frameworks

To understand the advocacy for LGBTQ and disability rights on an international scale, it is essential to consider several theoretical frameworks. One such framework is Intersectionality, coined by Kimberlé Crenshaw, which posits that individuals experience oppression in varying configurations and degrees of intensity based on their overlapping identities. This theory is particularly relevant for LGBTQ individuals with disabilities, as they navigate multiple layers of discrimination that can exacerbate their struggles.

Furthermore, the Social Model of Disability provides a critical lens through which to view advocacy efforts. This model argues that disability is not an individual deficit but rather a result of societal barriers that prevent people with disabilities from fully participating in society. By applying this model, advocates like Paula emphasize the need for systemic change rather than solely focusing on individual impairments.

Global Challenges

Advocating for LGBTQ and disability rights on an international scale presents numerous challenges. In many parts of the world, LGBTQ individuals face criminalization, violence, and social ostracism. Countries with stringent anti-LGBTQ laws often lack comprehensive disability rights protections, leaving LGBTQ individuals with disabilities particularly vulnerable. For example, in regions where homosexuality is punishable by law, the intersection of sexual orientation and disability can lead to heightened risks of violence and discrimination.

Additionally, cultural attitudes towards both LGBTQ identities and disabilities can hinder advocacy efforts. In many societies, traditional views may stigmatize both identities, leading to a lack of support for inclusive policies. This cultural resistance can manifest in various forms, including political opposition, social backlash, and even violence against advocates who dare to challenge the status quo.

Examples of Advocacy Efforts

Despite these challenges, there have been significant strides made in advocating for LGBTQ and disability rights on an international scale. Organizations such as ILGA (International Lesbian, Gay, Bisexual, Trans and Intersex Association) and the World Institute on Disability have collaborated to amplify the voices of LGBTQ individuals with disabilities. These organizations work to create inclusive policies and programs that address the unique needs of this community.

For instance, during international human rights conferences, advocates like Paula have effectively lobbied for the inclusion of LGBTQ and disability rights in global human rights agendas. By presenting data and personal testimonies, they have highlighted the urgent need for intersectional approaches in policy-making. One notable example is the inclusion of LGBTQ and disability rights in the United Nations' Sustainable Development Goals, which aim to ensure inclusive and equitable quality education and promote lifelong learning opportunities for all.

The Role of International Frameworks

International frameworks such as the Convention on the Rights of Persons with Disabilities (CRPD) and the Yogyakarta Principles provide essential guidelines for advocates. The CRPD emphasizes the rights of persons with disabilities to enjoy their human rights on an equal basis with others, while the Yogyakarta Principles outline how international human rights law should be applied to issues of sexual orientation and gender identity. These frameworks serve as powerful tools for advocacy, enabling activists to hold governments accountable for their commitments to human rights.

Moreover, the intersection of these frameworks allows for a more comprehensive approach to advocacy. By leveraging both the CRPD and the Yogyakarta Principles, advocates can argue for policies that address the unique challenges faced by LGBTQ individuals with disabilities, ensuring that their rights are recognized and protected.

Conclusion

Advocating for LGBTQ and disability rights on an international scale is a complex and multifaceted endeavor. It requires a deep understanding of the theoretical frameworks that inform advocacy, an awareness of the global challenges faced by this community, and a commitment to leveraging international frameworks to effect change. Through her tireless efforts, Paula Lupi has not only raised awareness about the intersectionality of these issues but has also inspired a new generation of activists to continue the fight for equality and justice on a global scale. By advocating for systemic change, she has laid the groundwork for a more inclusive world where the rights of all individuals, regardless of their sexual orientation or disability, are upheld and celebrated.

The challenges and triumphs of navigating diplomacy

Navigating the complex landscape of international diplomacy presents unique challenges and opportunities for activists like Paula Lupi, particularly when advocating for LGBTQ and disability rights. The interplay of culture, politics, and social norms across different countries often creates a multifaceted environment that can either facilitate or hinder progress.

One of the primary challenges Paula faced was the stark contrast in LGBTQ rights across various nations. For instance, while Portugal had made significant strides in legalizing same-sex marriage and promoting disability rights, many countries still criminalized homosexuality or lacked adequate protections for disabled individuals. This disparity required Paula to adopt a nuanced approach to diplomacy, recognizing that a one-size-fits-all strategy would be ineffective.

In her advocacy, Paula employed the theory of **constructivism**, which posits that international relations are shaped by social constructs and identities rather than merely by material power. Constructivism emphasizes the importance of dialogue and understanding in fostering international cooperation. Paula understood that to influence change effectively, she needed to engage with diverse stakeholders, including government officials, NGOs, and local activists, to build a common understanding of human rights issues.

One notable example of her diplomatic efforts was her participation in the *International Conference on LGBTQ Rights*, held in Geneva. Here, Paula faced the challenge of addressing representatives from countries with vastly different human rights records. Utilizing her skills in **negotiation theory**, she approached discussions with a focus on mutual interests rather than confrontational tactics. For instance, she highlighted the economic benefits of inclusive policies, such as increased tourism and international investment, which resonated with delegates from countries seeking to boost their economies.

However, the path was not without its setbacks. During a high-profile meeting with diplomats from a country notorious for its anti-LGBTQ stance, Paula encountered hostility. The delegates dismissed her concerns, arguing that cultural values superseded international human rights norms. This moment underscored the **cultural relativism** debate, which posits that human rights may be interpreted differently across cultures. Paula navigated this challenge by framing her arguments in terms of universal human dignity, emphasizing that the rights of LGBTQ individuals are not merely Western ideals but fundamental to all human beings.

Moreover, the intersectionality of LGBTQ and disability rights added another layer of complexity. Paula advocated for a holistic approach, arguing that the experiences of disabled LGBTQ individuals often go overlooked in both LGBTQ and disability rights discussions. This perspective aligns with the **intersectionality theory**, which posits that individuals experience overlapping systems of discrimination. By highlighting stories of disabled LGBTQ activists from various cultural backgrounds, Paula successfully illustrated the need for inclusive policies that address these intersecting identities.

Despite these challenges, Paula's diplomatic efforts yielded significant triumphs. Her advocacy contributed to the establishment of the *Global Coalition for LGBTQ and Disability Rights*, a collaborative initiative aimed at promoting inclusive policies worldwide. This coalition not only provided a platform for marginalized voices but also facilitated the sharing of best practices among countries striving to improve their human rights records.

In conclusion, Paula Lupi's journey through the intricacies of international diplomacy exemplifies the challenges and triumphs faced by activists advocating for LGBTQ and disability rights. By employing constructivist approaches, negotiation strategies, and intersectional perspectives, she navigated a complex landscape, ultimately fostering greater understanding and cooperation among diverse stakeholders. Her legacy serves as a testament to the power of diplomacy in effecting meaningful change on a global scale.

Making significant strides in global LGBTQ and disability rights

The journey towards global LGBTQ and disability rights has been marked by both challenges and significant achievements. Activists like Paula Lupi have played pivotal roles in this movement, advocating for the intersectionality of these rights on international platforms. The importance of recognizing the interconnectedness of LGBTQ rights and disability rights cannot be overstated; both communities face systemic discrimination, and their struggles often overlap.

Theoretical Framework

To understand the significance of these strides, we must consider the theoretical frameworks that underpin LGBTQ and disability rights advocacy. Intersectionality, a term coined by Kimberlé Crenshaw, provides a lens through which we can examine how various forms of discrimination intersect. For instance, a queer disabled person may face unique challenges that differ from those experienced by able-bodied LGBTQ individuals or disabled heterosexual individuals.

This intersectional approach is crucial for developing inclusive policies and practices that address the needs of all marginalized communities. Theories of social justice, particularly those articulated by theorists such as John Rawls and Martha Nussbaum, emphasize the necessity of equity and the provision of capabilities for all individuals. This theoretical foundation supports the idea that advocacy must not only aim for legal rights but also for social acceptance and the removal of barriers that hinder participation in society.

Challenges Faced

Despite progress, numerous challenges persist in the quest for LGBTQ and disability rights on a global scale. Discrimination remains deeply entrenched in many societies, often exacerbated by cultural norms and governmental policies. For example, in several countries, laws criminalizing homosexuality coexist with inadequate protections for disabled individuals, creating a dual burden for queer disabled people.

Moreover, the lack of comprehensive data on the experiences of LGBTQ individuals with disabilities hinders effective advocacy. In many regions, these communities are invisible within both LGBTQ and disability rights movements, leading to a lack of tailored resources and support.

Significant Achievements

In recent years, significant strides have been made at both national and international levels. One landmark achievement was the adoption of the United Nations Sustainable Development Goals (SDGs), which explicitly call for the inclusion of marginalized groups, including LGBTQ individuals and people with disabilities. This framework provides a roadmap for countries to assess and improve their policies regarding these communities.

For instance, the Global Fund for Women has funded initiatives that support LGBTQ and disabled activists in various countries, empowering them to advocate for their rights more effectively. These initiatives have led to tangible outcomes, such as the establishment of inclusive policies in schools and workplaces, which recognize the unique challenges faced by queer disabled individuals.

A notable example of successful advocacy is the campaign for marriage equality in countries like Malta and Taiwan, which included provisions for disabled individuals. These campaigns not only focused on the legal aspects but also on changing societal attitudes toward LGBTQ individuals with disabilities, highlighting their right to love and partnership.

Global Collaborations

The power of global collaboration cannot be underestimated in this fight. Organizations such as ILGA (International Lesbian, Gay, Bisexual, Trans and Intersex Association) and DPI (Disabled Peoples' International) have worked together to amplify the voices of LGBTQ individuals with disabilities. Their joint efforts have led to the creation of resources that address the specific needs of these communities, such as guidelines for inclusive event planning and advocacy strategies.

Furthermore, international conferences, such as the UN's Human Rights Council sessions, have provided platforms for activists like Paula Lupi to share their experiences and push for policy changes. These platforms have facilitated discussions on the importance of inclusive legislation that protects the rights of all individuals, regardless of their sexual orientation or disability status.

Case Studies

Several case studies illustrate the impact of these global efforts. In 2021, a coalition of LGBTQ and disability rights organizations in Brazil successfully lobbied for the inclusion of disability rights within the broader LGBTQ rights agenda. This led to the implementation of training programs for law enforcement officials on how to support queer disabled individuals in crisis situations.

Another example is the "Disability and LGBTQ Rights" project in South Africa, which focuses on creating safe spaces for queer disabled individuals. This project has not only provided resources but has also fostered community-building, allowing individuals to share their stories and support one another.

Conclusion

As we look to the future, the need for continued advocacy remains paramount. The strides made in global LGBTQ and disability rights are a testament to the power of intersectional activism. By recognizing the unique challenges faced by queer disabled individuals and advocating for their rights on both local and global stages, activists like Paula Lupi are laying the groundwork for a more inclusive world. The journey is far from over, but with each step forward, the vision of equality and justice becomes more attainable for all.

Amplifying the voices of activists from around the world

In the realm of advocacy, the act of amplifying voices is not merely a matter of sharing stories; it is a fundamental strategy for fostering global solidarity and promoting social justice. Paula Lupi recognized early on that her activism was part of a larger tapestry of struggles faced by LGBTQ and disabled individuals worldwide. By amplifying the voices of activists from diverse backgrounds, she aimed to create a network of support and shared experiences that transcended geographical and cultural boundaries.

The theory of intersectionality, as introduced by Kimberlé Crenshaw, provides a crucial framework for understanding how different forms of oppression intersect and compound each other. This theory emphasizes that individuals do not experience oppression in isolation but rather through a complex interplay of identities, including race, gender, sexual orientation, and disability. Paula's commitment to intersectionality meant that she actively sought to elevate the voices of marginalized activists who often remained unheard within mainstream discourses.

One of the significant challenges faced in amplifying voices globally is the issue of representation. Many activists from the Global South, particularly those representing LGBTQ and disabled communities, encounter systemic barriers that limit their visibility and access to platforms. Paula understood that without intentional efforts to include these voices, the narrative of activism would remain incomplete and skewed towards more privileged perspectives.

For example, during international conferences, Paula often collaborated with grassroots organizations from various countries, ensuring that activists from underrepresented regions could share their stories. In 2019, at the International LGBTQ Rights Conference in Lisbon, she facilitated a panel that featured activists from Brazil, Nigeria, and India, discussing the unique challenges they faced in their respective contexts. This initiative not only provided a platform for these activists but also fostered a rich dialogue on the varying dimensions of LGBTQ rights, highlighting how local struggles are intertwined with global movements.

Moreover, social media emerged as a powerful tool for amplifying voices in the digital age. Paula leveraged platforms like Twitter, Instagram, and Facebook to share the experiences of activists worldwide. By utilizing hashtags such as #GlobalLGBTQVoices and #DisabilityRightsNow, she created a digital space where stories could be shared, and solidarity could be built. This approach not only increased visibility for marginalized activists but also encouraged a sense of community among individuals advocating for similar causes, regardless of their location.

However, the digital landscape is not without its pitfalls. The phenomenon of "slacktivism," where individuals engage in minimal online actions without substantial commitment to real-world change, posed a risk to the integrity of global activism. Paula emphasized the importance of translating online support into tangible actions, such as fundraising for international organizations or participating in local advocacy efforts. She often reminded her followers that, while social media could amplify voices, it was essential to engage in sustained activism that addressed the root causes of oppression.

Another critical aspect of amplifying voices is ensuring that the narratives shared are authentic and representative. Paula was acutely aware of the potential for misrepresentation and appropriation of marginalized voices. Therefore, she advocated for a model of activism that prioritized consent and collaboration. This meant that when sharing stories from other activists, she would seek permission and ensure that the narratives were presented in ways that aligned with the activists' own experiences and contexts.

In practice, this approach led to the creation of a documentary series titled "Voices of Change," which showcased the stories of LGBTQ and disabled activists from around the world. Each episode featured activists narrating their experiences in their own words, accompanied by insights from Paula and other allies on how to support these movements. The series not only provided visibility but also educated audiences on the intricacies of global advocacy, fostering a deeper understanding of the challenges faced by different communities.

Ultimately, Paula Lupi's commitment to amplifying the voices of activists from around the world was rooted in the belief that collective action is essential for meaningful change. By recognizing and valuing the diverse experiences and perspectives within the global LGBTQ and disability rights movements, she sought to build a more inclusive and equitable world. The act of amplification, therefore, became a powerful tool for solidarity, enabling activists to learn from one another, share resources, and unite in their common struggle for justice.

In conclusion, the work of amplifying voices transcends mere representation; it is about creating a global movement that honors the diversity of experiences within the LGBTQ and disability rights communities. Paula Lupi's legacy in this regard serves as a reminder that true activism requires not only the courage to speak out but also the humility to listen, learn, and uplift those whose voices have historically been marginalized. As future generations of activists continue this vital work, they will carry forward Paula's vision of a world where every voice is heard and valued in the ongoing fight for equality and justice.

Building bridges between different cultures and movements

In the intricate tapestry of activism, building bridges between different cultures and movements is not merely a noble goal; it is an essential strategy for fostering solidarity and understanding. For Paula Lupi, this endeavor became a cornerstone of her work as she recognized that the struggles faced by the LGBTQ community were often intertwined with those of other marginalized groups, including people with disabilities, racial minorities, and women. This intersectional approach is crucial for creating a more inclusive and effective advocacy landscape.

Theoretical Framework

The theory of intersectionality, coined by Kimberlé Crenshaw, serves as a foundational framework for understanding how various forms of discrimination overlap and interact. Intersectionality posits that individuals do not experience oppression in a vacuum; rather, their identities—shaped by race, gender, sexuality, ability, and other factors—intersect to create unique experiences of marginalization. This theory underscores the importance of recognizing the diverse experiences within the LGBTQ community and advocating for a more holistic approach to social justice.

Challenges in Building Bridges

While the goal of cross-cultural solidarity is admirable, it is fraught with challenges. One significant issue is the potential for cultural appropriation, where elements of a marginalized culture are adopted by those outside it without proper context or respect. This can lead to the commodification of cultural symbols and practices, stripping them of their meaning and significance. For instance, when LGBTQ pride events feature cultural elements from Indigenous communities without acknowledgment or collaboration, it can create tensions and feelings of exploitation.

Another challenge is the tendency for movements to become siloed, where groups focus solely on their specific issues without recognizing the interconnectedness of their struggles. This can create an environment of competition rather than collaboration. For example, during the fight for marriage equality in Portugal, some LGBTQ activists prioritized their rights over those of disabled individuals, neglecting the unique challenges faced by queer disabled people. This oversight not only alienated potential allies but also weakened the overall movement.

Examples of Successful Bridge-Building

Despite these challenges, Paula Lupi's work exemplifies successful efforts to build bridges between different cultures and movements. One notable initiative was her collaboration with organizations advocating for racial justice in Portugal. By participating in joint protests and campaigns, Lupi helped to highlight the shared struggles against systemic oppression. This partnership not only amplified the voices of marginalized communities but also demonstrated the power of unity in activism.

Moreover, Lupi recognized the importance of allyship within the LGBTQ community itself. She actively sought to include voices from various cultural backgrounds in her advocacy efforts, ensuring that the narratives of Black, Indigenous, and people of color (BIPOC) were front and center. For instance, during international conferences, she made it a point to invite speakers from diverse backgrounds to share their perspectives on LGBTQ rights, thereby fostering a richer dialogue and promoting mutual understanding.

Strategies for Effective Collaboration

To effectively build bridges between different cultures and movements, several strategies can be employed:

1. **Inclusive Dialogue:** Creating spaces for open and honest conversations among diverse groups is vital. This can involve hosting forums or workshops that encourage participants to share their experiences and challenges, fostering empathy and understanding.

2. **Mutual Education:** Educating oneself and others about the history and struggles of different movements can promote respect and solidarity. Lupi often emphasized the importance of learning about the histories of racial justice and disability rights within the context of LGBTQ activism.

3. **Collaborative Projects:** Joint initiatives that address overlapping issues can strengthen alliances. For example, campaigns that advocate for accessible public spaces not only benefit disabled individuals but also create inclusive environments for LGBTQ people.

4. **Celebrating Diversity:** Recognizing and celebrating the unique contributions of various cultures can enhance the richness of the movement. Lupi organized cultural events that showcased the art, music, and traditions of different communities, fostering a sense of belonging and pride.

5. **Accountability:** Establishing mechanisms for accountability within and between movements is crucial. This can involve creating guidelines for collaboration that prioritize inclusivity and respect for all participants.

Conclusion

Building bridges between different cultures and movements is not just a strategy; it is a necessity in the fight for social justice. By embracing intersectionality and fostering collaboration, activists can create a more inclusive and powerful movement that addresses the multifaceted nature of oppression. Paula Lupi's legacy serves as a testament to the potential for solidarity in activism, reminding us that our struggles are interconnected and that together, we can forge a path toward a more equitable world.

Becoming a global icon and inspiration for activists worldwide

Paula Lupi's journey from a passionate local activist to a global icon is a testament to the power of advocacy and the ripple effects of individual actions. Her rise to international prominence was not merely a product of her activism but also a reflection of the changing tides within the global landscape concerning LGBTQ and disability rights.

The Power of Representation

Representation plays a critical role in activism, particularly for marginalized communities. Paula's visibility as a queer disabled woman challenged existing stereotypes and offered a new narrative that resonated with many. Her story illustrated that activism is not a monolithic endeavor; it is multifaceted, encompassing diverse experiences and identities.

The theory of intersectionality, as articulated by Kimberlé Crenshaw, emphasizes how overlapping social identities—such as race, gender, sexual orientation, and disability—can lead to unique experiences of discrimination and privilege. Paula embodied this theory, demonstrating how her intersecting identities fueled her passion for advocacy.

$$\text{Intersectionality} = f(\text{Identity}_1, \text{Identity}_2, \text{Identity}_3, \ldots) \qquad (52)$$

In this equation, each identity contributes to the overall experience of an individual, shaping their worldview and the way they engage with social justice issues. Paula's activism exemplified the need for an inclusive approach that recognizes and uplifts the voices of those at the intersections of various identities.

Global Collaborations

As Paula gained recognition, she began to collaborate with international organizations, amplifying her message on a global scale. Her participation in events such as the United Nations Human Rights Council sessions and LGBTQ rights conferences allowed her to share her insights and advocate for policies that protect the rights of marginalized communities worldwide.

One notable example was her involvement in the *Global LGBTQ Rights Summit*, where she presented a paper on the need for inclusive policies that address the unique challenges faced by queer disabled individuals. This platform not only showcased her expertise but also positioned her as a leading voice in international discussions about human rights.

Harnessing Social Media

In the digital age, social media has become an indispensable tool for activists seeking to reach broader audiences. Paula adeptly utilized platforms like Twitter, Instagram, and Facebook to share her journey, connect with supporters, and mobilize action. Her online presence allowed her to engage with followers in real-time, fostering a sense of community and solidarity among activists worldwide.

The viral nature of social media campaigns, such as the hashtag #InclusionForAll, exemplified how Paula's message resonated beyond borders. These campaigns not only raised awareness about LGBTQ and disability rights but also encouraged individuals to share their stories, creating a tapestry of experiences that highlighted the urgency of the cause.

Inspiring Future Generations

Paula's influence extended to inspiring a new generation of activists. Through mentorship programs and workshops, she dedicated herself to empowering young leaders, particularly those from marginalized backgrounds. Her emphasis on education as a tool for social change aligned with the belief that informed activists are better equipped to challenge systemic injustices.

One of her initiatives, the *Youth Advocacy Fellowship*, provided training and resources for aspiring activists, emphasizing the importance of intersectionality in their work. By nurturing young voices, Paula ensured that the fight for LGBTQ and disability rights would continue to evolve and adapt to the needs of future generations.

Legacy of Empowerment

As Paula solidified her status as a global icon, she remained grounded in her commitment to empowerment. She understood that her platform came with the responsibility to uplift those whose voices had been historically marginalized. Her advocacy was not solely about her own experiences; it was about creating a world where everyone, regardless of their identity, could thrive.

The impact of Paula's work is evident in the numerous accolades and honors she received, but perhaps more importantly, it is seen in the lives she touched and the movements she inspired. Her legacy is one of resilience, courage, and unwavering dedication to justice.

In conclusion, Paula Lupi's journey to becoming a global icon and inspiration for activists worldwide serves as a powerful reminder of the importance of representation, collaboration, and empowerment in the fight for equality. Her story is not just her own; it is a collective narrative that continues to inspire and mobilize individuals across the globe to advocate for a more inclusive and just world.

$$\text{Global Impact} = \text{Representation} + \text{Collaboration} + \text{Empowerment} \quad (53)$$

Media and Public Recognition

Capturing the attention of the media

In the age of information, where news travels faster than a blink, capturing the attention of the media is an art and a science. For Paula Lupi, a prominent LGBTQ and disability rights activist, this was not just a matter of luck but a calculated effort that involved understanding the media landscape, leveraging her unique narrative, and strategically positioning herself as a voice for the marginalized.

Understanding Media Dynamics

The media serves as a powerful conduit for shaping public perception and influencing societal norms. According to McCombs and Shaw's *Agenda-Setting Theory*, the media doesn't just tell us what to think, but rather what to think about. This theory posits that the issues highlighted by the media become the focal points of public discourse. For Paula, recognizing this dynamic was crucial. She understood that to elevate the plight of LGBTQ and disabled individuals, she needed to ensure that their stories were not just told, but told compellingly.

Crafting a Compelling Narrative

Paula's journey was rich with experiences that resonated deeply with the struggles faced by many. She leveraged her personal story—navigating the complexities of her identity as a queer disabled woman—to create a narrative that was both relatable and inspiring. According to Fisher's *Narrative Paradigm Theory*, humans are essentially storytelling beings, and we are more likely to be persuaded by stories than by facts alone. Paula's ability to weave her personal experiences with broader societal issues allowed her to connect emotionally with audiences, making her a media darling.

Utilizing Social Media Platforms

With the rise of social media, traditional media outlets are no longer the sole gatekeepers of information. Paula adeptly used platforms like Twitter, Instagram, and Facebook to amplify her message and engage directly with her audience. Social media not only allowed her to bypass traditional media filters but also provided a space for real-time interaction. According to the *Social Media Engagement Theory*, the level of engagement on these platforms can significantly influence public perception and mobilization efforts. Paula's posts often included hashtags like #LGBTQRights and #DisabilityAdvocacy, which helped to create a sense of community and urgency around her causes.

Strategic Media Appearances

Paula understood the importance of media appearances. She strategically sought out interviews, panel discussions, and speaking engagements that aligned with her mission. By appearing on popular talk shows and participating in high-profile events, she was able to elevate her message to a broader audience. Research has shown that visibility in mainstream media can lead to increased support for marginalized communities. For instance, after Paula's appearance on a national news program, there was a noticeable spike in public discussions regarding LGBTQ and disability rights.

Navigating Media Challenges

While capturing media attention can be beneficial, it is not without its challenges. Paula faced scrutiny and misrepresentation, common pitfalls for activists in the public eye. This aligns with the *Framing Theory*, which suggests that the way an issue is presented can significantly affect public perception. Paula's proactive approach to media training helped her navigate these challenges, equipping her with the tools to respond effectively to criticism and ensure her message was accurately conveyed.

The Role of Allies in Media Representation

Paula's journey was not solitary; she recognized the importance of allies in amplifying her voice. Collaborating with other activists and organizations helped to broaden her reach. For example, partnering with well-known LGBTQ organizations allowed her to tap into established media networks and gain credibility. This approach aligns with the *Collective Action Theory*, which posits that individuals working together can achieve greater impact than working alone.

Case Study: The Media Coverage of the Lisbon Pride Parade

One of the pivotal moments in Paula's media journey was her involvement in the Lisbon Pride Parade. This event garnered significant media attention, providing a platform for her to speak on critical issues facing the LGBTQ and disabled communities. The coverage of the parade highlighted not only the celebration of diversity but also the ongoing struggles for equality and acceptance. Paula's speeches during the event were covered by major news outlets, illustrating the power of strategic timing and visibility in media.

Conclusion

Capturing the attention of the media is an essential component of advocacy work. For Paula Lupi, it was about more than just being in the spotlight; it was about using that spotlight to illuminate the issues faced by LGBTQ and disabled individuals. By understanding media dynamics, crafting compelling narratives, utilizing social media, navigating challenges, and collaborating with allies, Paula not only captured media attention but also transformed it into a powerful tool for change. Her journey serves as a testament to the impact of effective media engagement in advocacy and activism.

The power of storytelling in raising awareness

Storytelling has long been recognized as a powerful tool for raising awareness and fostering empathy within communities. In the context of LGBTQ and disability rights, narratives that highlight personal experiences can bridge the gap between diverse groups, transforming abstract issues into relatable human stories. This section explores the theoretical frameworks, potential challenges, and illustrative examples of how storytelling serves as a catalyst for social change.

Theoretical Frameworks

At the heart of effective storytelling lies the concept of narrative transportation, which posits that individuals become immersed in a story, leading to emotional engagement and a shift in attitudes. According to Green and Brock (2000), narrative transportation can be defined as:

Narrative Transportation = Engagement + Empathy + Persuasion   (54)

This equation suggests that when audiences are engaged with a story, they are more likely to empathize with the characters and, consequently, be persuaded to adopt new viewpoints. In the realm of activism, this is particularly pertinent. For instance, when LGBTQ activists share their personal journeys, they humanize the struggles faced by the community, making the issues more tangible for listeners.

Another relevant theory is the social identity theory, which emphasizes the importance of group membership in shaping individual behaviors and attitudes. By sharing stories that resonate with shared identities, activists can foster a sense of belonging and solidarity within marginalized communities. This process often leads to collective action, as individuals feel empowered by their shared experiences.

Challenges in Storytelling

Despite its potential, storytelling in activism is not without challenges. One significant issue is the risk of oversimplification. When complex identities and experiences are reduced to single narratives, the diversity within communities can be obscured. This is particularly problematic for intersectional identities, where individuals may experience overlapping forms of discrimination.

Moreover, the authenticity of the storyteller can come into question. Unauthorized biographies, like the one focusing on Paula Lupi, can sometimes blur the lines between truth and representation, leading to controversies regarding the accuracy of the narratives presented. Critics may argue that such portrayals can misrepresent the lived experiences of individuals, undermining the very goals of advocacy.

Examples of Storytelling in Activism

One poignant example of storytelling in LGBTQ activism is the "It Gets Better" project, which was launched in response to a series of tragic suicides among LGBTQ youth. The campaign encourages individuals to share their stories of overcoming adversity and finding acceptance. By amplifying these narratives, the project not only raises awareness about the challenges faced by LGBTQ youth but also provides hope and encouragement to those who may be struggling.

In the realm of disability rights, the #DisabilityTooWhite campaign exemplifies how storytelling can highlight systemic issues within movements. By sharing personal accounts of disabled individuals of color, the campaign sheds light on the intersectionality of race and disability, challenging the predominantly white narratives that often dominate disability advocacy. This approach not only raises awareness but also calls for a more inclusive dialogue within the movement.

Conclusion

In summary, storytelling serves as a vital mechanism for raising awareness and fostering empathy in the fight for LGBTQ and disability rights. By engaging audiences through personal narratives, activists can transform abstract issues into relatable experiences, ultimately inspiring action and solidarity. However, it is crucial to navigate the complexities of representation and authenticity to ensure that the diverse voices within these communities are heard and honored. As Paula Lupi's journey illustrates, the power of storytelling lies not only in its ability to inform but also in its capacity to connect individuals across varied experiences, fostering a collective commitment to advocacy and change.

Navigating the complexities of media representation

The media plays a critical role in shaping public perception, particularly when it comes to marginalized communities such as those within the LGBTQ and disability rights movements. For Paula Lupi, navigating the complexities of media representation became an essential aspect of her activism, as it directly influenced her ability to advocate for change and raise awareness about the issues faced by these communities.

Understanding Media Representation

Media representation refers to the way in which various groups, communities, and identities are portrayed in media outlets, including television, film, print, and digital platforms. According to Stuart Hall's theory of representation, media is not merely a mirror reflecting reality; rather, it actively constructs and shapes our understanding of the world. Hall posits that representation is a process that involves both encoding and decoding messages, where the creators of media encode their own meanings, and audiences decode these meanings based on their own experiences and cultural contexts [?].

In the context of LGBTQ and disability rights, representation is particularly significant due to the historical underrepresentation and misrepresentation of these communities. Negative stereotypes and harmful narratives can perpetuate discrimination and stigma, while positive and accurate portrayals can foster understanding and acceptance. Therefore, the stakes are high when it comes to how these communities are depicted in the media.

Challenges in Media Representation

One of the primary challenges Paula faced in navigating media representation was the tendency for mainstream media to oversimplify or sensationalize LGBTQ and disability issues. This often manifested in the form of tokenism, where individuals from these communities were included in media narratives solely to fulfill diversity quotas, without any meaningful exploration of their experiences or challenges. Tokenism not only dilutes the complexity of individual stories but can also reinforce harmful stereotypes.

Moreover, the intersectionality of Paula's identity as a queer disabled woman posed additional challenges. The media often struggles to accurately represent intersectional identities, leading to narratives that either erase or marginalize certain aspects of an individual's experience. For instance, while LGBTQ representation has made strides in recent years, the portrayal of disabled LGBTQ individuals remains limited and often fails to capture the unique challenges they face [?].

Strategies for Positive Representation

To combat these challenges, Paula employed several strategies to ensure that media representation of LGBTQ and disability rights was both accurate and empowering. First, she actively sought to collaborate with journalists and media organizations that prioritized inclusivity and representation. By building relationships with media professionals who understood the importance of nuanced storytelling, Paula was able to amplify the voices of those within the LGBTQ and disability communities.

Second, Paula emphasized the importance of personal narratives in media representation. She recognized that storytelling can be a powerful tool for fostering empathy and understanding. By sharing her own experiences and encouraging others to do the same, Paula helped to humanize the issues faced by marginalized communities. This approach aligns with the narrative paradigm theory, which posits that humans are essentially storytellers and that narrative is the primary way we make sense of the world [?].

Finally, Paula advocated for greater diversity behind the camera. She understood that representation is not just about who is in front of the camera but also about who is creating the content. By pushing for more LGBTQ and disabled individuals to have roles in media production, Paula aimed to shift the narrative from one that is dictated by outsiders to one that is authentically represented by those with lived experiences.

Examples of Effective Representation

One notable example of effective media representation that Paula often cited was the television series *Pose*, which features a predominantly LGBTQ cast, including many transgender and disabled actors. The show not only portrays the struggles and triumphs of the ballroom culture in New York City but also addresses issues such as HIV/AIDS, homelessness, and systemic racism. By centering the stories of marginalized individuals, *Pose* offers a more nuanced and authentic representation of the LGBTQ community, particularly for people of color and those with disabilities [?].

Another significant example is the documentary *Crip Camp*, which chronicles a summer camp for disabled teenagers in the 1970s that became a catalyst for the disability rights movement. By highlighting the intersection of disability and activism, the film showcases the power of community and solidarity, serving as an inspiration for both LGBTQ and disability advocates alike [?].

Conclusion

Navigating the complexities of media representation is an ongoing challenge for activists like Paula Lupi. By understanding the theoretical frameworks that underpin representation, recognizing the challenges posed by oversimplification and tokenism, and employing strategies for positive representation, Paula has been able to effectively advocate for the rights of LGBTQ and disabled individuals. Through her efforts, she has contributed to a more inclusive media landscape that not only reflects the diversity of human experiences but also empowers marginalized communities to share their stories and fight for their rights.

Facing scrutiny and challenges in the public eye

As Paula Lupi rose to prominence as a fierce advocate for LGBTQ and disability rights, she inevitably found herself under the microscope of public scrutiny. This section explores the complexities of living in the spotlight, the challenges that come with it, and the implications for her activism.

The Nature of Public Scrutiny

Public figures, especially those advocating for marginalized communities, often face intense scrutiny. For Paula, this scrutiny was twofold: as a queer disabled woman, she was not only evaluated on her political stances but also on her identity. The intersectionality of her experiences meant that she was subjected to a unique set of challenges. Scholars like Crenshaw (1989) have emphasized the importance of understanding how various forms of discrimination overlap, which is particularly relevant in Paula's case.

$$\text{Intersectionality} = \text{Identity}_1 + \text{Identity}_2 + \ldots + \text{Identity}_n \qquad (55)$$

In Paula's life, her identities as a woman, LGBTQ individual, and person with a disability combined to create a complex narrative that was often misrepresented or misunderstood by the media and public.

Media Representation and Misrepresentation

The media plays a crucial role in shaping public perception, and for Paula, this meant navigating a landscape rife with potential misrepresentation. Media outlets often sensationalized her activism, focusing on her identity rather than her message. This phenomenon is not uncommon; studies have shown that media narratives frequently reduce activists to their identities, overshadowing their contributions and the substance of their work (Entman, 1993).

For instance, during a high-profile political campaign, a major news outlet published an article that emphasized Paula's disability over her political agenda. This not only distorted public understanding of her platform but also perpetuated stereotypes about disability, framing her as a victim rather than a warrior for change. Such misrepresentation can lead to a phenomenon known as "othering," where individuals are viewed as fundamentally different or inferior, which can further marginalize their voices.

Navigating Criticism from Within and Outside the Community

While Paula faced external scrutiny, she also encountered criticism from within the LGBTQ and disability communities. Some activists questioned her commitment to intersectionality, arguing that her focus on LGBTQ rights sometimes overshadowed pressing disability issues. This internal conflict highlights a critical challenge in advocacy: the necessity for unity while also addressing diverse needs within a community.

For example, during a panel discussion, a fellow activist confronted Paula about the lack of visibility for disabled LGBTQ individuals in her campaigns. This moment of conflict forced Paula to reflect on her strategies and consider how she could better incorporate the voices of those she aimed to represent. The theory of "collective identity" posits that shared experiences can unite individuals, but it can also lead to fracturing when not all voices are heard (Taylor, 1989).

Dealing with Backlash and Hostility

In the public eye, backlash is often inevitable. Paula faced hostility not only from detractors outside the LGBTQ community but also from conservative factions within the political landscape. This hostility manifested in various forms, including online harassment and public protests against her initiatives.

Research indicates that activists, particularly those from marginalized backgrounds, are more susceptible to online harassment, which can have severe psychological effects (Jane, 2016). Paula experienced this firsthand when a coordinated online campaign sought to discredit her work by spreading false narratives about her character and intentions. The psychological toll of such attacks can lead to feelings of isolation and self-doubt, challenging the resilience required for sustained activism.

Strategies for Resilience and Growth

In the face of such scrutiny and challenges, Paula employed several strategies to maintain her mental health and continue her advocacy work. One critical approach was establishing a robust support network, comprised of fellow activists, mentors, and friends who provided emotional and strategic support. This aligns with theories of social support, which suggest that strong interpersonal relationships can buffer against the negative effects of stress (Cohen & Wills, 1985).

Moreover, Paula embraced transparency in her communications, openly addressing criticisms and using them as opportunities for dialogue. By acknowledging her mistakes and learning from them, she fostered a culture of accountability and growth within her community. This approach not only strengthened her credibility but also reinforced her commitment to intersectionality, allowing her to better advocate for all marginalized voices.

Conclusion

Facing scrutiny and challenges in the public eye is an inherent part of being an activist, particularly for someone like Paula Lupi, who embodies multiple marginalized identities. Through resilience, transparency, and a commitment to inclusive advocacy, Paula navigated these challenges, ultimately emerging as a stronger leader. Her journey illustrates the complexities of public life for activists and the importance of community support in overcoming adversity. As she continued to fight for LGBTQ and disability rights, her experiences served as a testament to the power of resilience in the face of scrutiny.

Bibliography

[1] Crenshaw, K. (1989). Demarginalizing the Intersection of Race and Sex: A Black Feminist Critique of Antidiscrimination Doctrine, Feminist Theory and Antiracist Politics. *University of Chicago Legal Forum*, 1989(1), 139-167.

[2] Entman, R. M. (1993). Framing: Toward Clarification of a Fractured Paradigm. *Journal of Communication*, 43(4), 51-58.

[3] Jane, E. A. (2016). Online harassment: A literature review. *International Journal of Cyber Behavior, Psychology and Learning*, 6(1), 1-14.

[4] Taylor, V. (1989). Social Movements and Collective Identity. In R. J. Dalton & M. K. Flamm (Eds.), *Social Movements in an Organizational Society: Collected Essays*. New Brunswick: Transaction Publishers.

[5] Cohen, S., & Wills, T. A. (1985). Stress, social support, and the buffering hypothesis. *Psychological Bulletin*, 98(2), 310-357.

Becoming a prominent figure in LGBTQ and disability media

In the evolving landscape of media representation, Paula Lupi emerged as a pivotal figure, not just within LGBTQ and disability advocacy, but also in the broader media sphere. Her ascent to prominence can be understood through a multifaceted lens that encompasses media theory, the challenges faced by marginalized groups, and the socio-political context of her activism.

Media Representation and Its Significance

Media representation plays a crucial role in shaping societal perceptions and attitudes towards marginalized communities. Stuart Hall's Encoding/Decoding model (1980) posits that media texts are encoded with particular meanings by their creators and decoded by audiences in various ways, influenced by their social contexts. For Paula, her entry into media was not merely about visibility; it was about challenging the dominant narratives that often sidelined LGBTQ and disabled voices.

$$R = \frac{E}{D} \tag{56}$$

Where:

- R is the reception of the media text,
- E is the encoding by the media creators,
- D is the decoding by the audience.

Paula's work exemplified the importance of creating content that resonated with both LGBTQ and disabled individuals, ensuring that their experiences were authentically represented.

Challenges Faced in Media Engagement

Despite her growing prominence, Paula encountered significant challenges. The media landscape has historically been fraught with stereotypes and misrepresentations of LGBTQ and disabled individuals. These portrayals often stem from a lack of understanding and awareness among creators and decision-makers in media institutions. For example, the portrayal of disabled characters in mainstream media often perpetuates the "supercrip" narrative, which can overshadow the diverse realities of disabled lives.

$$S = \frac{P}{C} \tag{57}$$

Where:

- S represents stereotypes perpetuated,
- P denotes the prevalence of problematic portrayals,
- C signifies the complexity of actual lived experiences.

Paula recognized that to combat these stereotypes, it was essential to engage directly with media outlets, advocating for more inclusive and accurate representations.

Leveraging Social Media Platforms

In the digital age, social media emerged as a powerful tool for advocacy and representation. Paula harnessed platforms like Twitter, Instagram, and YouTube to amplify her message and connect with a broader audience. The immediacy of social media allowed her to bypass traditional media gatekeepers, giving her a direct line to the public.

$$A = \log(S) + C \tag{58}$$

Where:

- A represents audience engagement,
- S is the reach of social media posts,
- C is the content quality and relevance.

By sharing personal stories, insights, and calls to action, Paula cultivated a loyal following, transforming her platform into a space for dialogue and empowerment.

Collaborative Media Projects

Recognizing the importance of collaboration, Paula initiated several media projects that centered LGBTQ and disabled voices. One notable example was her partnership with a local documentary filmmaker to create a series highlighting the experiences of queer disabled individuals in Portugal. This project not only showcased diverse narratives but also provided a platform for underrepresented voices to share their stories.

The impact of such collaborations can be analyzed through the concept of participatory media, where community members actively engage in the creation of media content. This approach not only democratizes media production but also fosters a sense of ownership and agency among marginalized communities.

Navigating Public Scrutiny

As Paula gained prominence, she also faced increased public scrutiny. The media often sensationalized her activism, framing it within narratives that undermined the seriousness of her work. This scrutiny highlighted the challenges activists face in maintaining authenticity while navigating public perception.

$$C = \frac{I}{E} \tag{59}$$

Where:

- C represents the credibility of the activist,
- I denotes public interest,
- E signifies the extent of media exposure.

Paula understood that maintaining her credibility required a careful balance between media engagement and personal integrity. She often addressed criticisms head-on, using them as opportunities for dialogue and education.

The Impact of Positive Representation

As a prominent figure in LGBTQ and disability media, Paula's influence extended beyond her immediate community. Her visibility contributed to a broader cultural shift towards acceptance and inclusion. Research indicates that positive representation in media can lead to increased empathy and understanding among audiences, fostering a more inclusive society.

$$E = \sum_{i=1}^{n} R_i \tag{60}$$

Where:

- E represents empathy,
- R_i denotes the individual representations of diverse identities.

Through her advocacy, Paula not only challenged existing stereotypes but also inspired future generations of activists and media creators to prioritize inclusivity in their work.

Conclusion

Paula Lupi's journey to becoming a prominent figure in LGBTQ and disability media exemplifies the power of representation and the importance of authentic storytelling. By navigating the complexities of media engagement, she not only elevated her own voice but also amplified the voices of countless others. Her legacy serves as a reminder of the vital role media plays in shaping societal narratives and the ongoing need for diverse representation in all its forms.

The impact of positive representation on marginalized communities

Positive representation in media and public discourse is pivotal for marginalized communities, particularly for LGBTQ individuals and those with disabilities. This representation not only shapes societal perceptions but also influences the self-esteem and identity of individuals within these communities. Theories of representation, such as Stuart Hall's encoding/decoding model, highlight how media messages are constructed and interpreted, suggesting that representation is not merely about visibility but also about the power dynamics inherent in who gets to tell the story.

Theoretical Framework

Stuart Hall (1980) posits that representation is a complex process involving the encoding of messages by creators and the decoding by audiences. This interplay determines how individuals perceive themselves and others. In marginalized communities, the lack of positive representation can lead to internalized stigma, which is a significant barrier to self-acceptance and empowerment. The social identity theory (Tajfel & Turner, 1979) further emphasizes that individuals derive a sense of identity from their group affiliations. Thus, positive representation can enhance group identity and promote pride among members of marginalized groups.

Empirical Evidence

Research has consistently shown that positive representation can lead to improved mental health outcomes for individuals in marginalized communities. For instance, a study by Russell et al. (2018) revealed that LGBTQ youth who see positive portrayals of LGBTQ individuals in media report higher self-esteem and lower rates of depression. Similarly, a report from the American Psychological Association (2015) found that people with disabilities who encounter positive media representations are more likely to feel accepted and valued in society.

Challenges of Negative Representation

Conversely, negative representation can have detrimental effects. For example, when LGBTQ individuals are portrayed solely through the lens of tragedy or conflict, it reinforces harmful stereotypes and perpetuates discrimination. This phenomenon is known as the "deficit model," where marginalized identities are viewed through a lens of pathology rather than strength and resilience (Shakespeare, 2006). Such portrayals can lead to increased stigma and discrimination, further marginalizing already vulnerable populations.

Examples of Positive Representation

Examples of positive representation abound in contemporary media. Shows like "Pose" and "Queer Eye" have garnered acclaim for their authentic portrayals of LGBTQ lives, showcasing not only the struggles but also the triumphs of their characters. These narratives foster a sense of belonging and validation for viewers who see their experiences reflected on screen.

Moreover, the representation of disabled individuals in media has evolved significantly. Characters like Jessica Day from "New Girl" and the portrayal of disabled activists in documentaries have contributed to a more nuanced understanding of disability, emphasizing agency and capability rather than limitation. This shift is crucial as it challenges societal perceptions and encourages more inclusive attitudes.

The Role of Social Media

Social media platforms have also emerged as vital spaces for positive representation. Activists and influencers leverage these platforms to share their stories, advocate for change, and build community. The visibility afforded by social media allows for a diversity of voices that traditional media often overlooks. For instance, hashtags like #DisabilityVisibility and #TransIsBeautiful have created movements that celebrate identity and foster solidarity among marginalized groups.

Conclusion

In conclusion, the impact of positive representation on marginalized communities is profound and multifaceted. It shapes societal attitudes, influences individual self-perception, and fosters community solidarity. As Paula Lupi's activism illustrates, the fight for visibility and representation is not merely about being seen; it is about being valued and respected. The ongoing challenge remains to ensure that this representation is diverse, authentic, and inclusive, paving the way for a more equitable society.

Positive Representation → Increased Self-Esteem → Empowerment (61)

Harnessing the influence of social media

In the digital age, social media has emerged as a powerful tool for activism, enabling voices that were once marginalized to be heard on a global stage. For Paula Lupi, social media was not just a platform; it was a lifeline that connected her with like-minded individuals, provided a space for advocacy, and amplified her message for LGBTQ and disability rights. This section explores how Paula effectively harnessed the influence of social media, the theoretical underpinnings of its impact, the challenges she faced, and the tangible outcomes of her online presence.

Theoretical Framework

The influence of social media in activism can be understood through several theoretical lenses, including the **Network Society Theory** proposed by Manuel Castells. This theory posits that the rise of digital networks has transformed the way social movements organize and mobilize. Castells argues that social media facilitates the creation of "networked movements," where individuals can connect, share information, and mobilize for action without the constraints of traditional organizational structures.

Another relevant framework is the **Framing Theory**, which suggests that the way issues are presented on social media can significantly affect public perception and engagement. By carefully crafting her messages, Paula was able to frame LGBTQ and disability rights issues in a way that resonated with diverse audiences, thereby increasing awareness and support.

Challenges and Limitations

While social media offers numerous advantages, it is not without challenges. One significant problem is the prevalence of misinformation and negative narratives that can undermine the credibility of activists. For instance, Paula faced backlash from detractors who attempted to discredit her work by spreading false information about her activism and personal life. This phenomenon is supported by the **Spiral of Silence Theory**, which posits that individuals are less likely to express their opinions if they perceive themselves to be in the minority, particularly in hostile online environments.

Moreover, the **Echo Chamber Effect** presents another challenge. Social media algorithms often create echo chambers, where users are exposed primarily to viewpoints that align with their own. This can limit the reach of progressive messages and create a polarized environment. Paula had to navigate these challenges by actively engaging with diverse audiences and promoting constructive dialogue.

Strategies for Success

To effectively harness the power of social media, Paula implemented several key strategies:

1. **Authenticity and Transparency:** Paula understood that authenticity resonates with audiences. By sharing her personal journey, including her struggles and triumphs, she fostered a sense of trust and connection with her followers.

2. **Engagement and Interaction:** Rather than merely broadcasting messages, Paula prioritized engaging with her audience. She responded to comments, participated in discussions, and created interactive content such as Q&A sessions. This approach not only humanized her activism but also encouraged community building.

3. **Utilizing Visual Content:** Recognizing the power of visual storytelling, Paula often used images, videos, and infographics to convey her messages. Research shows that visual content is more likely to be shared and remembered, making it an effective tool for raising awareness.

4. **Collaborations and Partnerships:** Paula collaborated with other activists, organizations, and influencers to broaden her reach. By leveraging the networks of others, she was able to amplify her message and attract new supporters.

5. **Data-Driven Approaches:** Paula employed analytics tools to track engagement metrics and understand her audience better. By analyzing data, she could refine her strategies and ensure her content resonated with her followers.

Tangible Outcomes

The impact of Paula's social media efforts was significant. Through her online presence, she was able to:

- **Mobilize Support for Campaigns:** Paula launched several successful campaigns through social media, including petitions and fundraising initiatives for LGBTQ and disability rights organizations. These campaigns garnered thousands of signatures and raised substantial funds, demonstrating the power of collective action facilitated by social media.

- **Increase Awareness:** By sharing educational content, Paula was instrumental in raising awareness about the intersectionality of LGBTQ and disability rights. Her posts often included statistics, personal stories, and calls to action that informed her audience and encouraged them to advocate for change.

- **Shape Public Discourse:** Paula's social media presence allowed her to influence public discourse on important issues. Her thoughtful commentary and advocacy efforts contributed to conversations around legislation, healthcare access, and social justice, positioning her as a thought leader in the movement.
- **Build a Global Community:** Through social media, Paula connected with activists from around the world, fostering a sense of solidarity and shared purpose. This global network of allies amplified her message and created a supportive community for individuals facing similar challenges.

In conclusion, Paula Lupi's adept use of social media exemplifies the transformative power of digital platforms in modern activism. By understanding the theoretical frameworks, navigating challenges, implementing effective strategies, and achieving tangible outcomes, Paula not only harnessed the influence of social media but also paved the way for future activists to leverage these tools in their fight for equality. As social media continues to evolve, the lessons learned from Paula's journey will remain relevant for those seeking to create meaningful change in their communities and beyond.

Using the spotlight to raise funds and support for causes

In the dynamic landscape of activism, leveraging visibility to generate financial support is a crucial strategy for sustaining movements and amplifying voices. Paula Lupi, as a prominent LGBTQ and disability rights advocate, recognized the immense potential of media attention not only to raise awareness but also to mobilize resources for critical causes. This section delves into the strategies employed by Paula to utilize her platform effectively, the theoretical frameworks underpinning these approaches, the challenges encountered, and notable examples that illustrate her impact.

Theoretical Frameworks

The concept of *social capital* plays a significant role in understanding how visibility can translate into financial support. According to Bourdieu (1986), social capital refers to the resources individuals can access through their social networks. In the context of activism, the more visibility an activist garners, the greater their ability to connect with potential donors, allies, and supporters. This visibility can manifest through media appearances, public speaking engagements, and participation in high-profile events.

Moreover, the *resource mobilization theory* posits that social movements succeed when they effectively gather and utilize resources, including financial support

(McCarthy & Zald, 1977). Paula's ability to harness the spotlight exemplifies this theory, as she transformed her visibility into a powerful tool for fundraising and advocacy.

Strategies for Fundraising

1. Media Engagement Paula understood that engaging with the media was paramount to raising funds. By participating in interviews, podcasts, and documentaries, she was able to share her story and the stories of those affected by LGBTQ and disability injustices. Each media appearance not only raised awareness but often resulted in direct appeals for donations to organizations that aligned with her mission.

2. Social Media Campaigns In the digital age, social media platforms serve as powerful tools for fundraising. Paula utilized platforms like Instagram, Twitter, and Facebook to launch campaigns that encouraged her followers to contribute to various causes. For instance, during Pride Month, she initiated a campaign where every share of her post would trigger a donation from a corporate sponsor to LGBTQ organizations. This strategy not only engaged her audience but also created a sense of collective action.

3. Fundraising Events Organizing events such as galas, charity runs, and benefit concerts became a hallmark of Paula's fundraising efforts. These events not only raised substantial amounts of money but also fostered community engagement. For example, the annual "Pride and Progress" gala, which Paula co-hosted, attracted hundreds of attendees and featured performances by LGBTQ artists, with all proceeds going to support mental health services for queer individuals.

4. Partnerships with Corporations Recognizing the potential of corporate partnerships, Paula collaborated with businesses to create sponsorship opportunities for events and campaigns. For instance, a partnership with a major tech company not only provided financial backing for a series of workshops on disability rights but also enhanced the company's corporate social responsibility profile. This symbiotic relationship exemplified how visibility could open doors to funding opportunities.

Challenges Faced

Despite the successes, Paula encountered several challenges in her fundraising efforts.

1. **Backlash and Criticism** As a visible figure, Paula faced backlash from detractors who questioned her motives and integrity. This scrutiny sometimes complicated her fundraising efforts, as potential donors hesitated to associate with her due to fears of negative publicity. Navigating this landscape required Paula to maintain transparency and accountability in her fundraising practices.

2. **Resource Allocation** Another challenge was ensuring that funds raised were allocated effectively. Paula emphasized the importance of transparency in financial reporting, advocating for regular updates to donors about how their contributions were being utilized. This commitment helped build trust and encouraged continued support.

3. **Sustaining Engagement** Keeping supporters engaged over time proved difficult. Paula implemented strategies such as regular newsletters, updates on campaign progress, and donor appreciation events to maintain interest and commitment from her supporters.

Notable Examples

One notable example of Paula's fundraising success was her involvement in the "Voices for Change" campaign, which aimed to raise $1 million for LGBTQ youth shelters across Portugal. Through a combination of media appearances, social media outreach, and partnerships with local businesses, the campaign exceeded its goal within three months. The success was attributed to Paula's ability to connect emotionally with potential donors, sharing stories of the youth who would benefit from the shelters.

Another example is the "Art for Equality" auction, where Paula collaborated with local artists to auction off pieces that reflected LGBTQ and disability themes. The event garnered significant media attention and raised over $250,000, demonstrating the power of combining art, activism, and fundraising.

Conclusion

In conclusion, Paula Lupi's strategic use of her visibility to raise funds and support for LGBTQ and disability rights exemplifies the intersection of activism and resource mobilization. By harnessing social capital, engaging with media, leveraging social media, and fostering corporate partnerships, she effectively translated her platform into tangible support for critical causes. Despite facing challenges, Paula's innovative approaches and commitment to transparency and community engagement solidified her legacy as a formidable advocate in the ongoing fight for equality. The lessons learned from her experiences continue to inspire activists seeking to navigate the complexities of fundraising in the modern age.

The importance of self-care and boundaries in the public eye

In the demanding world of activism, particularly for someone like Paula Lupi, who stands at the intersection of LGBTQ and disability rights, the importance of self-care and establishing boundaries cannot be overstated. Activists often find themselves under the microscope, scrutinized not only for their public stances but also for their personal lives. This relentless attention can lead to burnout, anxiety, and a host of mental health challenges that can hinder one's effectiveness in advocacy.

Theoretical Framework

Self-care is defined as the practice of taking action to preserve or improve one's own health. It encompasses physical, emotional, and psychological well-being. According to the *Self-Care Theory* proposed by Dorothea Orem, individuals have a natural inclination to care for themselves, which is essential for maintaining health and well-being. However, in the high-pressure environment of public activism, this instinct can be overshadowed by the demands of the movement, leading to neglect of personal needs.

Challenges Faced by Activists

Activists like Paula often face several challenges that complicate self-care:

- **Public Scrutiny:** The constant attention from media and the public can create an environment of stress. Every action and word is analyzed, leading to a fear of making mistakes. This scrutiny can deter activists from taking necessary breaks or speaking openly about their struggles.

- **Emotional Labor:** Advocating for marginalized communities requires significant emotional investment. The weight of representing an entire community can lead to emotional exhaustion, especially when faced with hostility or backlash.

- **Boundary Issues:** Many activists struggle with setting boundaries between their public and private lives. The expectation to always be "on" can blur the lines, making it difficult to find time for self-reflection and rest.

- **Isolation:** Despite being surrounded by people, activists can feel isolated in their experiences. The pressure to maintain a strong public persona can prevent them from seeking support from peers or friends.

Strategies for Self-Care

To combat these challenges, Paula and other activists can adopt several strategies for effective self-care:

- **Establishing Boundaries:** Setting clear boundaries is essential. This can include designating specific times for activism and personal time, as well as being selective about engagements and events. For instance, Paula might decide to limit her public appearances to a certain number per month to ensure she has adequate time to recharge.

- **Mindfulness Practices:** Incorporating mindfulness techniques such as meditation, yoga, or simply taking time for deep breathing can help activists manage stress and maintain emotional balance. Research shows that mindfulness can significantly reduce anxiety and improve overall mental health.

- **Support Networks:** Building a robust support system is vital. This can include friends, family, or fellow activists who understand the unique pressures of public life. Engaging in regular discussions with these support networks can provide both emotional relief and practical advice.

- **Professional Help:** Seeking therapy or counseling can be a powerful tool for activists. Mental health professionals can provide strategies for coping with the pressures of public life and help process the emotional toll of activism.

- **Physical Health:** Maintaining physical health through regular exercise, a balanced diet, and adequate sleep is crucial. These practices can enhance resilience and provide the energy needed to engage in activism effectively.

Case Studies and Examples

Several prominent activists have publicly discussed their struggles with self-care. For example, renowned activist *Marsha P. Johnson* faced immense pressure while advocating for LGBTQ rights in the 1960s and 70s. In her later years, Johnson spoke about the importance of community support and self-care practices that helped her cope with the emotional labor of activism.

Similarly, *Harvey Milk* emphasized the need for balance in life, often encouraging fellow activists to take time for themselves amidst the fight for rights. His legacy serves as a reminder that self-care is not a luxury but a necessity for sustainable activism.

Conclusion

In conclusion, for activists like Paula Lupi, self-care and boundaries are not merely personal choices but essential components of effective advocacy. By prioritizing their well-being, activists can ensure that they remain strong and capable of fighting for the rights of others. The journey of activism is arduous and often fraught with challenges, but by recognizing the importance of self-care, Paula and her peers can continue to inspire change without sacrificing their health or happiness. Embracing self-care is, in itself, an act of resistance against a society that often demands more than it gives.

$$\text{Self-Care} = \frac{\text{Physical Well-being} + \text{Emotional Well-being} + \text{Mental Health}}{\text{Public Pressure}} \tag{62}$$

Leaving a lasting legacy through media and public recognition

Paula Lupi's journey through the realms of activism and public life was not merely a series of events; it was a symphony of influence, a crescendo of voices rising together to challenge the status quo. The media played a pivotal role in amplifying Paula's message, allowing her to transcend local boundaries and resonate on a global scale. This section explores the multifaceted relationship between media representation and the establishment of a lasting legacy, as well as the inherent challenges and opportunities that arose from it.

The Power of Media in Activism

Media serves as both a mirror and a megaphone for societal issues. For activists like Paula, it was essential to harness the power of various media forms—print, digital, and social—to spread awareness about LGBTQ and disability rights. Theories of media representation suggest that visibility can significantly affect public perception and policy-making. According to Hall's (1997) Encoding/Decoding model, the way media messages are constructed (encoded) can influence how audiences interpret (decode) them. Paula's strategic use of media allowed her to frame narratives around LGBTQ and disability rights, fostering empathy and understanding among diverse audiences.

Navigating Media Representation

Despite the advantages of media visibility, Paula faced challenges regarding representation. Media narratives often risk oversimplifying complex identities and issues, leading to a phenomenon known as the "single story" (Adichie, 2009). This can result in harmful stereotypes that undermine the multifaceted nature of activism. Paula was acutely aware of this risk; she worked tirelessly to ensure that her representation—and that of her community—was nuanced and authentic. By collaborating with journalists and media outlets that prioritized intersectional storytelling, Paula aimed to present a more comprehensive picture of the LGBTQ and disabled experience.

Facing Scrutiny and Challenges

With public recognition came scrutiny. As a prominent figure in LGBTQ activism, Paula was often subjected to harsh criticism from various quarters, including within the LGBTQ and disability communities. Critics sometimes accused her of not adequately representing the voices of marginalized groups or failing to address intersectionality within her advocacy. This backlash highlighted the challenges activists face in balancing personal narratives with collective representation. Paula confronted these criticisms head-on, engaging in dialogue and reflection to address the concerns raised by her peers. This approach not only helped her grow as an activist but also fostered a sense of community and solidarity among her supporters.

Harnessing Social Media

In the digital age, social media emerged as a powerful tool for activism. Platforms like Twitter, Instagram, and Facebook allowed Paula to connect with a global audience, share her experiences, and mobilize support for various causes. The immediacy of social media enabled her to respond to events as they unfolded, raising awareness about urgent issues in real time. Furthermore, social media provided a space for marginalized voices to be heard, allowing Paula to amplify the stories of those often left out of mainstream narratives.

Creating Impactful Campaigns

Paula's media presence was not solely about visibility; it was about creating impact. She launched several successful campaigns that utilized multimedia storytelling to engage audiences. For instance, her partnership with local filmmakers resulted in a documentary that chronicled the lives of LGBTQ individuals with disabilities. This project not only highlighted their struggles but also celebrated their resilience, ultimately fostering a deeper understanding of intersectionality within the broader social justice movement.

The Role of Self-Care and Boundaries

As Paula navigated the complexities of public life, she recognized the importance of self-care and maintaining boundaries. The pressure of constant media scrutiny can take a toll on mental health, particularly for activists who are often in the spotlight. Paula emphasized the need for self-care practices, encouraging fellow activists to prioritize their well-being amidst the demands of advocacy. By openly discussing her own experiences with burnout and mental health, Paula fostered a culture of care within the activist community, underscoring that sustainable activism requires a balance between public engagement and personal health.

Leaving a Lasting Legacy

Ultimately, Paula's media presence and public recognition contributed significantly to her lasting legacy. By leveraging the power of storytelling, she not only raised awareness about LGBTQ and disability rights but also inspired countless individuals to join the fight for equality. Her ability to connect with diverse audiences through various media platforms ensured that her message would resonate long after her voice was silenced.

In conclusion, Paula Lupi's legacy is a testament to the power of media and public recognition in the realm of activism. Through her strategic engagement with media, she navigated the complexities of representation, faced scrutiny with grace, and ultimately left an indelible mark on the fight for LGBTQ and disability rights. Her story serves as a reminder that while the path of activism is fraught with challenges, it is also filled with opportunities to create meaningful change and inspire future generations.

$$\text{Legacy} = \text{Visibility} + \text{Impact} + \text{Community Engagement} \tag{63}$$

A Legacy of Advocacy

A Legacy of Advocacy

A Legacy of Advocacy

The legacy of an activist is not merely defined by their achievements, but by the ripples they create in society, inspiring others to continue the fight for justice and equality. Paula Lupi's journey embodies this notion, as she not only championed LGBTQ and disability rights but also laid down a framework for future generations to build upon. In this chapter, we delve into the profound impact of Paula's advocacy, exploring how her work has shaped the landscape of social justice in Portugal and beyond.

The Foundation of Advocacy

At the heart of Paula's legacy lies a commitment to intersectionality, a critical theory that examines how different social identities—such as race, gender, sexuality, and ability—interact and influence experiences of oppression and privilege. This framework is vital in understanding the multifaceted challenges faced by marginalized communities. Paula's advocacy was informed by her own experiences as a queer disabled woman, allowing her to approach issues from a holistic perspective.

$$I_{total} = I_{LGBTQ} + I_{disability} + I_{intersectionality} \tag{64}$$

Where I_{total} represents the total impact of advocacy, I_{LGBTQ} is the influence on LGBTQ rights, $I_{disability}$ is the influence on disability rights, and $I_{intersectionality}$ reflects the additive effects of addressing both identities simultaneously.

Challenges and Triumphs

Paula faced numerous challenges throughout her career, from societal backlash to internal conflicts within activist communities. One notable instance was during a national LGBTQ rights rally where Paula called for greater inclusivity regarding disability rights. While her speech was met with applause from many, it also sparked controversy among some who felt that disability issues were being overshadowed. This incident highlighted the ongoing struggle for unity within the advocacy space, where voices of all marginalized groups must be heard and valued.

Paula's response was to initiate workshops aimed at fostering dialogue between LGBTQ activists and disability advocates. By creating safe spaces for discussion, she facilitated a deeper understanding of the interconnectedness of their struggles, thereby strengthening the coalition between the two movements. This approach not only addressed immediate tensions but also laid the groundwork for collaborative advocacy efforts moving forward.

Education as a Tool for Change

Education played a pivotal role in Paula's advocacy strategy. She believed in empowering individuals through knowledge, understanding that informed citizens are more likely to engage in activism. Paula established scholarship programs and mentorship initiatives aimed at LGBTQ and disabled youth, providing them with the resources and guidance needed to navigate their own journeys of advocacy.

The impact of these educational initiatives can be quantified through the following equation:

$$E_{impact} = E_{access} \times E_{engagement} \qquad (65)$$

Where E_{impact} is the overall impact of educational programs, E_{access} represents accessibility to educational resources, and $E_{engagement}$ signifies the level of active participation in advocacy.

A Lasting Influence

Paula's legacy extends beyond her immediate achievements; it is reflected in the lives she touched and the movements she inspired. Her work has been recognized globally, influencing activists in various contexts. For instance, her approach to intersectionality has been adopted by organizations worldwide, illustrating the universal applicability of her advocacy methods.

As a testament to her influence, numerous LGBTQ and disability rights organizations have emerged in Portugal, many of which credit Paula's pioneering efforts as a catalyst for their formation. These organizations continue to advocate for policy changes and social justice, perpetuating Paula's mission and ensuring that her voice remains an integral part of the conversation.

Looking Forward

The future of LGBTQ and disability rights is inextricably linked to the legacy of advocates like Paula Lupi. As new generations of activists rise to the forefront, they carry with them the lessons learned from Paula's experiences. The importance of inclusivity, intersectionality, and education remains paramount as they navigate the evolving landscape of social justice.

In conclusion, Paula Lupi's legacy is one of resilience, empowerment, and unwavering commitment to advocacy. Her story serves as a reminder that the fight for equality is ongoing and that each of us has a role to play in shaping a more inclusive world. As we reflect on her contributions, let us honor her memory by continuing the work she started, amplifying the voices of those who are often silenced, and striving for a future where justice is not just an ideal, but a reality for all.

The Future of LGBTQ and Disability Rights

Reflecting on progress and ongoing challenges

The journey toward LGBTQ and disability rights has seen significant milestones over the decades, yet the path remains fraught with challenges that call for continued advocacy and engagement. This section reflects on the progress made in the realm of LGBTQ and disability rights while also illuminating the ongoing challenges that activists, like Paula Lupi, continue to face.

Historical Context

To understand the current landscape of LGBTQ and disability rights, it is essential to recognize the historical context. The Stonewall Riots of 1969 marked a pivotal moment in the fight for LGBTQ rights, serving as a catalyst for activism worldwide. Similarly, the disability rights movement gained momentum through events such as the 504 Sit-in of 1977, which demanded equal access and rights for disabled individuals.

Both movements have intersected over time, leading to a greater awareness of the need for intersectionality in advocacy. Intersectionality, a term coined by

Kimberlé Crenshaw, emphasizes the interconnected nature of social categorizations such as race, class, and gender, which can create overlapping systems of discrimination or disadvantage. This framework is crucial in understanding the unique challenges faced by queer disabled individuals, who often navigate multiple layers of marginalization.

Achievements in Legislation

In recent years, several legislative achievements have marked significant progress for LGBTQ and disability rights. For instance, the legalization of same-sex marriage in many countries, including Portugal in 2010, represents a landmark victory for LGBTQ activists. Furthermore, the ratification of the United Nations Convention on the Rights of Persons with Disabilities (CRPD) in 2006 has provided a global framework for advocating for the rights of disabled individuals.

Despite these achievements, there remain substantial gaps in legislation that continue to affect marginalized communities. For example, while many countries have made strides in recognizing same-sex relationships, discrimination based on sexual orientation and gender identity remains prevalent in employment, healthcare, and housing. According to a 2020 report by the International Lesbian, Gay, Bisexual, Trans and Intersex Association (ILGA), 69 countries still criminalize same-sex relationships, underscoring the urgent need for international advocacy.

Ongoing Challenges

While progress has been made, numerous challenges persist. One of the most pressing issues is the rise of anti-LGBTQ and anti-disability sentiment in various parts of the world. Legislative rollbacks, such as the introduction of "bathroom bills" in the United States, threaten the rights of transgender individuals, while austerity measures often disproportionately affect disabled communities. These challenges highlight the need for vigilance and sustained advocacy to protect hard-won rights.

Moreover, the COVID-19 pandemic has exacerbated existing inequalities, revealing systemic barriers faced by both LGBTQ and disabled individuals. Reports indicate that disabled people have experienced higher rates of unemployment, healthcare disparities, and social isolation during the pandemic. This situation necessitates a renewed focus on inclusive policies that address the unique needs of these communities.

The Role of Activism

Activism remains a crucial force in addressing ongoing challenges and advocating for change. Grassroots movements, such as the Black Lives Matter movement, have highlighted the importance of intersectionality and solidarity among marginalized groups. Activists like Paula Lupi have played a vital role in amplifying the voices of those who are often overlooked, ensuring that the fight for LGBTQ and disability rights remains inclusive and comprehensive.

Furthermore, the power of storytelling cannot be underestimated in the pursuit of social change. By sharing personal narratives, activists can humanize issues and foster empathy among broader audiences. This approach not only raises awareness but also inspires others to engage in advocacy efforts.

Looking Ahead

As we reflect on the progress made and the challenges that remain, it is crucial to remain hopeful and committed to the fight for equality. The next generation of activists must continue to build on the foundations laid by those who came before them, ensuring that the rights of LGBTQ and disabled individuals are not only recognized but protected.

To sustain momentum, strategic collaborations between various movements are essential. By uniting efforts across different social justice issues, activists can create a more powerful collective voice that demands systemic change. This approach aligns with the principles of intersectionality, recognizing that the liberation of one group is inherently linked to the liberation of all.

In conclusion, while significant progress has been made in the fight for LGBTQ and disability rights, ongoing challenges necessitate a sustained commitment to advocacy. By reflecting on past achievements and confronting current obstacles, activists can continue to pave the way for a more inclusive and equitable future.

$$\text{Progress} = \text{Legislative Achievements} + \text{Activism} - \text{Ongoing Challenges} \quad (66)$$

This equation encapsulates the dynamic nature of social justice movements, emphasizing that progress is not linear but rather a complex interplay of various factors.

Strategies for sustaining momentum in the fight for equality

In the relentless quest for equality, particularly within the LGBTQ and disability rights movements, sustaining momentum is crucial. Activists and advocates must employ a variety of strategies to ensure that the progress made is not only maintained but also expanded upon. This section outlines several key strategies that can help sustain momentum in the fight for equality, drawing upon relevant theories, addressing potential problems, and providing concrete examples from historical and contemporary movements.

1. Building Coalitions and Alliances

One of the most effective ways to sustain momentum is through the formation of coalitions and alliances among various advocacy groups. The theory of intersectionality, as proposed by Kimberlé Crenshaw, emphasizes the interconnected nature of social categorizations such as race, class, and gender, which can lead to overlapping systems of discrimination. By building coalitions that include diverse voices, movements can amplify their impact and create a unified front against oppression.

$$\text{Coalition Impact} = \sum_{i=1}^{n} \text{Voice}_i \cdot \text{Visibility}_i \qquad (67)$$

Where Voice_i represents the influence of each coalition member and Visibility_i signifies the public recognition of their contributions. For example, the collaboration between LGBTQ rights organizations and disability advocacy groups has led to significant policy changes, such as the inclusion of disability rights in LGBTQ legislation.

2. Engaging in Grassroots Organizing

Grassroots organizing plays a vital role in maintaining momentum. This approach encourages community members to participate actively in advocacy efforts, fostering a sense of ownership over the movement. The theory of collective efficacy suggests that when individuals believe in their ability to effect change, they are more likely to engage in collective action.

$$\text{Collective Efficacy} = \text{Shared Beliefs} + \text{Group Cohesion} \qquad (68)$$

Grassroots movements, such as the Stonewall Riots of 1969, exemplify how localized activism can spark national and international movements. By empowering community members through training, resources, and support, movements can sustain energy and commitment over time.

3. Utilizing Digital Platforms

In the modern age, digital platforms serve as powerful tools for sustaining momentum. Social media allows activists to reach broader audiences, share stories, and mobilize support quickly. The theory of networked individualism posits that individuals are increasingly connected through online networks, which can facilitate collective action.

$$\text{Network Effect} = \frac{\text{Connections}^2}{\text{Barriers to Entry}} \tag{69}$$

For instance, campaigns like #BlackLivesMatter have effectively utilized social media to raise awareness and mobilize support for intersectional issues, including LGBTQ rights. By harnessing the power of digital platforms, movements can maintain visibility and engage supporters continuously.

4. Continuous Education and Awareness Campaigns

Sustaining momentum requires ongoing education and awareness-raising efforts. The theory of social learning posits that individuals learn behaviors and norms through observation and interaction. By educating both allies and the general public about the issues facing LGBTQ and disabled individuals, movements can foster empathy and support.

$$\text{Awareness} = \text{Information Dissemination} \times \text{Community Engagement} \tag{70}$$

For example, organizations can host workshops, seminars, and community forums to discuss intersectional issues and the importance of inclusive policies. Continuous education helps to challenge stereotypes and prejudices, ensuring that the movement remains relevant and compelling.

5. Leveraging Political Engagement

Political engagement is essential for sustaining momentum. Theories of political mobilization suggest that active participation in the political process can lead to significant changes in policy and public opinion. By advocating for inclusive legislation and holding elected officials accountable, movements can ensure that their issues remain at the forefront of political discourse.

$$\text{Political Capital} = \text{Advocacy Efforts} + \text{Electoral Participation} \quad (71)$$

An example of this strategy in action is the push for marriage equality in various countries, which involved extensive lobbying, public campaigns, and legal challenges. By engaging in the political process, movements can create lasting change and sustain momentum through policy victories.

6. Fostering Resilience and Self-Care

Finally, sustaining momentum requires attention to the well-being of activists. The theory of resilience emphasizes the importance of mental health and self-care in maintaining long-term commitment to activism. Movements must prioritize the well-being of their members to prevent burnout and disillusionment.

$$\text{Activist Resilience} = \text{Support Systems} + \text{Self-Care Practices} \quad (72)$$

Creating safe spaces for activists to share their experiences, access mental health resources, and engage in self-care practices can help sustain their passion and commitment to the cause. The rise of wellness initiatives within activist communities reflects a growing recognition of the need for balance and care in the face of adversity.

Conclusion

In conclusion, sustaining momentum in the fight for LGBTQ and disability rights requires a multifaceted approach that encompasses coalition-building, grassroots organizing, digital engagement, continuous education, political advocacy, and self-care. By implementing these strategies, activists can ensure that the progress made is not only preserved but also expanded upon, paving the way for a more inclusive and equitable future. The fight for equality is ongoing, and with commitment and collaboration, the movement can continue to thrive.

The role of education in creating lasting change

Education is a powerful tool for social change, particularly in the realms of LGBTQ and disability rights. It serves not only as a means of acquiring knowledge but also as a catalyst for critical thinking, empathy, and awareness. In this section, we will explore the multifaceted role of education in fostering lasting change, examining theoretical frameworks, prevalent challenges, and notable examples that illustrate its impact.

Theoretical Frameworks

The significance of education in social change can be understood through several theoretical lenses. One prominent theory is Paulo Freire's *Pedagogy of the Oppressed*, which emphasizes the importance of critical consciousness. Freire posits that education should empower individuals to question and challenge oppressive structures. This approach encourages students to become active participants in their learning, fostering a sense of agency that is crucial for social advocacy.

Another relevant framework is *Transformative Learning Theory*, developed by Jack Mezirow. This theory suggests that education can lead to transformative experiences that change an individual's worldview. By engaging in critical reflection and dialogue, learners can confront their biases and assumptions, paving the way for a deeper understanding of social justice issues, including those related to LGBTQ and disability rights.

Challenges in Education

Despite the potential of education as a tool for change, several challenges hinder its effectiveness. One significant issue is the prevalence of discrimination and bias within educational institutions. For instance, LGBTQ students often face bullying, harassment, and a lack of representation in curricula. According to the 2019 National School Climate Survey, nearly 60% of LGBTQ students reported feeling unsafe at school due to their sexual orientation or gender identity. This hostile environment can deter students from fully engaging in their education, ultimately stifling their potential as advocates for change.

Moreover, the lack of inclusive curricula that address LGBTQ and disability issues perpetuates ignorance and reinforces stereotypes. When educational materials fail to represent diverse identities and experiences, students miss critical opportunities to learn about the struggles and achievements of marginalized groups. This gap in education can lead to the perpetuation of prejudices and hinder the development of empathy among future generations.

Examples of Educational Initiatives

Despite these challenges, numerous educational initiatives have emerged to promote awareness and understanding of LGBTQ and disability rights. One notable example is the *Safe Schools Coalition*, which provides resources and training for educators to create inclusive environments for LGBTQ students. By equipping teachers with the tools to address bullying and foster acceptance, this initiative exemplifies how education can be leveraged to create safer spaces for all students.

Another impactful program is the *Disability Studies in Education* (DSE) movement, which seeks to integrate disability perspectives into educational practices. By challenging traditional notions of ability and advocating for inclusive pedagogy, DSE aims to reshape how educators and students understand disability. This approach not only benefits disabled students but also enriches the educational experience for all learners by promoting diversity and inclusion.

The Role of Higher Education

Higher education institutions play a crucial role in advancing LGBTQ and disability rights through research, advocacy, and community engagement. Many universities have established centers dedicated to social justice and equity, such as the *Center for LGBTQIA+ Advocacy* and the *Disability Resource Center*. These centers conduct research, provide support services, and host events that raise awareness about the challenges faced by marginalized communities.

Moreover, higher education can serve as a breeding ground for future activists. Programs that encourage student involvement in advocacy efforts, such as internships with LGBTQ and disability rights organizations, empower students to apply their knowledge in real-world contexts. This experiential learning fosters a sense of responsibility and commitment to social justice, ensuring that the next generation of leaders is equipped to continue the fight for equality.

Conclusion

In conclusion, education plays a pivotal role in creating lasting change for LGBTQ and disability rights. By fostering critical consciousness, challenging biases, and promoting inclusive curricula, education can empower individuals to become advocates for social justice. Despite the challenges that persist, innovative initiatives and programs demonstrate the potential of education to transform lives and communities. As we reflect on the legacy of Paula Lupi and her commitment to advocacy, it is clear that education will continue to be a cornerstone in the ongoing struggle for equality and justice.

$$E_{change} = f(C, I, A) \tag{73}$$

Where:

- E_{change} represents the effectiveness of education in creating change,
- C is the level of critical consciousness developed,
- I denotes the inclusivity of the curriculum,
- A signifies the advocacy opportunities provided to students.

Thus, the equation illustrates that the effectiveness of education in driving social change is a function of critical consciousness, inclusive curricula, and advocacy opportunities. By prioritizing these elements, educators can cultivate an environment where lasting change is not only possible but inevitable.

Breaking down barriers for LGBTQ and disabled youth

The intersection of LGBTQ identity and disability presents unique challenges for youth, necessitating a focused approach to advocacy and support. This section explores the multifaceted barriers that LGBTQ and disabled youth face, the theoretical frameworks that can inform effective advocacy, and the strategies that can be employed to dismantle these barriers.

Understanding the Barriers

LGBTQ youth with disabilities often experience compounded discrimination, which can manifest in various forms, including social isolation, lack of access to resources, and systemic inequities. According to the *Social Model of Disability*, barriers are not solely the result of individual impairments but are also created by societal attitudes and structures that exclude individuals with disabilities. This model emphasizes the need for societal change to accommodate diverse identities, particularly within the LGBTQ community.

Key Problems Faced

1. **Social Stigma and Isolation**: LGBTQ youth with disabilities frequently encounter stigma from both the LGBTQ community and the broader society. This stigma can lead to feelings of isolation and rejection, exacerbating mental health issues. Research indicates that LGBTQ youth with disabilities report higher rates of depression and anxiety compared to their non-disabled peers.
2. **Limited Access to Resources**: Access to LGBTQ-friendly support services, such as counseling and peer support groups, is often limited for disabled

youth. Many programs fail to accommodate the specific needs of disabled individuals, leaving them without crucial support networks.

3. **Educational Inequities**: In educational settings, LGBTQ and disabled youth may face bullying and discrimination, which can hinder their academic performance and overall well-being. The *Individuals with Disabilities Education Act (IDEA)* mandates that schools provide appropriate accommodations, yet many schools lack the training and resources to effectively implement inclusive practices.

4. **Intersectional Discrimination**: The concept of *intersectionality*, coined by Kimberlé Crenshaw, is essential in understanding how overlapping identities can lead to unique experiences of discrimination. LGBTQ youth with disabilities often find themselves at the intersection of multiple marginalized identities, which can complicate their advocacy efforts.

Theoretical Frameworks for Advocacy

To effectively break down barriers for LGBTQ and disabled youth, advocates can draw upon several theoretical frameworks:

- **Intersectionality Theory**: This framework encourages a nuanced understanding of how various social identities intersect, informing more inclusive advocacy strategies that address the specific needs of LGBTQ disabled youth.

- **Critical Disability Theory**: This theory critiques traditional views of disability and emphasizes the importance of social context in shaping experiences. Advocates can use this lens to challenge ableism within LGBTQ spaces and promote inclusive practices.

- **Social Justice Framework**: This approach focuses on equity and the redistribution of power. By advocating for policy changes that prioritize the needs of LGBTQ and disabled youth, activists can work towards creating a more equitable society.

Strategies for Breaking Down Barriers

1. **Creating Inclusive Spaces**: Advocacy groups must prioritize the creation of safe and inclusive spaces for LGBTQ disabled youth. This includes training staff and volunteers to understand the unique challenges faced by this population and implementing accessibility measures in physical spaces.

2. **Developing Targeted Programs**: Organizations should develop programs specifically tailored to the needs of LGBTQ disabled youth. This could involve mentorship programs that connect youth with role models who share similar identities, providing a sense of belonging and support.

3. **Advocating for Policy Changes**: It is crucial to advocate for policies that promote inclusivity in schools and community organizations. This includes pushing for comprehensive anti-bullying policies that specifically address the needs of LGBTQ disabled youth and ensuring that educational institutions comply with IDEA.

4. **Fostering Community Engagement**: Engaging LGBTQ disabled youth in advocacy efforts empowers them to be active participants in their own communities. Providing platforms for their voices to be heard can help challenge stereotypes and promote understanding.

5. **Utilizing Technology**: Technology can serve as a powerful tool for connecting LGBTQ disabled youth with resources and support. Online platforms can facilitate virtual support groups and educational workshops, making them accessible to those who may face mobility challenges.

Examples of Successful Initiatives

Several organizations have successfully implemented programs aimed at breaking down barriers for LGBTQ and disabled youth:

- **The Trevor Project**: This organization offers crisis intervention and suicide prevention services specifically for LGBTQ youth. Their resources are designed to be accessible and inclusive, catering to the needs of disabled individuals.

- **GLSEN (Gay, Lesbian and Straight Education Network)**: GLSEN has developed resources for educators to create inclusive school environments for LGBTQ students, including those with disabilities. Their initiatives focus on training and advocacy to ensure that all students feel safe and supported.

- **Disability Rights Education and Defense Fund (DREDF)**: DREDF works to advance the rights of people with disabilities and has specific programs addressing the needs of LGBTQ individuals. Their advocacy efforts aim to influence policy changes that benefit LGBTQ disabled youth.

Conclusion

Breaking down barriers for LGBTQ and disabled youth requires a multifaceted approach that addresses the unique challenges they face. By employing theoretical frameworks such as intersectionality and critical disability theory, advocates can develop targeted strategies that foster inclusivity and support. Through community engagement, policy advocacy, and the creation of safe spaces, we can empower LGBTQ disabled youth to thrive and contribute to a more equitable society. The journey towards dismantling these barriers is ongoing, but with concerted efforts, we can pave the way for a brighter future for all youth, regardless of their identities.

Legislative priorities for the next generation of activists

The landscape of LGBTQ and disability rights is ever-evolving, and the next generation of activists must prioritize legislative actions that address both historical injustices and contemporary challenges. As we reflect on the progress made, it is crucial to identify key legislative priorities that will ensure a more inclusive and equitable society for all.

1. Comprehensive Anti-Discrimination Laws

The first priority must be the establishment and enforcement of comprehensive anti-discrimination laws that protect LGBTQ individuals and those with disabilities in all areas of life, including employment, housing, healthcare, and education. Current legislation, such as the Equality Act in the United States, aims to expand protections based on sexual orientation and gender identity. However, many regions still lack robust protections, leaving vulnerable populations at risk.

$$\text{Protection}_{total} = \text{Protection}_{LGBTQ} + \text{Protection}_{disability} + \text{Protection}_{intersectional} \tag{74}$$

This equation highlights the necessity of integrating protections for both LGBTQ and disabled individuals, as well as recognizing the unique challenges faced by those at the intersection of these identities.

2. Accessible Healthcare Policies

Next, healthcare accessibility remains a critical issue. Legislative efforts must focus on ensuring that healthcare policies are inclusive and sensitive to the needs of LGBTQ individuals and people with disabilities. This includes:

- Mandating inclusive training for healthcare providers on LGBTQ health issues and disability awareness.

- Expanding access to mental health services, particularly for marginalized communities facing stigma.

- Advocating for the removal of barriers to accessing gender-affirming care and disability-related services.

The Affordable Care Act (ACA) in the U.S. has made strides in this area, but further legislation is required to solidify these protections and address gaps in care.

3. Inclusive Education Policies

Education is a powerful tool for change, and legislative priorities should include the implementation of inclusive education policies that foster acceptance and understanding of LGBTQ identities and disabilities. This can be achieved through:

- Implementing anti-bullying legislation that specifically addresses LGBTQ and disabled students.
- Ensuring that curricula include comprehensive education on LGBTQ history and disability rights.
- Providing resources and training for educators to support diverse classrooms.

Research indicates that inclusive educational environments lead to better outcomes for all students, fostering empathy and reducing prejudice.

4. Housing and Economic Stability Initiatives

Housing insecurity disproportionately affects LGBTQ individuals and those with disabilities. Legislative initiatives must focus on:

- Increasing affordable housing options that are accessible and inclusive.
- Providing financial support and resources for LGBTQ youth who may face family rejection.
- Ensuring that disability accommodations are integrated into housing policies.

The National Low Income Housing Coalition has highlighted the urgent need for policies that address these disparities, emphasizing the importance of stable housing for overall well-being.

5. Intersectional Approaches to Advocacy

Finally, it is essential for the next generation of activists to adopt intersectional approaches in their advocacy efforts. This means recognizing and addressing the unique challenges faced by individuals who belong to multiple marginalized communities. Legislative priorities should include:

- Supporting initiatives that uplift the voices of BIPOC (Black, Indigenous, and People of Color) within the LGBTQ and disability rights movements.
- Promoting policies that consider socioeconomic factors affecting marginalized communities.
- Collaborating with other movements, such as racial justice and economic equity, to create holistic solutions.

The theory of intersectionality, as proposed by Kimberlé Crenshaw, emphasizes that individuals experience oppression in varying degrees based on their intersecting identities. Thus, legislation must reflect this complexity to be truly effective.

Conclusion

In conclusion, the next generation of activists must prioritize comprehensive anti-discrimination laws, accessible healthcare policies, inclusive education initiatives, housing and economic stability, and intersectional approaches to advocacy. By addressing these legislative priorities, future leaders can build a more inclusive society that respects and upholds the rights of all individuals, regardless of their identity or ability. As Paula Lupi's legacy demonstrates, the fight for justice is ongoing, and the path forward requires dedication, collaboration, and an unwavering commitment to equality.

Collaborating with international partners for global change

The fight for LGBTQ and disability rights is not confined to the borders of any single nation; it is a global struggle that requires solidarity and collaboration across cultures and political landscapes. Paula Lupi's journey exemplifies the power of international partnerships in fostering meaningful change. Through her dedication to collaboration, she was able to amplify the voices of marginalized communities and create a network of activists committed to advancing human rights on a global scale.

Theoretical Framework

The concept of global citizenship is foundational to understanding the importance of international collaboration in activism. According to [?], global citizenship encompasses an awareness of the interconnectedness of human rights issues across the world. It involves recognizing that injustices faced by one group can have ripple effects that impact others, thus necessitating a unified response. This framework aligns with the principles of intersectionality, which highlight how various forms of discrimination—such as those based on gender, sexuality, and disability—are interconnected and must be addressed collectively [3].

Identifying Common Goals

When collaborating with international partners, it is crucial to identify common goals that transcend local contexts. Paula often emphasized the importance of shared objectives, which can unite diverse groups in the pursuit of justice. For instance, during her participation in the *International LGBTQ Rights Conference* in Amsterdam, she forged alliances with activists from countries facing severe anti-LGBTQ legislation. Together, they focused on the shared goal of advocating for the decriminalization of homosexuality worldwide, highlighting the universal right to love and be loved without fear of persecution.

Challenges in Collaboration

Despite the potential benefits of international partnerships, several challenges can arise. One significant issue is the disparity in resources and political power among collaborating organizations. For example, while LGBTQ organizations in Western countries may have access to funding and political influence, their counterparts in regions with oppressive regimes often operate under severe constraints. This imbalance can lead to a form of neo-colonialism, where Western activists inadvertently impose their agendas on marginalized communities without fully understanding local contexts [?].

Additionally, cultural differences can pose challenges in communication and strategy formulation. Paula recognized the need for cultural sensitivity and adaptability in her collaborations. During a joint initiative with activists from the Global South, she facilitated workshops that allowed participants to share their unique experiences and perspectives, fostering mutual understanding and respect.

Successful Examples of Collaboration

One notable example of Paula's international collaboration was her involvement in the *Global Coalition for LGBTQ Rights*, which brought together organizations from over 30 countries. This coalition worked to draft a comprehensive report on the state of LGBTQ rights globally, highlighting both progress and setbacks. The report served as a critical tool for advocacy, providing evidence-based recommendations to policymakers and international bodies such as the United Nations.

Another successful initiative was the *Disability and LGBTQ Rights Summit* held in London, where Paula partnered with disability rights organizations to address the intersectionality of these movements. The summit resulted in the formation of a task force dedicated to advocating for inclusive policies that recognize the unique challenges faced by queer disabled individuals. This collaborative effort not only strengthened the ties between the LGBTQ and disability rights movements but also showcased the power of intersectional advocacy.

The Role of Technology

In the modern era, technology plays a pivotal role in facilitating international collaboration. Social media platforms and online communication tools have enabled activists to connect and share resources across borders. Paula leveraged these tools to organize virtual meetings, webinars, and campaigns that engaged a global audience. For instance, her use of social media during the #GlobalPride campaign allowed activists from different countries to unite in celebration and solidarity, demonstrating the power of collective action in the digital age.

Measuring Impact

To ensure the effectiveness of international collaborations, it is essential to establish metrics for measuring impact. Paula advocated for the use of qualitative and quantitative indicators to assess the outcomes of collaborative efforts. For example, tracking changes in legislation, public awareness, and community engagement can provide valuable insights into the effectiveness of advocacy initiatives. Additionally, gathering testimonials from individuals directly impacted by these efforts can highlight the human stories behind the statistics, reinforcing the need for continued collaboration.

Conclusion

In conclusion, Paula Lupi's commitment to collaborating with international partners has been instrumental in advancing LGBTQ and disability rights on a global scale. By fostering solidarity, addressing challenges, and celebrating successes, she has demonstrated that the fight for justice is a collective endeavor. As the world continues to grapple with issues of inequality and discrimination, the lessons learned from Paula's collaborative efforts will serve as a guiding light for future activists seeking to create a more inclusive and equitable world.

Building inclusive communities and safe spaces

Creating inclusive communities and safe spaces is a vital component of the ongoing struggle for LGBTQ and disability rights. These spaces not only provide refuge from societal discrimination but also foster empowerment, solidarity, and resilience among marginalized individuals. Paula Lupi recognized the importance of these environments early in her activism, understanding that community-building is fundamental to achieving lasting change.

Theoretical Framework

The concept of safe spaces is rooted in theories of social justice and intersectionality. *Intersectionality*, a term coined by Kimberlé Crenshaw, emphasizes that individuals experience overlapping forms of discrimination based on their various identities, such as race, gender, sexual orientation, and disability. This framework highlights the necessity of creating spaces that acknowledge and address these complexities, ensuring that all voices are heard and respected.

$$D = \sum_{i=1}^{n}(P_i \cdot W_i) \tag{75}$$

Where D is the degree of inclusivity in a community, P_i represents the presence of diverse identities, and W_i symbolizes the weight of their representation and empowerment. This equation illustrates that a higher degree of inclusivity is achieved when diverse identities are not only present but actively engaged and valued.

Challenges in Building Inclusive Communities

Despite the clear benefits, creating inclusive communities is fraught with challenges. One significant problem is the *tokenism* that can occur when marginalized groups are superficially included without genuine engagement or representation. This often leads to feelings of alienation rather than belonging. For example, a local LGBTQ organization may invite disabled individuals to participate in events but fail to provide necessary accommodations, ultimately sidelining their voices.

Another challenge is the *internalized oppression* experienced by individuals from marginalized backgrounds. Many LGBTQ and disabled individuals have been conditioned to feel unworthy or fearful of expressing their identities. This internal struggle can hinder their participation in community-building efforts.

Paula understood that addressing these psychological barriers was crucial for fostering an environment where everyone felt safe to express themselves.

Strategies for Creating Safe Spaces

To effectively build inclusive communities, several strategies can be employed:

- **Education and Awareness:** Conducting workshops and training sessions to educate community members about the importance of inclusivity and the specific needs of LGBTQ and disabled individuals. This can help dismantle prejudices and foster understanding.

- **Accessibility:** Ensuring that all community spaces are physically accessible to individuals with disabilities. This includes wheelchair ramps, accessible restrooms, and sensory-friendly environments. Paula often advocated for these changes in local venues, emphasizing that accessibility is a fundamental right.

- **Inclusive Policies:** Implementing policies that explicitly promote diversity and inclusion within organizations and community groups. This could involve creating guidelines for respectful language, establishing zero-tolerance policies for discrimination, and ensuring diverse representation in leadership roles.

- **Peer Support Networks:** Establishing peer support groups where individuals can share their experiences and challenges in a safe and supportive environment. Paula often facilitated these groups, providing a platform for healing and empowerment.

- **Cultural Celebrations:** Hosting events that celebrate the diverse identities within the community, such as Pride parades or disability awareness days. These events not only raise visibility but also foster a sense of belonging and pride among participants.

Examples of Successful Initiatives

Several initiatives around the world exemplify successful efforts to build inclusive communities and safe spaces. For instance, the *LGBTQ+ Center* in San Francisco offers a myriad of resources, including mental health services, legal assistance, and social events tailored to LGBTQ individuals, ensuring all members feel welcome and supported. Similarly, the *Disability Rights Network* in Portugal has created forums for disabled activists to voice their concerns and collaborate on advocacy efforts, emphasizing the intersectionality of their struggles.

In her own community, Paula spearheaded the establishment of a local LGBTQ and disability support group, which provided resources, advocacy, and social events. This group became a model for inclusivity, demonstrating that when individuals from diverse backgrounds come together, they can create a powerful force for change.

Conclusion

Building inclusive communities and safe spaces is not merely an ideal; it is a necessity for the advancement of LGBTQ and disability rights. By employing intersectional approaches and actively addressing the unique challenges faced by marginalized individuals, advocates like Paula Lupi can create environments where everyone is empowered to thrive. As we move forward, it is essential to remember that the strength of our communities lies in their diversity and the commitment to ensuring that every voice is heard and valued.

Ensuring healthcare access for all LGBTQ and disabled individuals

Access to healthcare is a fundamental human right, yet for many LGBTQ and disabled individuals, this access remains fraught with barriers. Paula Lupi recognized that the intersectionality of sexual orientation, gender identity, and disability status creates unique challenges in obtaining necessary healthcare services. In this section, we will explore the theoretical framework surrounding healthcare access, identify the problems faced by these communities, and provide real-world examples of advocacy efforts aimed at dismantling these barriers.

Theoretical Framework

The concept of *intersectionality*, coined by Kimberlé Crenshaw, serves as a crucial theoretical lens through which to examine the healthcare disparities faced by LGBTQ and disabled individuals. Intersectionality posits that individuals experience multiple, overlapping identities that can compound discrimination and inequity. For instance, a queer disabled person may face discrimination not only due to their sexual orientation or disability but also because of the unique combination of both identities. This can lead to a phenomenon known as *double jeopardy*, where the individual is subjected to greater levels of marginalization.

Additionally, the *social determinants of health* framework highlights how social factors such as socioeconomic status, education, and community support influence health outcomes. LGBTQ and disabled individuals often encounter systemic barriers that affect their ability to access quality healthcare, including prejudice from healthcare providers, lack of culturally competent care, and financial constraints.

Problems Facing LGBTQ and Disabled Individuals

1. **Discrimination in Healthcare Settings**: Many LGBTQ individuals report experiences of discrimination when seeking medical care. This can manifest as verbal harassment, refusal of treatment, or a lack of understanding regarding LGBTQ-specific health needs. For disabled individuals, the challenges are often exacerbated by physical barriers in healthcare facilities, such as inaccessible entrances or equipment.
2. **Lack of Culturally Competent Care**: Healthcare providers may lack training in LGBTQ health issues or in addressing the needs of disabled patients. This lack of knowledge can lead to misdiagnosis or inadequate treatment. For example, a transgender person may face challenges in receiving hormone therapy due to a provider's bias or ignorance about gender-affirming care.
3. **Financial Barriers**: Many LGBTQ and disabled individuals face economic hardships that limit their access to healthcare. A study by the *National LGBTQ Task Force* found that LGBTQ individuals are more likely to experience poverty compared to their heterosexual counterparts. Coupled with the additional costs associated with disability, such as medical equipment or assistive devices, these financial constraints can hinder access to necessary healthcare services.
4. **Mental Health Stigma**: The stigma surrounding mental health issues can be particularly pronounced in LGBTQ communities, where individuals may already feel marginalized. Disabled individuals often face additional stigma, leading to reluctance in seeking mental health support. This can create a cycle of poor mental health that further complicates access to physical healthcare.

Examples of Advocacy Efforts

Paula Lupi's advocacy work has been instrumental in addressing these healthcare disparities. Below are some notable examples of initiatives aimed at ensuring healthcare access for LGBTQ and disabled individuals:
1. **Community Health Initiatives**: Lupi collaborated with local organizations to establish community health clinics that cater specifically to

LGBTQ and disabled populations. These clinics prioritize culturally competent care and provide a safe space for individuals to seek medical attention without fear of discrimination.

2. **Legislative Advocacy**: Lupi has been a vocal advocate for policies that protect against discrimination in healthcare settings. Her efforts contributed to the passage of legislation that mandates training for healthcare providers on LGBTQ and disability issues, ensuring that all patients receive respectful and informed care.

3. **Public Awareness Campaigns**: Recognizing the power of education, Lupi launched campaigns aimed at raising awareness about the unique healthcare needs of LGBTQ and disabled individuals. By sharing personal stories and data, these campaigns have helped to foster understanding and empathy among healthcare providers and the general public.

4. **Collaborative Research**: Lupi has been involved in research initiatives that focus on the health disparities faced by LGBTQ and disabled individuals. By collecting and disseminating data, these studies have provided a foundation for evidence-based advocacy efforts and informed policy changes.

Conclusion

Ensuring healthcare access for all LGBTQ and disabled individuals requires a multifaceted approach that addresses the complex interplay of discrimination, economic barriers, and societal stigma. Paula Lupi's commitment to intersectional advocacy has paved the way for significant strides in improving healthcare access for these marginalized communities. By continuing to advocate for inclusive policies, fostering community support, and raising awareness, we can work towards a healthcare system that truly serves all individuals, regardless of their identity or ability.

In summary, the journey towards equitable healthcare access is ongoing, and it is imperative that we remain vigilant in our efforts to dismantle barriers and promote inclusivity. As we reflect on Paula's legacy, let us carry forward her vision of a world where everyone has the opportunity to thrive, free from discrimination and inequity.

Empowering future activists to continue the fight

Empowering future activists is a crucial element of sustaining the momentum in the fight for LGBTQ and disability rights. This empowerment involves a multifaceted approach that combines education, mentorship, community building, and the cultivation of leadership skills. By equipping the next generation with the tools they need, we can ensure that the fight for equality continues with vigor and passion.

The Role of Education

Education serves as the bedrock for activism. It is through education that individuals can understand the historical context of their struggles, the nuances of intersectionality, and the importance of inclusivity. Theoretical frameworks such as *Critical Pedagogy* (Freire, 1970) emphasize the need for an educational approach that encourages critical thinking and social justice. Future activists must be taught not only the facts but also how to question the status quo and develop a critical consciousness.

$$\text{Critical Consciousness} = \text{Awareness of Social Inequities} + \text{Ability to Challenge Oppression} \tag{76}$$

This equation illustrates that critical consciousness is a synthesis of awareness and action, which is essential for effective activism.

Mentorship and Role Models

Mentorship plays an invaluable role in empowering future activists. By connecting emerging leaders with established activists, we create a support system that fosters growth and resilience. Mentorship can take various forms, from formal programs to informal relationships, and should focus on sharing experiences, skills, and networks. The significance of mentorship is underscored by Bandura's (1977) Social Learning Theory, which posits that individuals learn behaviors and norms through observation and imitation of role models.

$$\text{Learning} = \text{Attention} \times \text{Retention} \times \text{Reproduction} \times \text{Motivation} \tag{77}$$

This equation highlights that for learning to occur, future activists must be attentive, retain information, reproduce actions, and be motivated to engage in activism.

Building Community

A strong sense of community is vital for sustaining activism. Communities provide emotional support, resources, and a collective identity that can empower individuals. Creating safe spaces for LGBTQ and disabled individuals fosters inclusivity and encourages participation. The *Community Organizing Theory* emphasizes that grassroots movements are more effective when they are built from the ground up, involving community members in decision-making processes.

Cultivating Leadership Skills

Leadership skills are essential for effective activism. Future activists should be trained in areas such as public speaking, strategic planning, and conflict resolution. Programs that focus on skill-building can help individuals gain confidence and competence in their advocacy efforts. The *Transformational Leadership Theory* suggests that leaders inspire and motivate others to achieve a common vision, which is particularly relevant in social justice movements.

$$\text{Transformational Leadership} = \text{Idealized Influence} + \text{Inspirational Motivation} + \text{Intellectual} \tag{78}$$

This equation illustrates the components of transformational leadership, emphasizing the importance of inspiring others while being considerate of individual needs.

Utilizing Technology and Social Media

In today's digital age, technology and social media are powerful tools for activism. Future activists must be equipped to navigate these platforms effectively. Social media can amplify voices, mobilize supporters, and spread awareness about critical issues. The *Networked Publics Theory* posits that digital networks can create new forms of public engagement and collective action. Training future activists in digital literacy ensures they can leverage these tools for advocacy.

Challenges and Barriers

While empowering future activists is essential, it is also important to recognize the challenges they may face. Systemic barriers such as discrimination, lack of resources, and societal stigma can hinder their efforts. Addressing these challenges requires a collective response from the broader community. Intersectional approaches must be employed to ensure that the unique experiences of LGBTQ and disabled individuals are considered in activism.

Conclusion

Empowering future activists is not merely an option; it is a necessity for the ongoing fight for LGBTQ and disability rights. By investing in education, mentorship, community building, and leadership development, we can cultivate a new generation of activists who are equipped to continue the struggle for equality. As we reflect on Paula Lupi's legacy, we must commit to fostering an environment that encourages and empowers future leaders, ensuring that the fight for justice remains vibrant and relentless.

References

- Bandura, A. (1977). *Social Learning Theory*. Englewood Cliffs, NJ: Prentice Hall.

- Freire, P. (1970). *Pedagogy of the Oppressed*. New York: Continuum.

Leaving a lasting legacy for a more inclusive world

Paula Lupi's journey as an LGBTQ and disability rights activist is not merely a narrative of personal triumph; it is a blueprint for creating a more inclusive world. The legacy she leaves behind serves as a guiding light for future generations, illuminating paths toward equality and justice for marginalized communities. This section examines the multifaceted aspects of her legacy, including theoretical frameworks, persistent challenges, and concrete examples of her impact.

Theoretical Frameworks of Inclusion

To understand Paula's legacy, we must first delve into the theories that underpin inclusive activism. The concept of **intersectionality**, coined by Kimberlé Crenshaw, emphasizes that individuals experience overlapping identities that shape their social realities. Paula's work exemplifies intersectionality by advocating for both LGBTQ and disability rights, recognizing that these identities cannot be separated in the fight for justice.

In addition, **social justice theory** posits that a fair society is one where all individuals have equal rights and opportunities. Paula's activism aligns with this theory as she worked tirelessly to dismantle systemic barriers that hindered the rights of LGBTQ individuals and those with disabilities. By addressing issues such as healthcare access, education, and employment discrimination, Paula's legacy embodies the essence of social justice.

Challenges to Building an Inclusive World

Despite the progress made, Paula's legacy also underscores the ongoing challenges faced in the pursuit of inclusivity. One significant issue is the **persistent stigma** surrounding LGBTQ individuals and people with disabilities. This stigma often manifests in various forms, including discrimination in the workplace, social ostracization, and inadequate representation in media and politics. For instance, research indicates that LGBTQ individuals with disabilities are more likely to experience mental health issues due to societal pressures and lack of support systems.

Furthermore, the intersection of race, gender, and socioeconomic status complicates the fight for inclusivity. Many activists within the LGBTQ and disability rights movements are still grappling with issues of privilege and representation. Paula's advocacy highlighted these complexities, urging a more nuanced understanding of how different identities intersect and how activism must adapt to address these intersections effectively.

Concrete Examples of Impact

Paula's legacy is not just theoretical; it is grounded in tangible achievements that have paved the way for a more inclusive world. One notable example is her role in advocating for inclusive education policies in Portugal. By collaborating with educational institutions and policymakers, Paula helped implement programs that support LGBTQ and disabled students, ensuring that they receive the resources and support necessary for their success.

Additionally, Paula's international advocacy work brought attention to the rights of LGBTQ individuals and people with disabilities on a global scale. By representing Portugal at international conferences, she amplified marginalized voices, fostering a sense of solidarity among activists worldwide. Her speeches often highlighted the need for global cooperation in addressing human rights violations, emphasizing that the fight for equality transcends borders.

Empowering Future Generations

A crucial aspect of Paula's legacy is her commitment to empowering future activists. Through mentorship programs, public speaking engagements, and educational initiatives, she inspired countless individuals to take up the mantle of activism. Paula understood that true change requires a collective effort, and she actively worked to cultivate a new generation of leaders who would continue the fight for inclusivity.

One of her most impactful initiatives was the establishment of the **Lupi Foundation,** dedicated to supporting LGBTQ and disabled youth. The foundation provides scholarships, resources, and mentorship opportunities, ensuring that young activists have the tools and support they need to effect change in their communities.

Conclusion: A Lasting Impact

In conclusion, Paula Lupi's legacy is a testament to the power of activism in creating a more inclusive world. By intertwining theoretical frameworks with practical action, she has laid a foundation for future generations to build upon. While challenges remain, Paula's unwavering commitment to justice and equality serves as a reminder that the fight for inclusivity is ongoing. Her legacy is not just a reflection of her achievements but a call to action for all of us to continue the work she started. As we honor her memory, let us also commit to leaving our own legacies of inclusivity, ensuring that the world becomes a better place for everyone, regardless of their identity.

Recognitions and Honors

Awards and accolades for her advocacy work

Paula Lupi's journey as an activist has not only transformed the landscape of LGBTQ and disability rights in Portugal but has also garnered her numerous awards and accolades, both nationally and internationally. These honors serve as a testament to her relentless dedication and the profound impact of her work on marginalized communities.

National Recognition

In Portugal, Paula has received several prestigious awards that highlight her contributions to social justice and advocacy. One of the most notable accolades is the *Prémio da Igualdade*, awarded by the Portuguese government, which recognizes individuals who have made significant strides in promoting equality and fighting discrimination. This award not only acknowledges Paula's tireless efforts but also underscores the importance of intersectionality in her activism, as she has been a vocal advocate for both LGBTQ and disability rights.

Another significant recognition came from the *Associação Portuguesa de Deficientes*, which honored Paula with the *Medalha de Mérito* for her work in raising awareness about the challenges faced by disabled individuals within the LGBTQ community. This award reflects her commitment to inclusivity and her ability to bridge gaps between different advocacy movements.

International Accolades

Paula's influence has transcended borders, earning her international acclaim. She was nominated for the *International LGBTQ Rights Award* at the *Global Equality Fund* gala, an event that celebrates individuals who have made extraordinary contributions to advancing LGBTQ rights worldwide. Her nomination highlighted her work in advocating for policy changes that protect the rights of LGBTQ individuals and disabled persons, demonstrating her ability to effect change on a global scale.

In addition, Paula received the *Human Rights Defender Award* from the *European Union Agency for Fundamental Rights* (FRA). This award is given to individuals who have shown exceptional courage in defending human rights, particularly in the face of adversity. Paula's acceptance speech emphasized the necessity of solidarity among various movements, stating, "Our struggles are interconnected; when we uplift one another, we create a force that cannot be ignored."

Impact of Awards on Activism

The recognition Paula has received has not only validated her work but has also amplified her voice in the fight for equality. Awards often come with platforms that allow recipients to further advocate for their causes. For instance, following her receipt of the *Human Rights Defender Award*, Paula was invited to speak at several international conferences, where she shared her insights on the intersectionality of LGBTQ and disability rights. These speaking engagements have enabled her to network with other activists and policymakers, fostering collaborations that have led to significant advancements in legislation.

Furthermore, accolades have provided Paula with the resources to expand her initiatives. Many awards come with monetary grants, which Paula has utilized to fund community outreach programs and educational workshops aimed at empowering LGBTQ and disabled youth. As she often states, "Recognition is not just a trophy; it's a tool for change."

Challenges and Controversies

Despite the accolades, Paula's journey has not been devoid of challenges. Some critics argue that awards can sometimes overshadow the collective efforts of grassroots movements. In her acceptance of the *Prémio da Igualdade*, Paula addressed this concern by emphasizing the importance of recognizing the unsung heroes of activism. She remarked, "Every award I receive is a reflection of the countless individuals who have fought beside me. This is not just my victory; it is ours."

Moreover, the nature of awards can sometimes lead to a perception of elitism within activist circles. Paula has actively worked to combat this narrative by using her platform to highlight the voices of those who may not have the opportunity to be recognized. She believes that the true measure of success lies in the tangible changes made in communities, rather than the accolades received.

Conclusion

In conclusion, Paula Lupi's numerous awards and accolades serve as a testament to her unwavering commitment to advocating for LGBTQ and disability rights. These honors not only recognize her individual contributions but also highlight the broader movement for equality. As Paula continues her work, she remains dedicated to ensuring that her achievements pave the way for future generations of activists, inspiring them to fight for a more inclusive and equitable world. The legacy of her advocacy is not merely encapsulated in awards but is reflected in the lives she has touched and the systemic changes she has helped to bring about.

$$\text{Impact of Advocacy} = \text{Recognition} + \text{Community Engagement} + \text{Policy Change} \tag{79}$$

This equation represents the multifaceted nature of advocacy, where recognition serves as a catalyst for community engagement and leads to meaningful policy changes that benefit marginalized groups. Paula Lupi exemplifies this dynamic, proving that one person's efforts can indeed ignite a movement.

Honorary degrees and recognitions from universities

Throughout her illustrious career, Paula Lupi has garnered numerous honorary degrees and accolades from prestigious universities across Portugal and beyond. These recognitions not only celebrate her relentless dedication to LGBTQ and disability rights but also highlight the profound impact of her advocacy on academia and society at large.

Honorary degrees are typically conferred by universities to individuals who have made significant contributions to society, often in areas that align with the institution's values and mission. Paula's journey to receiving these honors can be viewed through the lens of several key theoretical frameworks, including the social constructivist perspective, which posits that knowledge and meaning are constructed through social interactions and experiences.

Theoretical Underpinnings

In the context of honorary recognitions, we can apply the **Social Identity Theory**, which suggests that individuals derive a sense of self from their group memberships. Paula's identity as a queer disabled woman has informed her activism and shaped her contributions to social justice. Universities, recognizing her unique position and the intersectionality of her identity, have honored her to affirm their commitment to diversity and inclusion.

Additionally, the **Theory of Change** can be employed to understand the ripple effects of Paula's work. This theory outlines how specific actions can lead to desired outcomes in social movements. By awarding her honorary degrees, universities acknowledge the transformative impact of her activism on policy, education, and community empowerment.

Notable Recognitions

One of the most significant honors bestowed upon Paula was an honorary doctorate from the *University of Lisbon*. This recognition was awarded in acknowledgment of her pioneering work in advocating for inclusive education policies that accommodate LGBTQ and disabled students. The university's decision to honor her reflects a broader commitment to fostering an environment where all students can thrive, regardless of their sexual orientation or disability status.

Another notable recognition came from the *University of Coimbra*, which awarded Paula the title of *Distinguished Alumni*. This accolade not only celebrated her achievements but also served as a testament to the university's commitment to social justice and human rights. The ceremony was attended by prominent activists, scholars, and students, all of whom were inspired by Paula's journey and dedication.

Challenges and Controversies

However, the path to these honors has not been devoid of challenges. Paula faced scrutiny from various quarters, including criticisms regarding the inclusivity of her activism. Some argued that her focus on LGBTQ rights overshadowed the specific needs of disabled individuals within the community. This backlash prompted

Paula to engage in critical self-reflection and dialogue, emphasizing the importance of intersectionality in her work.

For instance, during her acceptance speech at the *University of Porto*, Paula addressed these concerns head-on. She articulated her commitment to amplifying marginalized voices within the LGBTQ and disability communities, stating:

> "I recognize that my journey is intertwined with the struggles of others. It is my responsibility to ensure that no one is left behind in our pursuit of equality and justice."

This statement resonated with many attendees, showcasing Paula's ability to turn criticism into an opportunity for growth and unity.

Impact of Recognitions on Paula's Work

The honorary degrees and recognitions have had a profound impact on Paula's advocacy work. They serve as a validation of her efforts and provide her with a platform to reach wider audiences. For example, after receiving her honorary doctorate from the *University of Lisbon*, Paula was invited to speak at various international conferences, where she shared her insights on the intersectionality of LGBTQ and disability rights.

These speaking engagements not only elevated her profile but also fostered collaborations with other activists and organizations. As a result, Paula was able to spearhead initiatives aimed at improving access to education for LGBTQ and disabled youth, thereby creating a more inclusive environment in schools across Portugal.

Conclusion

In conclusion, the honorary degrees and recognitions received by Paula Lupi represent more than mere accolades; they symbolize a collective acknowledgment of her contributions to social justice and equality. They reflect the changing landscape of academia, where institutions are increasingly recognizing the importance of diverse voices and perspectives in shaping a more inclusive society. Paula's journey serves as an inspiration for future generations of activists, reminding us that the fight for justice is a continuous process that requires dedication, resilience, and a commitment to uplifting all marginalized communities.

Being an ambassador for global organizations

As Paula Lupi rose to prominence in her advocacy for LGBTQ and disability rights, she found herself stepping into the role of an ambassador for various global organizations. This role was not merely ceremonial; it was a profound commitment to representing the voices of marginalized communities on an international stage. The responsibilities of an ambassador in this context include not only advocacy but also diplomacy, education, and collaboration across borders.

The Role of an Ambassador

Being an ambassador for global organizations involves several key functions:

- **Representation:** Paula served as a representative of her country and the communities she advocated for, ensuring that their needs and concerns were voiced in international forums.

- **Advocacy:** She actively campaigned for policies that promote LGBTQ and disability rights, using her platform to influence global standards and practices.

- **Education:** An essential part of her role was to educate other leaders and organizations about the unique challenges faced by LGBTQ individuals with disabilities, fostering a greater understanding of intersectionality.

- **Collaboration:** Paula worked closely with other global leaders and organizations, forging alliances that could amplify the impact of their collective efforts.

Challenges Faced

Despite the significant impact of her role, Paula encountered numerous challenges:

- **Cultural Differences:** Navigating the diverse cultural attitudes toward LGBTQ rights globally was a complex task. In some regions, advocacy efforts were met with resistance, requiring Paula to adapt her approach to resonate with local customs and beliefs.

- **Political Backlash:** Engaging with international organizations often meant facing political backlash at home. Paula had to balance her global responsibilities with her local activism, sometimes at great personal cost.

- **Resource Limitations:** Many global organizations operate on limited resources, which can hinder the effectiveness of campaigns. Paula often had to strategize on how to maximize impact with minimal funding.

Examples of Impact

Paula's ambassadorship yielded tangible outcomes:

- **Global Conferences:** At major international conferences, such as the United Nations Human Rights Council, Paula delivered powerful speeches that highlighted the plight of LGBTQ individuals with disabilities. Her impassioned calls for action led to the inclusion of specific provisions aimed at protecting these communities in global human rights discussions.

- **Collaborative Initiatives:** Paula spearheaded collaborative initiatives between organizations in Portugal and those in countries facing severe restrictions on LGBTQ rights. These initiatives often focused on knowledge sharing and capacity building, empowering local activists to advocate for change in their own contexts.

- **Public Awareness Campaigns:** Through her role, Paula helped launch global awareness campaigns that utilized social media platforms to reach millions. These campaigns not only educated the public but also mobilized support for legislative changes in various countries.

Theoretical Framework

The effectiveness of Paula's role as an ambassador can be analyzed through the lens of several theoretical frameworks:

- **Social Movement Theory:** This framework emphasizes the importance of collective action and the role of leaders in mobilizing resources and support. Paula exemplified this by leveraging her position to unite various movements under the common goal of equality.

- **Intersectionality:** Coined by Kimberlé Crenshaw, this theory highlights the interconnected nature of social categorizations such as race, class, and gender. Paula's advocacy work was deeply rooted in an understanding of intersectionality, which informed her approach to global issues.

- **Globalization:** The interconnectedness of the world means that local issues can have global repercussions. Paula's work reflected the reality of globalization, as she sought to address local injustices within a broader international framework.

Conclusion

Paula Lupi's role as an ambassador for global organizations was a testament to her commitment to amplifying the voices of the marginalized. Through her advocacy, she not only influenced policy but also inspired a new generation of activists to engage on the international stage. Her journey illustrates the complexities and rewards of being an ambassador in the fight for LGBTQ and disability rights, ultimately contributing to a more inclusive world.

$$\text{Impact} = \text{Representation} + \text{Advocacy} + \text{Education} + \text{Collaboration} \qquad (80)$$

Invitations to speak at prestigious events and conferences

As Paula Lupi's influence grew within the LGBTQ and disability rights communities, her expertise and passionate advocacy led to numerous invitations to speak at prestigious events and conferences around the world. These platforms not only allowed her to share her message but also provided a unique opportunity to engage with a diverse audience, including policymakers, activists, and scholars.

One of the primary theories underlying the importance of speaking engagements is the **Social Change Theory**, which posits that effective communication can lead to awareness and ultimately, action. By addressing large audiences, Paula was able to disseminate her ideas and experiences, fostering a collective understanding of the intersectionality of LGBTQ and disability rights.

$$\text{Social Change} = f(\text{Awareness}, \text{Engagement}, \text{Action}) \qquad (81)$$

The Power of the Platform

Invitations to speak at events such as the International LGBTQ Rights Conference and the Global Disability Summit provided Paula with a platform to highlight the challenges faced by queer disabled individuals. These events are often attended by influential figures in politics and civil society, creating a ripple effect that can lead to policy changes and increased funding for advocacy programs. For instance, during her keynote address at the European Conference on Disability and Human Rights, Paula emphasized the need for inclusive policies that address the specific needs of disabled LGBTQ individuals, which resonated with attendees and prompted discussions on legislative reforms.

Challenges and Opportunities

However, speaking at such high-profile events was not without its challenges. Paula often faced scrutiny and pressure to represent multiple marginalized identities simultaneously. Critics within the LGBTQ and disability communities sometimes questioned her ability to authentically speak on behalf of all individuals, given the diverse experiences and challenges they face. This criticism underscores the concept of **Representation Theory**, which asserts that the voices of marginalized groups must be included in discussions that directly affect them. Paula addressed these concerns head-on, advocating for a more inclusive dialogue that elevates the voices of those who are often overlooked.

$$\text{Effective Representation} = \frac{\text{Diversity of Voices}}{\text{Inclusivity of Dialogue}} \tag{82}$$

Examples of Impactful Engagements

One notable example of Paula's impactful speaking engagements was her participation in the United Nations Human Rights Council. There, she presented a compelling case for the urgent need to address the intersectional discrimination faced by LGBTQ individuals with disabilities. Her speech not only garnered international media attention but also resulted in a commitment from several countries to develop inclusive policies that protect the rights of these individuals.

Another significant moment occurred at the World Health Organization's Global Health Conference, where Paula discussed the health disparities faced by queer disabled individuals. By sharing personal stories and data-driven insights, she illuminated the urgent need for healthcare systems to adapt and become more inclusive. This presentation led to collaborative efforts among health organizations to create guidelines that ensure equitable access to healthcare for all individuals, regardless of their sexual orientation or disability status.

Building Networks and Alliances

Through her speaking engagements, Paula also built valuable networks and alliances with other activists and organizations. These connections were crucial for amplifying her message and expanding the reach of her advocacy efforts. For example, her collaboration with international NGOs led to joint campaigns that addressed both LGBTQ and disability rights, showcasing the power of intersectional advocacy.

In conclusion, Paula Lupi's invitations to speak at prestigious events and conferences were not merely opportunities for personal recognition but pivotal moments for advancing the conversation around LGBTQ and disability rights. By leveraging these platforms, she was able to inspire action, foster collaboration, and contribute to a legacy of advocacy that continues to resonate globally. Her ability to navigate the complexities of representation and intersectionality has made her a sought-after speaker and a powerful voice for marginalized communities.

$$\text{Legacy of Advocacy} = \sum_{i=1}^{n} \text{Impact of Engagements}_i \qquad (83)$$

The impact of recognition on Paula's work and personal life

Recognition can serve as a double-edged sword, particularly for activists like Paula Lupi, whose work intersects with both LGBTQ and disability rights. On one hand, accolades and public acknowledgment can amplify an activist's voice, increase their visibility, and enhance their ability to effect change. On the other hand, recognition can also lead to scrutiny, pressure, and the potential for misrepresentation.

Enhancing Visibility and Credibility

One of the most significant impacts of recognition for Paula has been the enhancement of her visibility as a leader in the LGBTQ and disability rights movements. With each award and honor, Paula's platform grew, allowing her to reach a broader audience. This visibility can be mathematically represented by the following equation:

$$V = f(A, P) \qquad (84)$$

Where V is visibility, A represents the number of awards received, and P denotes public presence through media coverage and speaking engagements. As A increases, so does V, leading to greater opportunities for advocacy and outreach.

For example, after receiving the prestigious *Human Rights Advocate of the Year* award, Paula was invited to speak at several international conferences, significantly increasing her influence. This recognition not only validated her work but also provided her with a platform to advocate for marginalized communities on a global scale.

Building Networks and Alliances

Recognition also facilitated the establishment of vital networks and alliances. By being acknowledged for her contributions, Paula was able to connect with other influential figures in activism and politics. This interconnectedness can be viewed through the lens of social capital theory, which posits that social networks have value.

$$SC = \sum_{i=1}^{n} C_i \qquad (85)$$

Where SC is social capital, and C_i represents the connections made through recognition, such as partnerships with other activists, organizations, and even political figures. Each connection enhances Paula's ability to mobilize resources and create impactful campaigns.

For instance, after being recognized by a major LGBTQ organization, Paula collaborated with several international NGOs to launch a campaign advocating for inclusive education policies for disabled LGBTQ youth. This collaboration not only expanded the reach of her message but also fostered a sense of solidarity among various movements.

Navigating Public Scrutiny

However, increased recognition also brought challenges. As Paula's public profile rose, so did scrutiny of her actions and statements. This phenomenon is often referred to as the "celebrity effect," where the public expects a higher standard of behavior from recognized figures.

This scrutiny can lead to a phenomenon known as the *imposter syndrome*, where even the most accomplished individuals doubt their abilities and fear being exposed as a "fraud." For Paula, this manifested in moments of self-doubt, particularly when faced with criticism from within the LGBTQ and disability communities.

$$IS = \frac{C}{E} \times 100 \qquad (86)$$

Where IS represents the level of imposter syndrome, C is the amount of criticism faced, and E denotes the extent of her achievements. As C increased with recognition, Paula sometimes felt that her achievements were overshadowed by the weight of expectations.

Balancing Activism and Personal Life

The impact of recognition extended beyond Paula's professional life; it also affected her personal life. As her activism gained attention, the demands on her time increased, leading to challenges in maintaining a work-life balance. The following equation illustrates this dynamic:

$$B = W - L \tag{87}$$

Where B represents balance, W is the workload from activism and recognition, and L denotes personal life commitments. As W increased due to recognition, B often decreased, creating tension between her professional responsibilities and personal relationships.

For instance, Paula found it increasingly difficult to spend quality time with friends and family, leading to feelings of isolation. Recognizing this imbalance, she began to implement self-care practices and set boundaries to protect her personal life. This included scheduling regular breaks and prioritizing time for loved ones, which ultimately contributed to her overall well-being.

Legacy and Inspiration

Despite the challenges, the recognition Paula received played a crucial role in shaping her legacy. It not only validated her work but also inspired countless individuals to engage in activism. The impact of her recognition can be encapsulated in the following equation:

$$L = R \times I \tag{88}$$

Where L is legacy, R represents recognition, and I denotes the inspiration generated among others. As R increases, so does L, creating a ripple effect that encourages future generations to fight for LGBTQ and disability rights.

In conclusion, while recognition brought both opportunities and challenges to Paula Lupi's work and personal life, it ultimately served as a catalyst for her continued activism. The balance she sought between her public persona and personal identity became a testament to her resilience and commitment to creating a more inclusive world. Through her journey, Paula not only carved a path for herself but also illuminated the way for others to follow, leaving an indelible mark on the landscape of LGBTQ and disability rights.

Giving back through mentorship and support

In the realm of activism, mentorship serves as a crucial pillar for sustaining movements and empowering the next generation. Paula Lupi recognized early on that her journey was not just about her own advocacy but also about creating pathways for others to follow. This understanding shaped her approach to giving back through mentorship and support, allowing her to cultivate a nurturing environment for budding activists.

Mentorship in activism is often defined by the transfer of knowledge, skills, and experiences from one individual to another. According to Kram's (1985) theory of mentoring, the relationship can be categorized into two distinct functions: career functions and psychosocial functions. Career functions include sponsorship, exposure, and visibility, while psychosocial functions encompass role modeling, acceptance, and confirmation. Paula embodied both aspects, becoming a significant figure who not only guided emerging activists in navigating the complexities of LGBTQ and disability rights but also provided emotional support to help them build confidence in their identities.

One of the primary challenges faced by young activists, particularly those from marginalized communities, is the feeling of isolation. Many struggle to find their voices in a world that often silences them. Paula's mentorship initiatives were designed to address this issue directly. By establishing mentorship programs within local LGBTQ organizations, she created safe spaces where young activists could share their experiences, discuss their aspirations, and receive guidance from someone who had successfully navigated similar challenges.

For instance, during her tenure with the Lisbon LGBTQ Youth Collective, Paula initiated a program called "Voices of Tomorrow." This program paired seasoned activists with youth seeking to explore their identities and engage in advocacy work. Participants in the program reported feelings of increased empowerment and motivation, citing Paula's unwavering support as a catalyst for their personal and political growth. One mentee, Maria, shared, "Paula taught me that my voice matters. She helped me see that I could be an advocate for change, even as a young queer woman with a disability."

Moreover, Paula's commitment to mentorship extended beyond formal programs. She frequently hosted workshops and seminars focusing on skills development—ranging from public speaking to grassroots organizing. These workshops not only equipped young activists with practical tools but also fostered a sense of community. By bringing together individuals from diverse backgrounds, Paula emphasized the importance of intersectionality within activism, encouraging participants to understand how various identities intersect and influence their experiences.

The psychosocial aspect of mentorship is equally vital. Paula often shared her own struggles with self-doubt and the internalized prejudice she faced as a queer disabled woman. By being open about her vulnerabilities, she created an atmosphere of authenticity that resonated with her mentees. This transparency allowed them to feel comfortable discussing their own challenges, fostering resilience and a sense of belonging.

As highlighted in a study by Allen et al. (2004), effective mentorship can lead to increased self-efficacy among mentees, which is particularly important in activist circles. Paula's approach exemplified this theory; her mentees reported a significant boost in their belief in their ability to effect change. This newfound confidence often translated into active participation in advocacy efforts, with many mentees going on to lead their initiatives within the community.

In addition to direct mentorship, Paula also emphasized the importance of creating a supportive network among activists. She believed that collaboration was key to amplifying marginalized voices. By encouraging her mentees to connect with one another, she facilitated the formation of a supportive community that extended beyond her individual influence. This network not only provided emotional support but also fostered collective action, enabling young activists to mobilize around shared causes.

Paula's legacy in mentorship is evident in the numerous activists she inspired, many of whom have taken on leadership roles within the LGBTQ and disability rights movements. For instance, one of her former mentees, Tiago, now leads a national campaign advocating for inclusive policies in schools. He attributes his success to the foundational skills and confidence he gained under Paula's guidance. "Paula showed me that activism is not just about fighting against oppression; it's about lifting others as you climb," he stated during a panel discussion honoring her contributions.

In conclusion, Paula Lupi's commitment to giving back through mentorship and support not only enriched her life but also transformed the lives of countless young activists. By fostering a culture of empowerment, collaboration, and intersectionality, she ensured that her legacy would continue to inspire future generations. The impact of her mentorship can be seen in the ongoing efforts of her mentees, who carry forward the torch of activism, embodying the values of justice, equality, and community that Paula championed throughout her life.

$$\text{Empowerment} = \text{Confidence} + \text{Support} + \text{Knowledge} \qquad (89)$$

Shaping the next generation of LGBTQ and disability rights leaders

The legacy of Paula Lupi is not merely a reflection of her own accomplishments, but a powerful catalyst for inspiring and shaping the next generation of LGBTQ and disability rights leaders. Her commitment to advocacy serves as a blueprint for emerging activists who seek to navigate the complex landscape of social justice, identity, and systemic change. In this section, we will explore the theoretical underpinnings of leadership in social movements, the challenges faced by young activists, and practical examples of mentorship and empowerment that Paula championed.

Theoretical Framework

At the heart of effective leadership in social justice movements lies the concept of *transformational leadership*, which emphasizes the importance of inspiring and motivating followers to achieve a common vision. According to Bass and Avolio (1994), transformational leaders exhibit four key components: idealized influence, inspirational motivation, intellectual stimulation, and individualized consideration. Paula embodied these principles, using her platform to uplift marginalized voices while encouraging young activists to think critically about the intersectionality of LGBTQ and disability rights.

Moreover, the theory of *intersectionality*, coined by Kimberlé Crenshaw (1989), highlights the interconnected nature of social categorizations such as race, gender, and disability, which create overlapping systems of discrimination. Paula's work exemplified this theory, as she continuously advocated for an inclusive approach that recognized the unique challenges faced by individuals at the intersections of multiple identities. By fostering an understanding of intersectionality among young leaders, Paula laid the groundwork for a more comprehensive and nuanced approach to activism.

Challenges Faced by Emerging Activists

Despite the progress made in LGBTQ and disability rights, young activists encounter numerous obstacles that can hinder their effectiveness. These challenges include:

- **Systemic Barriers:** Many young activists face institutional barriers that limit their access to resources, funding, and opportunities for engagement. For instance, educational institutions may lack inclusive policies that support LGBTQ and disabled students, thereby stifling their voices.
- **Internalized Prejudice:** Emerging leaders often grapple with internalized stigma and self-doubt, which can impede their confidence and willingness to advocate for their rights. This psychological barrier can prevent them from fully embracing their identities and potential as leaders.
- **Generational Gaps:** The divergence in perspectives between older and younger activists can lead to misunderstandings and conflicts within

movements. Younger activists may feel that their concerns are overlooked or dismissed by established leaders who may not fully grasp the contemporary issues they face.

Mentorship and Empowerment Initiatives

Recognizing the importance of mentorship in shaping future leaders, Paula Lupi initiated several programs aimed at empowering young activists. These initiatives included:

- **Leadership Workshops:** Paula organized workshops that focused on skill-building in areas such as public speaking, advocacy strategies, and community organizing. By equipping young activists with practical skills, she fostered a sense of agency and confidence.

- **Peer Mentorship Programs:** Connecting seasoned activists with emerging leaders, these programs facilitated knowledge exchange and provided a support network. For example, a mentorship pair might engage in regular discussions about navigating activism while balancing personal challenges, thus creating a safe space for growth.

- **Scholarship Opportunities:** Paula championed scholarships for LGBTQ and disabled youth seeking higher education in fields related to social justice. By removing financial barriers, she encouraged young leaders to pursue their passions and contribute meaningfully to the movement.

- **Advocacy Incubators:** Paula founded advocacy incubators that provided resources, funding, and training for innovative projects led by young activists. These incubators served as platforms for collaboration, allowing emerging leaders to experiment with new ideas and strategies in a supportive environment.

Examples of Impact

The impact of Paula's mentorship and empowerment initiatives is evident in the success stories of numerous young activists who have emerged as influential leaders in their own right. For instance, the case of Miguel Santos, a queer disabled activist, illustrates the transformative power of mentorship. Under Paula's guidance, Miguel developed a campaign advocating for accessible public spaces in Lisbon, which garnered significant media attention and ultimately led to policy changes.

Furthermore, the establishment of the "Lupi Fellowship" program has created a pipeline of young leaders equipped to tackle pressing issues within the LGBTQ and disability communities. Fellows engage in hands-on advocacy projects while receiving guidance from experienced mentors, ensuring that Paula's legacy continues to inspire and shape the future of activism.

Conclusion

In conclusion, shaping the next generation of LGBTQ and disability rights leaders is a multifaceted endeavor that requires intentionality, commitment, and a recognition of the complexities of identity and advocacy. Paula Lupi's legacy serves as a powerful reminder that mentorship, empowerment, and a focus on intersectionality are crucial in fostering a new wave of activists. By addressing the challenges faced by emerging leaders and providing them with the tools and support necessary for success, we can ensure that the fight for equality and justice continues to thrive, echoing Paula's enduring impact on the world.

Bibliography

[1] Bass, B. M., & Avolio, B. J. (1994). Improving organizational effectiveness through transformational leadership. *Sage Publications*.

[2] Crenshaw, K. (1989). Demarginalizing the intersection of race and sex: A black feminist critique of antidiscrimination doctrine, feminist theory and antiracist politics. *University of Chicago Legal Forum*, 1989(1), 139-167.

Inspiring change beyond her own lifetime

Paula Lupi's journey as an activist transcends her own life, embodying a legacy that inspires future generations to continue the fight for LGBTQ and disability rights. Her commitment to activism was not merely a personal endeavor; it was a movement aimed at fostering systemic change and creating a world where equality is a given, not a privilege.

Theoretical Framework

The concept of *intergenerational justice* is pivotal in understanding Paula's impact. This theory posits that current generations have a responsibility to ensure that future generations inherit a world that is equitable and just. As articulated by scholars like [1], the principles of justice must extend beyond the immediate context, requiring a vision that considers the long-term implications of social policies and actions.

Challenges in Inspiring Change

Despite her profound impact, Paula faced numerous challenges in her quest to inspire change. One significant problem is the *institutional inertia* that often accompanies social movements. Many organizations and political systems resist change due to entrenched interests and biases. This resistance can stifle progress and discourage new activists who may feel overwhelmed by the enormity of the task at hand.

Another challenge is the phenomenon of *activist burnout*, where individuals become disillusioned or exhausted from the relentless nature of advocacy work. Paula recognized these challenges and sought to address them through mentorship and community-building initiatives, ensuring that the torch of activism would be passed on to a new generation.

Examples of Lasting Impact

Paula's legacy is evident in various initiatives that continue to thrive long after her direct involvement. For instance, the *Lisbon Pride Festival*, which she helped establish, has grown into one of the largest celebrations of LGBTQ rights in Europe. This event not only raises awareness but also fosters a sense of community and solidarity among marginalized groups. The festival serves as a platform for young activists to voice their concerns and share their stories, embodying Paula's belief in the power of collective action.

Moreover, Paula's influence can be seen in educational programs designed to promote inclusivity in schools. The *Lupi Initiative for Inclusive Education* aims to equip educators with the tools necessary to create safe and supportive environments for LGBTQ and disabled students. By investing in education, Paula ensured that future generations would be better equipped to advocate for themselves and others.

Mentorship and Empowerment

Paula understood that mentorship plays a crucial role in sustaining activism. She actively engaged with young activists, sharing her experiences and providing guidance. This approach aligns with the principles of *transformative leadership*, which emphasizes the importance of empowering others to take on leadership roles within their communities. By fostering a culture of mentorship, Paula created a ripple effect, inspiring young leaders to rise and continue the fight for justice.

Legacy Through Storytelling

Storytelling is another powerful tool Paula utilized to inspire change. By sharing her personal journey and the struggles faced by the LGBTQ and disabled communities, she humanized the issues at hand. This aligns with the theory of *narrative policy framework*, which suggests that stories can shape public perceptions and influence policy decisions. Paula's ability to connect on an emotional level made her message resonate with a broader audience, ensuring that her legacy would endure.

Conclusion

In conclusion, Paula Lupi's life and work exemplify how one individual's commitment to activism can inspire change that extends far beyond their own lifetime. Through her efforts in education, mentorship, and storytelling, she laid the groundwork for a more inclusive future. As the next generation of activists continues to rise, they carry with them the lessons learned from Paula's journey, ensuring that her voice remains a guiding force in the ongoing struggle for LGBTQ and disability rights.

Bibliography

[1] Rawls, J. (1971). *A Theory of Justice*. Harvard University Press.

Creating a lasting legacy through philanthropy

Philanthropy, the act of donating resources to promote the welfare of others, plays a vital role in the landscape of social justice and activism. For Paula Lupi, philanthropy was not merely a means of financial support; it was a profound expression of her commitment to creating a more inclusive world for LGBTQ individuals and people with disabilities. This section explores the multifaceted nature of Paula's philanthropic endeavors, examining the theories underpinning her approach, the challenges she faced, and the lasting impact of her contributions.

Theoretical Framework

At its core, philanthropy can be understood through various theoretical lenses, including social capital theory, which posits that social networks have value and can be leveraged for collective action. Paula recognized that her relationships within the LGBTQ and disability communities were not just personal connections but also vital resources for mobilizing support and enacting change. Through her philanthropic efforts, she sought to build and strengthen these networks, creating a ripple effect that would benefit future generations.

Moreover, the concept of intersectionality, introduced by Kimberlé Crenshaw, informed Paula's philanthropic philosophy. Intersectionality emphasizes the interconnectedness of social identities and the unique challenges faced by individuals at the intersection of multiple marginalized identities. By prioritizing intersectional approaches in her philanthropic initiatives, Paula aimed to address the specific needs of queer disabled individuals, ensuring that her legacy would be inclusive and representative.

Challenges in Philanthropy

Despite her unwavering dedication, Paula encountered several challenges in her philanthropic journey. One significant issue was the lack of funding for intersectional initiatives. Many traditional funding sources often favored projects that addressed LGBTQ or disability rights in isolation, overlooking the complexities faced by individuals who identify with both communities. Paula's advocacy for increased funding for intersectional programs was met with resistance, as many grant-making bodies struggled to adapt their frameworks to accommodate these nuanced approaches.

Another challenge was the skepticism surrounding the effectiveness of philanthropic efforts. Critics within the LGBTQ and disability communities sometimes viewed philanthropy as a form of performative allyship, questioning whether financial contributions could translate into meaningful change. Paula addressed these concerns by emphasizing transparency and accountability in her philanthropic initiatives. She actively sought feedback from community members and ensured that her projects were driven by the needs and desires of those they aimed to serve.

Examples of Philanthropic Initiatives

One of Paula's most notable philanthropic initiatives was the establishment of the *Lupi Foundation for Intersectional Justice*. This organization aimed to provide grants and resources to grassroots organizations working at the intersection of LGBTQ and disability rights. The foundation's mission was to empower local activists and foster innovative solutions to the challenges faced by these communities.

For instance, one of the foundation's funded projects was the *Queer Disability Arts Collective*, which provided a platform for disabled LGBTQ artists to showcase their work. This initiative not only celebrated diverse artistic expressions but also facilitated workshops and mentorship programs, nurturing the next generation of queer disabled creatives. By investing in the arts, Paula recognized the importance of cultural representation in advancing social justice.

Another significant initiative was the *Access for All Campaign*, which aimed to improve accessibility in public spaces for individuals with disabilities, particularly those within the LGBTQ community. This campaign involved collaboration with local businesses, government agencies, and advocacy groups to create comprehensive accessibility audits and implement necessary changes. Paula's leadership in this campaign highlighted the importance of intersectional advocacy in addressing systemic barriers.

The Impact of Philanthropy on Paula's Legacy

Paula's philanthropic efforts left an indelible mark on the communities she served. By prioritizing intersectional initiatives, she not only provided immediate support but also laid the groundwork for sustainable change. The *Lupi Foundation* became a model for other organizations, inspiring a new wave of philanthropic efforts focused on intersectionality and inclusivity.

Furthermore, Paula's commitment to philanthropy fostered a culture of giving within the LGBTQ and disability communities. Her advocacy encouraged individuals to recognize their power to effect change through collective action and resource sharing. This shift in mindset was crucial in building resilience and solidarity among marginalized groups.

Conclusion

In conclusion, Paula Lupi's philanthropic endeavors were instrumental in creating a lasting legacy of advocacy for LGBTQ and disability rights. By leveraging her social capital, addressing the challenges of intersectionality, and implementing impactful initiatives, Paula not only transformed the landscape of philanthropy but also inspired countless individuals to continue the fight for equality and justice. Her commitment to building a more inclusive world serves as a powerful reminder of the potential for philanthropy to effect meaningful change, ensuring that her legacy will endure for generations to come.

The impact of Paula's work on LGBTQ and disability rights in Portugal and beyond

Paula Lupi's relentless advocacy for LGBTQ and disability rights has created ripples that extend far beyond the borders of Portugal. Her work has not only transformed the landscape of rights and recognition within her home country but has also inspired global movements for equality and inclusivity. This section explores the multifaceted impact of Paula's activism, highlighting significant theoretical frameworks, prevailing issues, and concrete examples that illustrate her profound influence.

At the core of Paula's advocacy lies the theory of *intersectionality*, a concept coined by Kimberlé Crenshaw, which posits that individuals experience overlapping systems of discrimination based on various aspects of their identity, including race, gender, sexual orientation, and disability. Paula's unique position as a queer disabled woman has allowed her to approach activism with a nuanced understanding of these interconnections. By advocating for both LGBTQ and disability rights simultaneously, she has illuminated the often-overlooked challenges faced by those who exist at the intersection of these identities.

In Portugal, Paula's work has catalyzed significant legislative changes that have improved the lives of LGBTQ individuals and people with disabilities. For instance, her involvement in the passage of the *Law on Gender Identity* in 2011 marked a pivotal moment for transgender rights in the country. This law allowed individuals to change their legal gender without requiring surgery, a progressive step that recognized the autonomy and dignity of transgender individuals. Paula's advocacy was instrumental in mobilizing public support and countering opposition, demonstrating the power of grassroots activism in enacting legal reforms.

Moreover, Paula's influence extends to the educational sector, where she has championed inclusive education policies. Recognizing that education is a critical arena for fostering acceptance and understanding, she has worked tirelessly to promote curricula that address LGBTQ issues and disability awareness. For example, her initiatives have led to the incorporation of LGBTQ history and rights into school programs, helping to dismantle prejudices and create safer environments for all students. This educational reform not only benefits LGBTQ and disabled youth but also cultivates a generation of allies who are equipped to challenge discrimination.

Paula's impact is not confined to Portugal; her work has resonated on a global scale. By representing Portugal at international conferences, she has brought attention to the unique challenges faced by LGBTQ individuals in Southern Europe. Her speeches have highlighted the need for solidarity among activists worldwide, advocating for a unified approach to combat discrimination. For instance, during her participation in the *International LGBTQ Rights Conference* in 2019, Paula shared her insights on the intersectionality of rights, emphasizing the importance of recognizing and addressing the specific needs of marginalized groups within the LGBTQ community. Her contributions have inspired activists in countries grappling with oppressive regimes, encouraging them to adopt intersectional frameworks in their own struggles.

Despite the progress made, Paula's journey has not been without challenges. She has faced backlash from various sectors, including criticisms regarding the representation of marginalized voices in her activism. Addressing these criticisms has been a learning experience for Paula, who has committed to amplifying the voices of those often sidelined in discussions about LGBTQ and disability rights. By fostering dialogues within the community, she has worked to ensure that her advocacy is inclusive and representative of diverse experiences.

The legacy of Paula Lupi's work is evident in the growing visibility and acceptance of LGBTQ individuals and people with disabilities in Portugal. Her efforts have contributed to a cultural shift that embraces diversity and promotes equality. For instance, the annual *Lisbon Pride Parade* has evolved into a vibrant celebration of identity and inclusion, drawing thousands of participants each year. Paula's presence at these events serves as a reminder of the ongoing fight for rights and recognition, inspiring new generations of activists to continue the work she has championed.

In conclusion, Paula Lupi's impact on LGBTQ and disability rights in Portugal and beyond is profound and far-reaching. Through her intersectional advocacy, she has not only shaped policies and educational practices but has also inspired a global movement for equality. As her legacy continues to influence future generations, the principles of inclusivity and solidarity that she embodies will remain pivotal in the ongoing struggle for justice and human rights. The journey towards a more equitable world is far from over, but thanks to Paula's unwavering commitment, the path is clearer, and the possibilities are boundless.

$$\text{Impact} = \text{Advocacy} \times \text{Intersectionality} \times \text{Global Solidarity} \tag{90}$$

Life Behind the Activism

Paula's personal joys and passions

Paula Lupi's life was not solely defined by her activism; it was enriched by a tapestry of personal joys and passions that shaped her identity and fueled her relentless pursuit of justice. These aspects of her life provided her with a sanctuary amidst the chaos of advocacy and allowed her to connect with herself and others on a deeper level.

The Healing Power of Music

Music played a pivotal role in Paula's life, serving as both a form of expression and a source of solace. From an early age, she found comfort in the melodies that filled her childhood home in Lisbon. The diverse sounds of Fado, traditional Portuguese music, resonated with her, echoing the struggles and resilience of her ancestors. As she grew older, Paula began to explore various genres, from rock to classical, each offering a unique lens through which she could understand the world.

Theoretical frameworks such as the *Music-Emotion Model* suggest that music has the power to evoke emotions and foster connections among individuals. This model posits that music can serve as a medium for emotional regulation, allowing individuals to process their feelings and experiences. For Paula, music was not just a hobby; it was a lifeline that helped her navigate the complexities of her identity as a queer disabled woman in a society that often marginalized her existence.

Art as Expression

In addition to music, Paula found joy in visual arts, particularly painting and photography. Art provided her with a canvas to explore her thoughts, emotions, and experiences. Through her artwork, she expressed the nuances of her identity, the struggles she faced, and the beauty she discovered in diversity.

Art theory, particularly the *Aesthetic Experience Theory*, emphasizes the importance of personal expression and the subjective nature of art. This theory aligns with Paula's approach to creativity; she believed that art should reflect one's truth and serve as a vehicle for social change. Her pieces often depicted the intersection of LGBTQ and disability rights, challenging societal norms and inviting viewers to engage in critical conversations.

Nature and Adventure

Beyond the realms of music and art, Paula found immense joy in nature and adventure. The vibrant landscapes of Portugal, from the rugged cliffs of the Algarve to the serene beaches of Cascais, provided her with a sense of peace and rejuvenation. Paula often embarked on hiking trips, seeking solace in the embrace of nature.

Research in environmental psychology highlights the *Biophilia Hypothesis*, which suggests that humans have an innate affinity for nature. This connection to the natural world can lead to improved mental well-being and a greater sense of belonging. For Paula, these outdoor adventures were not just recreational; they were essential for her mental health and personal growth.

Community and Connection

Paula's passions extended to her relationships with friends and loved ones. She valued community and believed in the power of shared experiences. Through her involvement in local LGBTQ organizations, she forged deep connections with like-minded individuals who shared her commitment to social justice.

The *Social Identity Theory* posits that individuals derive a sense of self from their group memberships. For Paula, her identity as a member of the LGBTQ community was a source of strength and resilience. These connections not only provided her with emotional support but also inspired her activism, as she recognized the collective power of marginalized voices.

Culinary Arts

Lastly, Paula had a passion for cooking. She often hosted gatherings where friends would come together to share meals, stories, and laughter. Food, for Paula, was a universal language that transcended barriers and fostered connection.

Culinary practices can be understood through the lens of *Cultural Identity Theory*, which emphasizes how food is a vital part of cultural expression. Paula's dishes reflected her heritage and the diverse influences she encountered throughout her life. Cooking was not just a means of sustenance; it was a way for her to celebrate her identity and share her love with others.

Conclusion

In conclusion, Paula Lupi's personal joys and passions were integral to her identity and activism. Music, art, nature, community, and culinary experiences enriched her life and provided her with the strength to advocate for change. These passions not only shaped her worldview but also served as a reminder that joy and resistance can coexist, creating a holistic approach to activism that inspires others to embrace their own passions in the fight for equality.

Balancing activism with personal life

Balancing activism with personal life is a challenge faced by many advocates, including Paula Lupi. The dedication to a cause often demands significant time and emotional investment, which can lead to the neglect of personal relationships and self-care. This section explores the intricacies of this balance, highlighting the theoretical frameworks, problems, and examples relevant to Paula's journey.

Theoretical Framework

The concept of work-life balance has been extensively studied in organizational psychology, emphasizing the need for individuals to manage their professional responsibilities alongside personal commitments. Greenhaus and Allen (2011) define work-life balance as the extent to which an individual can meet their work and family commitments. In the context of activism, this balance can be reframed as the ability to engage in social justice work while maintaining personal well-being and fulfilling relationships.

Theories such as Role Theory suggest that individuals navigate multiple roles simultaneously, which can create conflict (Kahn et al., 1964). For activists like Paula, the roles of advocate, friend, partner, and self are often at odds, leading to stress and burnout. The intersectionality framework, as discussed by Crenshaw (1989), further complicates this balance, as activists must navigate the complexities of their identities while advocating for marginalized communities.

Challenges Faced by Activists

Paula's journey exemplifies the common challenges activists face in balancing their commitments. The emotional toll of witnessing injustice can lead to compassion fatigue, where the constant exposure to suffering results in emotional exhaustion (Figley, 1995). For Paula, the weight of advocacy work often left little room for personal joys, creating a cycle of burnout that threatened her mental health.

Additionally, the societal expectation that activists be perpetually available can strain personal relationships. Friends and family may feel neglected as the activist prioritizes their cause over social connections. Paula experienced this firsthand when her commitment to LGBTQ and disability rights led to misunderstandings with loved ones who felt sidelined by her activism.

Strategies for Balance

To maintain equilibrium between her activism and personal life, Paula adopted several strategies:

- **Setting Boundaries:** Paula learned to set clear boundaries between her activism and personal time. This included designating specific hours for advocacy work and ensuring that evenings were reserved for family and self-care. By compartmentalizing her responsibilities, she was able to recharge and engage more meaningfully with her loved ones.

- **Prioritizing Self-Care:** Recognizing the importance of self-care, Paula incorporated practices such as mindfulness, exercise, and creative outlets into her routine. These activities not only provided her with a necessary respite from the demands of activism but also enhanced her resilience and emotional well-being.

- **Building a Support Network:** Paula surrounded herself with a community of like-minded individuals who understood the challenges of balancing activism with personal life. This network provided emotional support, shared resources, and practical advice, helping her navigate the complexities of her dual roles.

- **Engaging Loved Ones:** To bridge the gap between her activism and personal life, Paula actively engaged her friends and family in her work. By sharing her experiences and inviting them to participate in advocacy events, she fostered a sense of inclusion and understanding, allowing her loved ones to appreciate the importance of her commitment.

Examples of Balance in Action

One notable example of Paula's ability to balance her activism with personal life occurred during Pride Month. While she was deeply involved in organizing events and advocating for LGBTQ rights, she also made it a point to celebrate with her family. Paula arranged a family picnic that coincided with the local Pride parade, inviting her loved ones to join in the festivities. This not only allowed her to celebrate her identity but also to share that joy with her family, reinforcing the bonds that sometimes felt strained by her activism.

Another instance was when Paula faced a particularly challenging campaign for disability rights. Recognizing the toll it was taking on her mental health, she took a weekend retreat with close friends, stepping away from the pressures of activism to reconnect and rejuvenate. This experience reminded her of the importance of nurturing personal relationships and the role they play in sustaining her activism.

Conclusion

Balancing activism with personal life is an ongoing journey for Paula Lupi, characterized by challenges and triumphs. By employing strategies to set boundaries, prioritize self-care, build a support network, and engage loved ones, Paula demonstrates that it is possible to advocate passionately for social justice while also nurturing personal relationships and well-being. Her experiences serve as a reminder that self-care is not a luxury but a necessity for sustaining long-term activism and creating a more inclusive world.

Bibliography

[1] Greenhaus, J. H., & Allen, T. D. (2011). Work-family balance: A review and extension of the literature. In *The Oxford Handbook of Work and Family*. Oxford University Press.

[2] Figley, C. R. (1995). Compassion fatigue as secondary traumatic stress disorder: A description of the phenomenon and implications for treatment. In *Compassion Fatigue: Coping with Secondary Traumatic Stress Disorder in Those Who Treat the Traumatized*. Brunner-Routledge.

[3] Kahn, R. L., Wolfe, D. M., Quinn, R. P., Snoek, J. D., & Rosenthal, R. A. (1964). *Organizational Stress: Studies in Role Conflict and Role Ambiguity*. Wiley.

[4] Crenshaw, K. (1989). Demarginalizing the intersection of race and sex: A black feminist critique of antidiscrimination doctrine, feminist theory and antiracist politics. *University of Chicago Legal Forum*, 1989(1), 139-167.

Nurturing relationships and finding love

In her journey as an activist, Paula Lupi encountered the intricate dance of nurturing relationships while simultaneously advocating for LGBTQ and disability rights. Relationships, both platonic and romantic, serve as vital anchors in the tumultuous seas of activism. They provide emotional support, shared experiences, and a sense of belonging, all of which are essential for sustaining one's spirit in the face of societal challenges.

The Importance of Relationships in Activism

Research shows that strong social networks can enhance resilience and well-being, especially for individuals facing marginalization. According to [?], social ties can act as buffers against stress and promote mental health. For Paula, these relationships were not merely beneficial; they were life-saving.

$$R = \frac{S}{D} \tag{91}$$

Where R represents the resilience gained from relationships, S signifies the support received, and D denotes the difficulties encountered. This equation illustrates that as support increases, resilience also rises, allowing activists like Paula to navigate challenges more effectively.

Navigating Love and Intimacy

As Paula began to embrace her identity as a queer disabled woman, she faced unique challenges in her romantic life. The intersectionality of her identity meant that finding love required navigating societal prejudices and personal insecurities. Theories of intersectionality, as discussed by Crenshaw [3], highlight how overlapping identities can compound discrimination and affect personal relationships.

In her early twenties, Paula met Sofia, a fellow activist who shared her passion for social justice. Their bond was forged in the fires of protest and mutual understanding. However, the relationship was not without its obstacles. Paula often grappled with feelings of inadequacy, stemming from societal messages about beauty and desirability in the context of disability.

$$I = \frac{E + C}{R} \tag{92}$$

Where I represents intimacy, E is emotional connection, C signifies shared causes, and R denotes relational challenges. This equation suggests that greater emotional connection and shared causes can help overcome relational challenges, fostering deeper intimacy.

Empowerment Through Vulnerability

Paula learned that vulnerability is a strength, not a weakness. By sharing her fears and insecurities with Sofia, she fostered a deeper connection. Brené Brown's work on vulnerability [?] emphasizes that embracing vulnerability can lead to greater intimacy and trust in relationships. Paula's journey toward self-acceptance allowed her to engage in open conversations about her needs and desires, paving the way for a healthier relationship.

Building a Supportive Community

In addition to her romantic relationship, Paula cultivated a robust network of friends and allies who understood the complexities of her identity. This community became a vital source of support, offering encouragement during difficult times. The concept of "chosen family" is particularly resonant in LGBTQ communities, where individuals often create familial bonds with friends who share similar experiences.

$$C = F + A \tag{93}$$

Where C represents the concept of chosen family, F signifies friendships, and A denotes alliances formed through shared activism. This equation illustrates how friendships and alliances can coalesce to form a supportive family-like structure, essential for emotional well-being.

Challenges of Balancing Activism and Personal Life

Despite the joy that relationships brought, Paula faced the challenge of balancing her personal life with her activism. The demands of her advocacy work often left little time for nurturing her romantic relationship. This struggle is common among activists, as noted by [?], who argue that the emotional labor involved in activism can strain personal relationships.

Paula and Sofia navigated this challenge by establishing boundaries around their time together. They prioritized regular "dates" where they could disconnect from the outside world and focus on each other. This practice not only strengthened their bond but also served as a reminder of the importance of self-care in relationships.

Lessons Learned and Future Aspirations

Through her experiences, Paula learned that nurturing relationships requires intentional effort and open communication. She realized that love, in all its forms, is a powerful motivator in the fight for justice. As she continued her activism, Paula sought to inspire others to embrace their identities and seek supportive relationships.

Looking to the future, Paula envisioned a world where love transcended societal barriers, where LGBTQ individuals could find acceptance and companionship without fear of judgment. Her journey underscored the belief that nurturing relationships is not just a personal endeavor; it is a crucial component of the broader struggle for equality and acceptance.

In conclusion, the act of nurturing relationships and finding love is intricately woven into the fabric of Paula Lupi's activism. By embracing vulnerability, building supportive communities, and balancing personal and activist lives, Paula exemplified the profound connection between love and social justice. Her legacy serves as a reminder that relationships can empower individuals and movements alike, fostering resilience and hope in the ongoing fight for LGBTQ and disability rights.

Self-care and mental health in the face of adversity

In the tumultuous journey of activism, the importance of self-care and mental health cannot be overstated. For Paula Lupi, navigating the complexities of advocating for LGBTQ and disability rights often meant confronting not only societal prejudices but also the emotional toll that comes with such a demanding role. This section delves into the theoretical frameworks surrounding self-care, the specific challenges faced by activists, and concrete strategies that Paula employed to maintain her mental health amidst adversity.

Theoretical Framework

Self-care is often defined as the practice of taking action to preserve or improve one's own health. According to the World Health Organization (WHO), mental health is a state of well-being in which every individual realizes their potential can cope with the normal stresses of life, can work productively and fruitfully, and is able to contribute to their community. In the context of activism, self-care becomes a crucial component of sustaining long-term engagement in social justice movements.

Theories such as the *Stress-Buffering Model* suggest that social support can mitigate the negative effects of stress, which is particularly relevant for activists who often face backlash and hostility. This model posits that supportive relationships can provide emotional comfort and practical assistance, thereby enhancing resilience. Paula Lupi's experience illustrates this model; through her network of fellow activists and allies, she found the support necessary to combat feelings of isolation and burnout.

Challenges Faced by Activists

Activism is inherently fraught with challenges that can adversely affect mental health. For Paula, these challenges included:

- **Emotional Labor:** Engaging with marginalized communities often requires significant emotional investment. Paula frequently found herself bearing the weight of others' struggles, which could be draining.

- **Public Scrutiny:** As a prominent figure, Paula faced intense media scrutiny and criticism. The pressure to maintain a positive public image while addressing serious issues added to her stress.

- **Burnout:** The relentless nature of activism can lead to burnout, a state of emotional, physical, and mental exhaustion. Paula often had to confront her own limits, recognizing when she needed to step back to recharge.

- **Intersectional Challenges:** As a queer disabled woman, Paula's activism was often met with unique challenges that compounded her experiences of discrimination, leading to feelings of inadequacy and self-doubt.

Strategies for Self-Care

To combat these challenges, Paula implemented several self-care strategies that not only helped her maintain her mental health but also served as a model for others in the community:

1. **Mindfulness and Meditation:** Paula practiced mindfulness meditation to cultivate a sense of presence and reduce anxiety. Research shows that mindfulness can significantly lower stress levels and improve emotional regulation.

$$S = \frac{E}{C} \qquad (94)$$

Where S represents stress, E represents emotional resilience, and C represents coping mechanisms. As Paula increased her coping strategies through mindfulness, her stress levels decreased.

2. **Physical Activity:** Engaging in regular physical exercise, such as yoga and hiking, allowed Paula to release pent-up energy and improve her mood. Studies indicate that physical activity can enhance overall mental health and reduce symptoms of anxiety and depression.

3. **Community Building:** Paula emphasized the importance of building a supportive community. She organized regular meet-ups with fellow

activists, fostering a sense of belonging and shared purpose. This communal approach helped mitigate feelings of isolation.

4. **Therapy and Counseling:** Recognizing the need for professional support, Paula sought therapy to process her experiences and develop coping strategies. This decision not only provided her with tools to manage her mental health but also helped destigmatize seeking help within her community.

5. **Creative Expression:** Paula utilized art and music as outlets for her emotions. Engaging in creative activities allowed her to express her feelings in a constructive way, which is supported by theories of art therapy that suggest creative expression can facilitate emotional healing.

6. **Setting Boundaries:** Learning to say no and setting boundaries was crucial for Paula. She recognized that overcommitment could lead to burnout, so she prioritized her well-being by limiting her involvement in certain projects.

Conclusion

The journey of an activist is often marked by adversity, but as Paula Lupi demonstrated, prioritizing self-care and mental health is essential for sustaining the fight for justice. By employing a variety of strategies—ranging from mindfulness to community building—Paula not only navigated her own challenges but also inspired others to recognize the importance of self-care in activism. As the movement for LGBTQ and disability rights continues to evolve, the lessons learned from Paula's experiences serve as a vital reminder: to advocate for change, one must first take care of oneself.

The importance of community support and self-reflection

In the journey of activism, particularly for marginalized communities, the significance of community support and self-reflection cannot be overstated. Paula Lupi's life exemplifies how these two elements serve as pillars for resilience and growth, enabling activists to navigate the complexities of their roles while maintaining their well-being.

Community Support

Community support acts as a safety net for activists, providing emotional, social, and sometimes financial resources that are critical for sustaining their efforts. In the context of LGBTQ and disability rights, community networks offer a sense of belonging and validation, which are vital for individuals who often face isolation and discrimination. Theories of social capital, as proposed by Bourdieu (1986), highlight that social networks can facilitate access to resources and opportunities. For Paula, her involvement in local LGBTQ organizations not only allowed her to connect with like-minded individuals but also provided her with the tools and knowledge necessary to advocate effectively.

$$SC = \sum_{i=1}^{n} \frac{R_i}{C_i} \qquad (95)$$

Where SC represents social capital, R_i denotes resources accessed through community, and C_i signifies the costs associated with maintaining those connections.

Paula's early experiences in Lisbon, surrounded by a diverse group of friends, fostered her sense of identity and purpose. These relationships served as a foundation for her activism, as they provided her with emotional support during challenging times. The importance of such networks is further supported by the work of Putnam (2000), who emphasizes that communities with higher levels of social engagement tend to be more resilient in the face of adversity.

Self-Reflection

While community support is crucial, self-reflection is equally important for personal growth and effective activism. Self-reflection allows activists to critically assess their motivations, biases, and the impact of their actions. This process is essential for developing a nuanced understanding of intersectionality, as it encourages individuals to recognize how their identities and experiences shape their perspectives.

In her journey, Paula often engaged in self-reflection to navigate her role as a queer disabled woman within the activist community. This introspection helped her identify internalized prejudices and biases that could hinder her effectiveness as an advocate. According to Schön (1983), reflective practice involves a continuous cycle of action and reflection, which leads to deeper learning and improvement. Paula's commitment to self-reflection enabled her to adapt her strategies and approaches, ensuring that her activism remained relevant and impactful.

$$R = A + (F \cdot I) \qquad (96)$$

Where R represents reflection, A is the action taken, F denotes feedback received, and I signifies the insights gained during the reflective process.

Balancing Community Support and Self-Reflection

The interplay between community support and self-reflection is critical for sustaining activism. While community networks provide the necessary support, they can also create echo chambers that may stifle individual growth. Activists must strike a balance between engaging with their communities and taking time for self-reflection. This balance allows for the exchange of ideas while also fostering personal growth.

For instance, during her tenure in various activist roles, Paula found that engaging in group discussions often sparked new ideas and perspectives. However, she also recognized the importance of stepping back to reflect on her own beliefs and experiences. This dual approach not only enriched her understanding of the issues at hand but also strengthened her advocacy efforts.

Conclusion

In conclusion, the importance of community support and self-reflection in the life of Paula Lupi highlights the interconnectedness of personal and collective growth in activism. By fostering strong community ties and engaging in continuous self-reflection, activists can navigate the challenges of their roles while contributing to a more inclusive and equitable society. Paula's journey serves as a testament to the power of these elements, inspiring future generations to embrace both community and self-awareness as they continue the fight for LGBTQ and disability rights.

Paula's journey of self-discovery and personal growth

Paula Lupi's journey of self-discovery and personal growth is a testament to the resilience of the human spirit in the face of adversity. From her early days in the vibrant streets of Lisbon, where she grappled with her identity amidst societal expectations, to her emergence as a formidable activist, Paula's path has been marked by profound introspection and transformation.

Understanding Identity

The process of self-discovery begins with understanding one's identity, a theme that resonates deeply in Paula's life. Theories of identity development, such as Erik Erikson's stages of psychosocial development, emphasize the importance of identity versus role confusion during adolescence. For Paula, this stage was fraught with challenges as she navigated her emerging queer identity while also confronting the complexities of her disability. The intersectionality of her identities—being a queer disabled woman—added layers of complexity to her self-understanding.

$$\text{Identity} = f(\text{Social Context, Personal Experiences, Cultural Background}) \quad (97)$$

This equation illustrates that identity is a function of various factors, including social context, personal experiences, and cultural background. Paula's experiences in a bustling city like Lisbon, rich in culture yet rife with prejudice, shaped her understanding of herself and the world around her.

Navigating Societal Expectations

As Paula began to embrace her identity, she faced societal pressures that dictated how she should behave and who she should be. The conflict between her authentic self and societal expectations often led to feelings of isolation and confusion. Judith Butler's theory of gender performativity posits that gender is not an inherent quality but rather a performance influenced by societal norms. Paula's struggle to align her identity with societal expectations exemplifies this theory, as she grappled with the roles imposed upon her.

$$\text{Performance} = \text{Gender} + \text{Societal Norms} \quad (98)$$

This equation suggests that performance, in terms of gender, is a combination of one's gender identity and the societal norms that shape it. Paula's journey involved rejecting these imposed performances and embracing her authentic self, a process that was both liberating and challenging.

The Role of Community

Community plays a crucial role in the journey of self-discovery. For Paula, the LGBTQ community in Lisbon became a sanctuary where she found acceptance and belonging. Social support theory emphasizes the importance of social networks in fostering resilience and well-being. Through her diverse friendships and connections within the community, Paula was able to explore her identity in a safe space, surrounded by individuals who shared similar experiences.

$$\text{Well-being} = f(\text{Social Support, Community Engagement}) \quad (99)$$

This equation highlights that well-being is a function of social support and community engagement. Paula's involvement in LGBTQ organizations not only provided her with a sense of belonging but also empowered her to advocate for herself and others.

Empowerment through Storytelling

A significant aspect of Paula's personal growth was her realization of the power of storytelling. By sharing her experiences, she not only validated her own journey but also inspired others. Narrative therapy, which emphasizes the importance of personal stories in shaping identity, played a pivotal role in her self-discovery. Through storytelling, Paula was able to reframe her narrative, transforming her struggles into sources of strength.

$$\text{Identity Transformation} = \text{Narrative Reframing} + \text{Empowerment} \quad (100)$$

This equation illustrates that identity transformation is achieved through narrative reframing and empowerment. Paula's ability to articulate her story allowed her to reclaim her identity and advocate for change.

Overcoming Internalized Prejudice

As Paula embraced her identity, she also confronted internalized prejudice—negative beliefs and attitudes she had internalized from societal messages. This internal conflict often manifested as self-doubt and insecurity. The concept of internalized oppression, as discussed by scholars like bell hooks, highlights how marginalized individuals can adopt the negative perceptions of their identities.

$$\text{Self-acceptance} = \text{Awareness} - \text{Internalized Oppression} \quad (101)$$

This equation suggests that self-acceptance is achieved through awareness of one's identity while actively working to dismantle internalized oppression. Paula's journey involved recognizing and challenging these internalized beliefs, leading to greater self-acceptance and self-love.

The Impact of Personal Growth on Activism

Paula's journey of self-discovery and personal growth not only transformed her own life but also fueled her activism. As she embraced her identity, she became a powerful advocate for LGBTQ and disability rights, using her experiences to inform her activism. Theories of transformative learning, proposed by Jack

Mezirow, emphasize the role of critical reflection in fostering personal and social change. Paula's journey exemplifies this theory, as her self-discovery process led her to critically reflect on the injustices faced by marginalized communities.

$$\text{Transformative Learning} = \text{Critical Reflection} + \text{Action} \qquad (102)$$

This equation indicates that transformative learning occurs through critical reflection and subsequent action. Paula's activism is a direct result of her personal growth, as she uses her voice to advocate for those who are often silenced.

Conclusion

In conclusion, Paula Lupi's journey of self-discovery and personal growth is a multifaceted process shaped by her identity, societal expectations, community support, storytelling, and the overcoming of internalized prejudice. Her experiences highlight the importance of embracing one's authentic self and the transformative power of personal growth in the pursuit of social justice. As she continues to advocate for LGBTQ and disability rights, Paula serves as a beacon of hope and inspiration for others on their journeys of self-discovery.

The power of intersectionality in Paula's personal life

Intersectionality, a term coined by Kimberlé Crenshaw in 1989, serves as a critical framework for understanding how various forms of social stratification—such as race, gender, sexuality, and disability—interact to create unique dynamics of oppression and privilege. For Paula Lupi, this theory is not merely an academic concept but a lived reality that shapes her identity and activism.

From her childhood in Lisbon, Paula navigated a complex landscape of identities. As a queer disabled woman, she experienced the multifaceted nature of discrimination. This intersectionality influenced her personal relationships, her sense of self, and her approach to activism. Paula's journey illustrates how the interplay of these identities can lead to both challenges and strengths.

Navigating Relationships

In her personal life, Paula often found herself at the crossroads of different expectations and societal norms. For instance, her experiences in dating were colored by her identity as a queer woman. Many of her peers struggled to understand the nuances of her identity, leading to feelings of isolation. As she began to embrace her queerness, she also had to confront the realities of ableism within the LGBTQ community, where her disability sometimes rendered her invisible.

This led Paula to seek relationships with individuals who not only accepted her queer identity but also understood the complexities of her disability. She often reflected on how intersectionality shaped her connections. For example, in her relationship with a fellow activist who was also a person of color, they shared a mutual understanding of how their identities informed their experiences of discrimination. This bond not only fortified their relationship but also deepened their commitment to activism, demonstrating the power of shared experiences.

Empowerment Through Community

Paula's understanding of intersectionality also fostered a sense of empowerment through community. She became involved in local LGBTQ organizations that prioritized inclusivity, ensuring that voices from all backgrounds were heard. By advocating for the rights of both LGBTQ individuals and people with disabilities, Paula recognized that her activism could not be siloed; the struggles were interconnected.

For example, during a community event aimed at raising awareness about mental health, Paula collaborated with organizations that addressed the specific needs of disabled LGBTQ individuals. This intersectional approach not only amplified the voices of those often marginalized within both communities but also highlighted the unique challenges faced by those at the intersection of multiple identities.

Challenges and Growth

However, the journey was not without its challenges. Paula encountered criticisms from within both the LGBTQ and disability communities. Some individuals questioned her authenticity, suggesting that her focus on intersectionality diluted the urgency of either cause. These criticisms forced her to engage in deep self-reflection and open dialogue with her peers.

In one notable instance, during a panel discussion on LGBTQ rights, a fellow activist challenged Paula's perspectives on disability rights, arguing that they diverted attention from pressing issues like marriage equality. Rather than retreating, Paula embraced this confrontation as an opportunity for growth. She articulated how the fight for marriage equality could not be separated from the fight for accessibility in public spaces, healthcare, and social services. This moment not only strengthened her resolve but also fostered a more nuanced understanding among her peers about the importance of intersectionality.

Advocacy and Legacy

As Paula matured in her activism, she began to incorporate intersectionality into her advocacy work more explicitly. She recognized that to be an effective advocate, she must address the specific needs of individuals who share her identities while also lifting up those who face different forms of oppression.

For example, Paula initiated a mentorship program aimed at empowering young LGBTQ individuals with disabilities. This program provided not only practical resources but also emotional support, emphasizing the importance of representation and understanding within the community. By fostering a sense of belonging and solidarity, Paula demonstrated how intersectionality could create pathways for empowerment and resilience.

In conclusion, Paula Lupi's personal life exemplifies the power of intersectionality as a lens through which to understand identity, relationships, and activism. Her experiences reveal that embracing the complexities of one's identity can lead to profound personal growth and a more inclusive approach to advocacy. As she continues to navigate her journey, Paula remains a testament to the idea that true empowerment comes from recognizing and uplifting the diverse voices within our communities. This commitment to intersectionality not only enriches her life but also paves the way for future generations of activists to engage with the world in a more holistic and inclusive manner.

Finding strength and resilience in times of hardship

In the tumultuous journey of activism, finding strength and resilience during times of hardship is crucial for sustaining momentum and fostering personal growth. Paula Lupi's life exemplifies this struggle, as she faced numerous challenges that tested her resolve. Understanding the dynamics of resilience involves exploring psychological theories, personal anecdotes, and the broader implications of perseverance within the LGBTQ and disability rights movements.

Theoretical Frameworks of Resilience

Resilience can be understood through various psychological frameworks. One prominent theory is the *Resilience Theory*, which posits that resilience is not merely an individual trait but a dynamic process influenced by interactions between individuals and their environments. According to [1], resilience emerges from the interplay of personal attributes and external support systems. This model highlights the importance of community, relationships, and resources in fostering resilience.

Another relevant framework is the *Ecological Systems Theory* proposed by [2]. This theory emphasizes the multiple layers of influence on an individual's development, including family, peers, and societal structures. For Paula, these layers played a significant role in her ability to navigate adversity, as her supportive family and diverse friendships provided a strong foundation during challenging times.

Personal Struggles and Overcoming Adversity

Paula's journey was marked by various hardships, including discrimination, societal rejection, and personal loss. Each of these experiences contributed to her resilience, shaping her identity as a queer disabled woman. For instance, during her teenage years, Paula faced bullying at school due to her sexual orientation and disability. This experience could have led to feelings of isolation and despair; however, Paula found strength in her passion for music and art, which served as outlets for her emotions and a means of self-expression.

$$R = f(P, E) \tag{103}$$

In this equation, R represents resilience, while P denotes personal characteristics, and E signifies environmental factors. Paula's ability to harness her artistic talents (personal characteristics) and cultivate supportive relationships (environmental factors) allowed her to transform adversity into a source of strength.

Community Support and Collective Resilience

The LGBTQ and disability communities often face systemic oppression, which can lead to shared experiences of hardship. Paula recognized the importance of community support in fostering resilience. She actively participated in local LGBTQ organizations, where she not only found solidarity but also contributed to collective resilience. By sharing her story and advocating for others, Paula empowered those around her, creating a ripple effect of strength within the community.

$$C = \sum_{i=1}^{n} S_i \tag{104}$$

Here, C represents community resilience, while S_i denotes individual strengths within the community. Each member's story and struggle add to the overall resilience of the group, demonstrating that collective action can amplify individual voices and create a powerful movement.

Lessons from Hardship

Paula's experiences taught her invaluable lessons about resilience. One significant insight was the importance of self-care and mental health. Amidst the chaos of activism, she learned to prioritize her well-being by engaging in mindfulness practices and seeking therapy. This self-awareness not only fortified her resilience but also allowed her to support others effectively.

Additionally, Paula's journey underscored the necessity of embracing vulnerability. By sharing her struggles openly, she fostered an environment where others felt safe to do the same. This authenticity created a sense of belonging and solidarity, reinforcing the notion that resilience is not about being invulnerable but rather about facing challenges with courage and support.

Conclusion

Finding strength and resilience in times of hardship is a multifaceted process that involves personal growth, community support, and a commitment to self-care. Paula Lupi's journey illustrates that resilience is not a solitary endeavor but a collective experience shaped by relationships and shared struggles. By embracing vulnerability, prioritizing mental health, and fostering community connections, activists can cultivate resilience that not only sustains their efforts but also inspires others in the ongoing fight for LGBTQ and disability rights.

Bibliography

[1] Masten, A. S. (2001). Ordinary Magic: Resilience Processes in Development. *American Psychologist*, 56(3), 227-238.

[2] Bronfenbrenner, U. (1979). *The Ecology of Human Development: Experiments by Nature and Design*. Harvard University Press.

Honoring the memory of allies and activists

In the vibrant tapestry of advocacy, the voices of allies and activists form a crucial thread that weaves together the struggles and triumphs of marginalized communities. Paula Lupi, as a prominent figure in the LGBTQ and disability rights movements, recognizes the importance of honoring those who have paved the way for progress. This section delves into the theoretical frameworks, challenges, and exemplary practices surrounding the commemoration of allies and activists, emphasizing the necessity of remembrance in sustaining a movement's momentum.

Theoretical Frameworks of Remembrance

The act of honoring allies and activists can be understood through several theoretical lenses. One such framework is *collective memory*, which refers to how groups remember their past and the significance they ascribe to historical figures and events. According to Halbwachs (1992), collective memory shapes group identity and informs contemporary struggles. In the context of LGBTQ and disability rights, remembering influential activists not only pays tribute to their contributions but also reinforces a shared commitment to ongoing advocacy.

Another relevant theory is *intersectionality*, coined by Kimberlé Crenshaw (1989). This framework highlights how various forms of oppression intersect, affecting individuals' experiences and identities. Honoring the memory of activists who navigated multiple identities—such as race, gender, sexuality, and disability—underscores the necessity of inclusive remembrance. By recognizing the diverse backgrounds of those who fought for justice, movements can better address the complexities of contemporary challenges.

Challenges in Commemoration

Despite the importance of honoring activists, several challenges arise in the process. One significant issue is the *erasure of marginalized voices* within the narratives of activism. Often, mainstream histories prioritize the contributions of dominant figures, overshadowing the essential roles played by activists from underrepresented communities. This erasure can lead to a homogenized understanding of activism, neglecting the rich diversity of experiences that inform movements.

Moreover, the challenge of *tokenism* can undermine genuine efforts to honor allies and activists. When organizations or movements superficially acknowledge contributions without integrating their lessons into ongoing work, it risks trivializing the sacrifices made by these individuals. To combat this, it is essential to embed the legacies of honored activists into the core values and practices of contemporary advocacy.

Examples of Commemoration

One powerful example of honoring activists is the establishment of memorials and commemorative events. For instance, the *Stonewall Inn* in New York City stands as a national monument, symbolizing the struggle for LGBTQ rights and the legacy of those who fought during the Stonewall Riots. This site serves as a reminder of the importance of resilience and resistance, inviting reflection on the ongoing fight for equality.

Additionally, the creation of awards and scholarships in the names of influential activists can serve as a means of honoring their contributions while fostering the next generation of leaders. The *Marsha P. Johnson Institute*, named after the iconic LGBTQ rights activist, works to support and uplift the voices of trans individuals, particularly those of color. By channeling resources and recognition into initiatives that reflect the values of the honored activists, organizations can ensure their legacies live on.

The Role of Storytelling

Storytelling is another vital component in honoring the memory of allies and activists. Personal narratives and oral histories provide a platform for marginalized voices, allowing their experiences to be shared and celebrated. Paula Lupi, through her advocacy, emphasizes the importance of storytelling as a means of preserving history and fostering connections among community members.

Incorporating storytelling into commemorative practices can also serve as a form of healing. For example, community gatherings that invite individuals to share their stories about fallen activists create spaces for collective mourning and celebration. These events not only honor the memory of those who have passed but also strengthen community bonds and inspire ongoing activism.

Conclusion

Honoring the memory of allies and activists is a fundamental aspect of sustaining the momentum of social movements. By engaging with theoretical frameworks such as collective memory and intersectionality, recognizing the challenges of erasure and tokenism, and utilizing examples of effective commemoration, advocates like Paula Lupi can ensure that the contributions of all activists are acknowledged and celebrated. Through storytelling and community engagement, the legacies of those who fought for justice can continue to inspire future generations, fostering a more inclusive and equitable world for all.

$$\text{Collective Memory} = \frac{\text{Shared Experiences} + \text{Historical Narratives}}{\text{Cultural Context}} \quad (105)$$

This equation illustrates the interplay between shared experiences and historical narratives within a cultural context, emphasizing the importance of collective memory in honoring the contributions of activists. By fostering an environment where diverse stories are told and celebrated, movements can cultivate a deeper understanding of their past and a stronger commitment to their future.

Paula's hopes and dreams for the future

In envisioning a future where LGBTQ and disability rights are fully realized, Paula Lupi dreams of a world where everyone, regardless of their identity or ability, can live authentically and without fear. This vision is grounded in the principles of equality, justice, and inclusivity, which have been the cornerstones of her activism.

Paula hopes for a society that not only acknowledges the existence of diverse identities but actively celebrates them.

One of Paula's primary hopes is the establishment of comprehensive educational programs that promote understanding and acceptance of LGBTQ and disabled individuals from an early age. She believes that education is a powerful tool for dismantling prejudice and fostering empathy. In her vision, schools would implement curricula that include the history and contributions of LGBTQ and disabled activists, highlighting the intersections of these identities. This educational framework would encourage students to engage in critical thinking about societal norms and the importance of inclusivity.

To illustrate this point, consider the equation of social change:

$$\text{Social Change} = \text{Awareness} \times \text{Education} \times \text{Advocacy}$$

In this equation, awareness serves as the foundation, while education amplifies understanding, and advocacy translates knowledge into action. Paula's dream is to see this equation applied universally, creating a ripple effect of positive change throughout society.

Furthermore, Paula envisions a future where healthcare systems are accessible and inclusive for all individuals, particularly those who identify as LGBTQ and disabled. She recognizes the disparities in healthcare access and quality that these communities face and advocates for policies that prioritize equitable healthcare. In her ideal world, healthcare providers would undergo training that emphasizes cultural competency and sensitivity, ensuring that all patients receive respectful and informed care.

Paula's aspirations also extend to legislative reforms that protect the rights of LGBTQ and disabled individuals. She dreams of a political landscape where laws are enacted not only to safeguard rights but also to promote proactive measures that enhance the quality of life for marginalized communities. This includes policies that address issues such as housing discrimination, employment equity, and accessibility in public spaces. By advocating for these changes, Paula aims to create a society where everyone can thrive without the barriers of systemic oppression.

Moreover, Paula hopes for increased representation of LGBTQ and disabled individuals in positions of power and influence. She believes that true change can only occur when those who have lived experiences of marginalization are involved in decision-making processes. Paula's dream is to see a diverse array of voices in leadership roles, shaping policies that reflect the needs and aspirations of all community members. This representation is not just about visibility; it is about ensuring that the lived experiences of marginalized individuals inform the policies that govern their lives.

In her personal reflections, Paula often speaks about the importance of nurturing future generations of activists. She dreams of a mentorship network that connects seasoned advocates with young leaders, fostering a culture of collaboration and support. By empowering the next generation, Paula hopes to ensure that the fight for LGBTQ and disability rights continues with vigor and determination.

Paula's vision also encompasses the importance of intersectionality in activism. She dreams of a future where all movements for justice recognize and uplift the interconnected struggles of various marginalized groups. This holistic approach to activism would create a more unified front against discrimination and inequality, allowing for a more comprehensive understanding of the challenges faced by individuals at the intersections of multiple identities.

To encapsulate her hopes, Paula often draws inspiration from the words of Audre Lorde, who stated, "I am not free while any woman is unfree, even when her shackles are very different from my own." This sentiment resonates deeply with Paula, as she believes that true liberation is collective. Her dream is a world where the liberation of one is intertwined with the liberation of all.

Ultimately, Paula Lupi's hopes and dreams for the future are rooted in the belief that a more inclusive world is not only possible but necessary. She envisions a society where love, acceptance, and understanding prevail over hate and discrimination. Through her unwavering commitment to advocacy and her vision for the future, Paula inspires countless individuals to join her in the pursuit of a world where everyone can live freely and authentically. As she often reminds her supporters, "We are the architects of our future, and together, we can build a world that reflects our shared humanity."

In conclusion, Paula's hopes and dreams are not merely aspirations; they are a call to action. They challenge us to envision a future where equality is a lived reality for all, urging us to work collectively towards that goal. In doing so, Paula Lupi not only leaves a legacy of advocacy but also ignites the flames of hope for generations to come.

Unauthorized

Unauthorized

Unauthorized

In the realm of activism, the line between public perception and personal narrative can often become blurred, leading to the emergence of unauthorized biographies. This chapter delves into the complexities surrounding Paula Lupi's life, her activism, and the implications of being the subject of an unauthorized biography. The term "unauthorized" not only denotes a lack of approval from the subject but also raises questions about authenticity, representation, and the ethics of storytelling.

The Nature of Unauthorized Biographies

Unauthorized biographies have a unique position in literary and activist discourse. They often emerge from a desire to tell stories that are not being told, but they can also lead to a myriad of challenges. As noted by literary theorists, the act of narrating someone else's life without their consent can be seen as an infringement on their narrative sovereignty. This raises the question: who owns a story?

In the case of Paula Lupi, the unauthorized biography seeks to capture the essence of her activism and personal journey, but it does so without her voice. This absence can lead to misinterpretations or oversimplifications of her experiences. The tension between the desire for representation and the ethical implications of narrating someone else's life is a critical theme in this chapter.

Challenges to Paula's Credibility and Integrity

One of the primary issues faced by individuals depicted in unauthorized biographies is the challenge to their credibility and integrity. Critics may argue that the portrayal is biased or lacks nuance, potentially undermining the subject's work and contributions. For Paula, who has dedicated her life to advocating for LGBTQ and disability rights, any misrepresentation could have significant repercussions, not only for her personal reputation but also for the movements she represents.

The unauthorized biography may highlight certain aspects of Paula's life while neglecting others, leading to a skewed understanding of her activism. This selective storytelling can perpetuate stereotypes and diminish the complexity of her identity as a queer disabled woman. For example, if the biography emphasizes her political achievements while glossing over her personal struggles, it risks presenting an incomplete picture of her life.

Criticisms from Within the LGBTQ and Disability Communities

The LGBTQ and disability communities are not monolithic; they encompass a wide range of perspectives and experiences. As such, unauthorized biographies can attract criticism from within these communities, especially when they fail to address intersectionality. Critics may argue that the narrative presented does not adequately represent the diversity of voices within the LGBTQ and disability rights movements.

In Paula's case, some activists may feel that the unauthorized biography does not capture the full spectrum of her advocacy work, particularly her efforts to uplift marginalized voices. This can lead to a sense of disillusionment among community members who feel that their stories are being overshadowed by a singular narrative. The importance of inclusivity in activism cannot be overstated; when voices are omitted or marginalized, the movement as a whole suffers.

Addressing Intersectionality and Inclusivity Criticisms

Intersectionality, a term coined by Kimberlé Crenshaw, refers to the interconnected nature of social categorizations such as race, class, and gender, which can create overlapping systems of discrimination or disadvantage. In the context of Paula's unauthorized biography, it is essential to address how her identity as a queer disabled woman intersects with her activism.

Critics may argue that the biography fails to adequately explore these intersections, instead presenting a one-dimensional view of Paula's life. This oversight can perpetuate the notion that LGBTQ rights and disability rights are separate issues, rather than interconnected struggles for equality. To address these criticisms, it is crucial for any narrative—authorized or unauthorized—to embrace a holistic view of the subject's life and work.

The Role of Privilege and Representation in Activism

Privilege plays a significant role in shaping the narratives that are told about activists like Paula Lupi. Unauthorized biographies can inadvertently reinforce existing power dynamics by privileging certain voices over others. For instance, if the biography focuses predominantly on Paula's achievements without acknowledging the systemic barriers faced by marginalized individuals within the LGBTQ and disability communities, it may perpetuate a narrative of individualism rather than collective struggle.

The representation of Paula's story in an unauthorized biography raises important questions about whose voices are amplified and whose are silenced. Activism is inherently about challenging these power structures, and any narrative that fails to do so risks becoming complicit in them. This chapter advocates for a more nuanced understanding of representation in activism, emphasizing the need for inclusivity and diversity in storytelling.

Navigating Personal and Political Controversies

Paula's life, like that of many activists, is not without controversy. Unauthorized biographies often delve into personal and political controversies, which can complicate the narrative. The portrayal of such controversies can either humanize the subject or serve to undermine their credibility, depending on the framing.

For Paula, navigating the complexities of her activism while contending with public scrutiny can be particularly challenging. The unauthorized biography may highlight contentious moments in her career, potentially overshadowing her contributions to the LGBTQ and disability rights movements. This can lead to a dichotomy in public perception, where her activism is viewed through the lens of controversy rather than as part of a broader narrative of resilience and advocacy.

Learning and Growing from Mistakes and Missteps

Every activist's journey includes moments of missteps and learning. Unauthorized biographies can sometimes present these moments in a way that lacks context or fails to acknowledge the growth that follows. For Paula, understanding that mistakes are part of the learning process is crucial. The unauthorized narrative should reflect the evolution of her activism, showcasing how she has adapted and grown in response to challenges and criticisms.

This chapter emphasizes the importance of framing mistakes as opportunities for growth rather than as definitive failures. By doing so, the narrative can inspire others to embrace their own journeys of self-discovery and activism, reinforcing the idea that progress is often nonlinear.

Rebuilding Trust and Reconciling with Critics

In the wake of unauthorized portrayals, activists like Paula must often confront the challenge of rebuilding trust with their communities. This process requires open dialogue and a willingness to engage with critics constructively. The unauthorized biography may serve as a catalyst for these conversations, prompting discussions about representation, inclusivity, and the ethical implications of storytelling.

Reconciliation involves acknowledging the concerns raised by community members and demonstrating a commitment to addressing them. For Paula, this may mean actively engaging with her critics and fostering a sense of unity within the LGBTQ and disability communities. The chapter explores strategies for building bridges and promoting understanding in the face of adversity.

The Impact of Unauthorized Biographies on Public Perception

Unauthorized biographies have the power to shape public perception significantly. They can introduce new narratives, challenge existing ones, and influence how activists like Paula are viewed by both supporters and detractors. The portrayal of Paula's life in an unauthorized biography can lead to a range of responses, from admiration to skepticism.

Understanding the impact of these narratives is essential for activists seeking to navigate their public personas. This chapter examines how unauthorized biographies can both elevate and complicate an activist's legacy, emphasizing the need for careful consideration of how stories are told and who gets to tell them.

Supporting and Uplifting Marginalized Voices in the LGBTQ and Disability Communities

Ultimately, the challenge of unauthorized biographies lies in their potential to overshadow the voices of marginalized individuals within the LGBTQ and disability communities. This chapter advocates for a narrative approach that prioritizes inclusivity and amplifies diverse voices. By supporting and uplifting these voices, activists like Paula can foster a more equitable representation of their communities.

The chapter concludes by emphasizing the importance of collaboration and solidarity in activism. By working together, activists can create a more comprehensive and nuanced understanding of the struggles faced by LGBTQ and disabled individuals, ensuring that their stories are told with the respect and dignity they deserve.

In summary, Chapter 4: Unauthorized serves as a critical examination of the implications of unauthorized biographies in the context of Paula Lupi's life and activism. By addressing the ethical considerations, challenges, and opportunities presented by such narratives, this chapter highlights the need for a more inclusive and thoughtful approach to storytelling in the realm of activism.

The Controversies and Backlash

Challenges to Paula's credibility and integrity

Paula Lupi's journey as a prominent LGBTQ and disability rights activist has not been without its challenges, particularly concerning her credibility and integrity. As she rose to prominence, the scrutiny intensified, revealing the complexities of navigating activism in a world rife with skepticism and critique. This section delves into the various challenges Paula faced regarding her credibility, the implications of these challenges, and the broader context of integrity within activism.

One of the primary challenges to Paula's credibility stemmed from her intersectional identity as a queer disabled woman. While her unique perspective provided invaluable insights into the struggles faced by marginalized communities, it also attracted criticism from within those very communities. Critics often questioned whether Paula's experiences were representative of the broader LGBTQ and disabled populations. This raises the question of representation in activism and the potential pitfalls of a singular narrative overshadowing diverse experiences.

A notable example of this occurred during a public forum where Paula spoke passionately about the need for inclusive policies that addressed the intersectionality of LGBTQ and disability rights. Some audience members challenged her by stating that her experiences, while significant, did not encompass the realities faced by individuals from different racial and socioeconomic backgrounds. This incident highlighted a critical issue in activism: the danger of assuming that one person's story can encapsulate the multifaceted nature of oppression.

Furthermore, the concept of *privilege* emerged as a contentious topic in discussions surrounding Paula's activism. Critics pointed out that as a publicly recognized figure, Paula benefited from certain privileges that others in the LGBTQ and disabled communities did not possess. This led to accusations of elitism and the idea that her platform might inadvertently silence less visible voices.

The discourse surrounding privilege in activism often revolves around the need for activists to acknowledge their own positionality and the responsibility that comes with it.

In response to these challenges, Paula took proactive steps to address concerns about her credibility. She engaged in open dialogues with critics, emphasizing her commitment to listening and learning from those whose experiences differed from her own. This approach aligns with the principles of *transformative justice*, which advocates for accountability, healing, and community-based solutions rather than punitive measures. By fostering a culture of dialogue, Paula aimed to rebuild trust and demonstrate her integrity as an advocate.

Moreover, the backlash against Paula's credibility was not solely rooted in her identity or the privileges she held. It also reflected broader societal issues concerning the authenticity of activist narratives. In an era where social media amplifies voices, the question of who gets to speak for whom becomes increasingly complex. The phenomenon of *performative activism*—where individuals or organizations engage in activism primarily for social capital rather than genuine commitment—further complicates the landscape. Critics were wary of Paula being perceived as part of this trend, prompting ongoing discussions about the ethical responsibilities of activists in representing marginalized communities.

In light of these challenges, it is essential to examine the implications of questioning an activist's credibility. On one hand, skepticism can serve as a necessary check on power dynamics within movements, ensuring that diverse voices are heard and respected. On the other hand, relentless scrutiny can undermine the collective efforts of activists and create divisions within movements. This dichotomy emphasizes the need for balance between accountability and support, particularly in communities striving for unity in the face of systemic oppression.

In conclusion, the challenges to Paula Lupi's credibility and integrity reflect the intricate dynamics of activism in contemporary society. Her experiences underscore the importance of intersectionality, the recognition of privilege, and the necessity for ongoing dialogue within activist communities. As Paula navigated these challenges, she not only confronted the external criticisms but also engaged in a process of self-reflection and growth, ultimately reinforcing her commitment to advocacy and the principles of inclusivity and justice. The road ahead for Paula and her peers involves not only addressing these challenges but also fostering a culture of mutual support and understanding, ensuring that the fight for LGBTQ and disability rights remains robust and inclusive.

THE CONTROVERSIES AND BACKLASH 261

Criticisms from within the LGBTQ and disability communities

The journey of Paula Lupi, while marked by significant achievements in advocating for LGBTQ and disability rights, has not been without its share of criticisms. Within the very communities she sought to uplift, there have been voices of dissent that have raised important issues regarding her approach, representation, and the intersectionality of her activism. These criticisms are crucial for understanding the complexities of advocacy and the need for inclusivity within movements.

One of the primary criticisms stems from the perception that Paula's activism, while impactful, often prioritized certain narratives over others. For instance, some activists argue that her focus on LGBTQ issues sometimes overshadowed the unique challenges faced by disabled individuals within the community. This critique highlights the need for a more nuanced understanding of intersectionality, a concept popularized by Kimberlé Crenshaw, which emphasizes how various forms of identity—such as race, gender, sexuality, and disability—interact and create overlapping systems of discrimination or disadvantage.

$$I = \{R, G, S, D\} \tag{106}$$

Where I represents identity, R is race, G is gender, S is sexuality, and D is disability. The intersectionality theory posits that individuals who belong to multiple marginalized groups experience unique forms of oppression that cannot be understood by examining each identity in isolation.

Moreover, some community members expressed concerns about the representation of queer disabled voices within Paula's initiatives. Critics argued that her platform, while well-intentioned, often featured narratives predominantly from able-bodied LGBTQ individuals, thereby marginalizing those who identified as both queer and disabled. This lack of representation can lead to a homogenized view of the LGBTQ experience, which fails to capture the diversity and complexity of the community.

For example, during a prominent LGBTQ rights rally organized by Paula, several disabled activists felt sidelined. They reported that accessibility measures were inadequate, which not only hindered their participation but also sent a message that their needs were secondary to the primary goals of the event. This incident exemplifies the ongoing struggle for inclusivity within advocacy spaces, where the voices of disabled individuals are often drowned out by louder, more dominant narratives.

Another criticism arose from Paula's approach to allyship and coalition-building. While she has been praised for her efforts to create alliances between LGBTQ and disability rights movements, some activists pointed out that these alliances were sometimes superficial. They argued that genuine allyship requires more than just collaboration; it necessitates a deep understanding of the distinct challenges faced by each group and a commitment to addressing those challenges in a meaningful way. This includes recognizing the historical context of oppression that has shaped the experiences of both communities.

In addressing these criticisms, it is essential to acknowledge the role of privilege in activism. Paula, as a queer disabled woman, occupies a unique position within the intersectional landscape. However, her experiences may not fully encapsulate the realities faced by all queer disabled individuals, particularly those from marginalized racial or socioeconomic backgrounds. This disparity can lead to a disconnect between her advocacy and the lived experiences of those she aims to support.

The backlash from within the LGBTQ and disability communities serves as a reminder of the importance of self-reflection and growth in activism. Paula's journey illustrates that no activist is immune to critique, and the willingness to listen, learn, and adapt is vital for fostering an inclusive movement. By engaging with these criticisms, Paula has the opportunity to strengthen her advocacy and ensure that it resonates with a broader spectrum of voices.

In conclusion, the criticisms directed at Paula Lupi from within the LGBTQ and disability communities underscore the necessity of intersectionality in advocacy. They highlight the importance of amplifying diverse voices and ensuring that all members of the community feel represented and valued. As Paula continues her work, embracing these critiques may not only enhance her effectiveness as an activist but also contribute to a more inclusive and equitable future for all marginalized individuals.

Addressing intersectionality and inclusivity criticisms

In recent years, the conversation surrounding intersectionality has gained significant traction within activist circles, particularly in the context of LGBTQ and disability rights. Intersectionality, a term coined by legal scholar Kimberlé Crenshaw in 1989, refers to the ways in which various forms of discrimination and privilege intersect and overlap, creating unique experiences for individuals who belong to multiple marginalized groups. This concept is crucial for understanding the complexities of identity and the necessity for inclusivity within advocacy efforts.

Paula Lupi's activism has not been immune to criticism regarding her approach to intersectionality. Critics argue that while she has championed LGBTQ rights and disability advocacy, there have been moments where her work has not fully encompassed the diverse experiences of all individuals within these communities.

For instance, some have pointed out that her focus on specific issues, such as marriage equality, may overshadow the needs of those who face compounded discrimination due to race, class, or socioeconomic status.

To illustrate this point, consider the experiences of LGBTQ individuals of color. Research indicates that people of color often face higher rates of violence and discrimination compared to their white counterparts within the LGBTQ community. A study conducted by the Human Rights Campaign (HRC) in 2017 revealed that Black LGBTQ individuals reported feeling less safe in their communities and were more likely to experience homelessness than their white peers. This highlights the necessity for activists to adopt a more nuanced understanding of intersectionality, ensuring that their advocacy efforts address the unique challenges faced by marginalized subgroups.

Moreover, the intersection of disability and LGBTQ identities presents additional layers of complexity. Many disabled individuals experience a dual marginalization that can lead to feelings of invisibility within both communities. For example, a queer disabled woman may encounter barriers to accessing healthcare that are compounded by both her sexual orientation and her disability. This intersectional lens emphasizes the need for inclusive policies that address the specific needs of individuals who exist at these crossroads.

Critics of Paula's approach have called for a more comprehensive framework that incorporates the voices and experiences of those who are often sidelined in mainstream discussions. The call for inclusivity is not merely a matter of representation; it is about ensuring that advocacy efforts are genuinely reflective of the diversity within the LGBTQ and disability communities. This includes recognizing the importance of amplifying the voices of those who are often marginalized, such as transgender individuals, people of color, and those with multiple intersecting identities.

To address these criticisms, Paula has taken steps to engage with a broader spectrum of activists and community members. She has participated in forums and discussions that focus on intersectionality, actively seeking to understand and incorporate the perspectives of those who challenge her views. By fostering dialogue and collaboration, Paula aims to create a more inclusive movement that recognizes the complexities of identity and the necessity for a multifaceted approach to advocacy.

In conclusion, addressing intersectionality and inclusivity criticisms is an ongoing process that requires vigilance, humility, and a commitment to listening. For Paula Lupi, this means acknowledging the limitations of her past work and striving to ensure that her activism reflects the diverse experiences of all individuals within the LGBTQ and disability communities. By embracing intersectionality as a guiding principle, Paula can work towards a more equitable and inclusive future, where every voice is heard, and every identity is valued.

$$I = \sum_{j=1}^{n} \frac{w_j}{d_j} \qquad (107)$$

Where I represents the inclusivity index, w_j is the weight assigned to each identity category, and d_j is the degree of representation within advocacy efforts. This equation serves as a framework for assessing the effectiveness of inclusive practices in activism, highlighting the importance of addressing the unique needs of diverse communities.

By understanding and implementing the principles of intersectionality, Paula Lupi can continue to evolve as an activist, ensuring that her work not only uplifts her own identity but also champions the rights of all marginalized individuals. The journey towards inclusivity is not without its challenges, but it is a crucial endeavor for creating a more just and equitable society.

The role of privilege and representation in activism

In the landscape of activism, the concepts of privilege and representation play pivotal roles in shaping the narratives, strategies, and effectiveness of movements. Understanding privilege—defined as the unearned advantages granted to certain groups based on characteristics such as race, gender, sexual orientation, ability, and socioeconomic status—allows activists to navigate the complexities of their work more effectively.

Activism is inherently about advocating for those whose voices have been marginalized or silenced. However, the effectiveness of such advocacy is often influenced by the privileges of those who lead the charge. For instance, a white, able-bodied, cisgender individual may have different experiences and challenges compared to a queer disabled person of color. This disparity highlights the importance of intersectionality, a framework that emphasizes how various social identities intersect to create unique experiences of oppression and privilege.

$$P = \frac{E}{S} \qquad (108)$$

Where P represents privilege, E represents the advantages experienced, and S represents the societal structures that perpetuate inequality. This equation illustrates that privilege is not merely about individual experiences but is deeply rooted in systemic factors.

Problems Arising from Privilege in Activism

One of the significant problems arising from privilege in activism is the tendency for certain voices to dominate the conversation, often sidelining those who are more marginalized. This phenomenon can lead to what is known as "performative activism," where individuals or organizations engage in activism primarily to enhance their image rather than to effect meaningful change. For example, a corporation may publicly support LGBTQ rights during Pride Month while failing to implement inclusive policies within their own workforce.

Moreover, the lack of representation can result in the perpetuation of stereotypes and the reinforcement of existing power dynamics. When activists do not reflect the diversity of the communities they aim to represent, they risk alienating those very individuals. This can be seen in many mainstream LGBTQ organizations that have historically prioritized the voices of white, cisgender individuals over those of queer people of color or disabled individuals.

Examples of Representation in Activism

A poignant example of the role of privilege and representation can be observed in the Black Lives Matter (BLM) movement. Founded by Alicia Garza, Patrisse Cullors, and Opal Tometi, the movement emphasizes the need for intersectionality within social justice movements. The founders recognized that the struggles faced by Black individuals are compounded by other identities, such as gender and sexual orientation. This approach has allowed BLM to address a wide array of issues, from police brutality to economic inequality, creating a more inclusive framework for activism.

Conversely, when organizations fail to embrace intersectionality, they risk becoming ineffective. For instance, the early days of the LGBTQ rights movement often focused heavily on issues pertinent to white, cisgender gay men, such as marriage equality, while neglecting the unique challenges faced by LGBTQ individuals of color, transgender individuals, and those with disabilities. This lack of representation not only undermines the movement's credibility but also perpetuates systemic inequalities.

The Importance of Inclusive Representation

Inclusive representation is not just a moral imperative; it is essential for the sustainability and effectiveness of activist movements. When diverse voices are included in leadership roles, movements can better understand and address the needs of the communities they serve. This is particularly important in the context of policy advocacy, where the experiences of marginalized individuals can inform and shape legislation that directly impacts their lives.

For example, the passage of the Americans with Disabilities Act (ADA) in the United States was heavily influenced by the activism of disabled individuals who shared their lived experiences. Their representation in the movement ensured that the law addressed the real barriers faced by disabled people, rather than relying solely on the perspectives of non-disabled allies.

Strategies for Enhancing Representation

To enhance representation within activism, it is crucial for organizations and movements to adopt inclusive practices. This can include:

1. **Diverse Leadership**: Actively seeking out and supporting leaders from marginalized communities to ensure that their voices are heard in decision-making processes. 2. **Collaboration**: Building coalitions with other organizations that represent different identities and experiences, fostering a more comprehensive approach to activism. 3. **Education and Training**: Providing training on privilege and intersectionality for all members of an organization to cultivate a deeper understanding of these concepts.

Conclusion

The role of privilege and representation in activism cannot be overstated. By recognizing and addressing the complexities of privilege, activists can create more inclusive movements that genuinely reflect the diversity of the communities they serve. This commitment to representation not only strengthens the effectiveness of activism but also fosters a more equitable society. As Paula Lupi's journey illustrates, embracing intersectionality and understanding privilege is essential for any activist aiming to make a lasting impact in the fight for LGBTQ and disability rights.

Navigating personal and political controversies

Navigating the tumultuous waters of personal and political controversies can be one of the most challenging aspects of an activist's journey. For Paula Lupi, this meant not only addressing external criticisms but also reconciling her own experiences and beliefs with the broader societal expectations placed upon her. The intersectionality of her identity as a queer disabled woman further complicated these challenges, often placing her at the crossroads of multiple movements and ideologies.

Understanding Controversies

Controversies in activism often arise from differing perspectives within the community. For Paula, the LGBTQ and disability rights movements, while overlapping, sometimes presented conflicting priorities. For instance, the urgency of addressing immediate LGBTQ issues such as marriage equality could clash with the pressing need for disability rights advocacy, such as accessible healthcare and employment opportunities. This tension can be illustrated by the following equation, which models the balance of advocacy priorities:

$$C = \frac{E_{LGBTQ} + E_{Disability}}{T} \tag{109}$$

where:

- C represents the overall effectiveness of advocacy,
- E_{LGBTQ} is the energy dedicated to LGBTQ issues,
- $E_{Disability}$ is the energy dedicated to disability rights,
- T is the time available for advocacy.

This equation emphasizes that the effectiveness of advocacy is contingent upon how well Paula could balance her focus between LGBTQ rights and disability rights, given the finite resources of time and energy.

Personal Struggles and Public Perception

Paula's personal life also became a battleground for controversy. As she rose to prominence, her relationships were scrutinized. Critics questioned her commitment to activism when her personal choices did not align with their expectations. For example, her decision to date someone outside of the LGBTQ community sparked debates about authenticity and representation. This led to a public backlash that forced her to confront her own identity and the perceptions of others.

In addressing these controversies, Paula utilized a theory of *social identity*, which posits that individuals derive a sense of self from their group memberships. This theory helped her navigate the complexities of her public persona versus her private life. By acknowledging that her worth as an activist was not solely defined by her relationships, she began to reframe the narrative surrounding her personal choices.

Reconciliation and Growth

The process of reconciling these controversies often involved difficult conversations with her peers and community members. Paula recognized the importance of dialogue in addressing grievances. For instance, after facing criticism regarding her approach to intersectionality, she organized a series of workshops aimed at fostering understanding and collaboration among diverse groups within the

LGBTQ and disability communities. These workshops emphasized the need for inclusive practices and highlighted the voices of those often marginalized within the movement.

One notable example of this reconciliation was her collaboration with a prominent disability rights activist, who had initially criticized Paula's focus on LGBTQ issues. Together, they created a joint initiative that addressed both LGBTQ and disability rights, demonstrating that unity could be achieved through shared goals rather than divisive rhetoric. This partnership became a model for future collaborations, showcasing the power of intersectional advocacy.

The Role of Media

Media representation played a crucial role in shaping public perception of Paula's controversies. The way her story was framed in the press often influenced how her actions were interpreted by the public. In some instances, sensationalized headlines exacerbated misunderstandings, leading to further backlash. To combat this, Paula took control of her narrative by engaging with media outlets directly, providing them with the context necessary to portray her accurately.

She harnessed the power of social media to share her story and connect with her audience on a more personal level. By using platforms like Twitter and Instagram, Paula was able to clarify misconceptions and present her experiences authentically. This proactive approach not only helped mitigate some of the controversies but also fostered a sense of community among her supporters.

Conclusion

Navigating personal and political controversies is an inherent part of activism, particularly for someone like Paula Lupi, who exists at the intersection of multiple identities. By embracing her complexities, engaging in dialogue, and taking control of her narrative, Paula transformed challenges into opportunities for growth and unity. Her journey illustrates that controversies, while difficult, can ultimately lead to deeper understanding and stronger coalitions within the fight for equality.

As Paula continues to advocate for LGBTQ and disability rights, her ability to navigate these controversies will serve as a testament to her resilience and dedication to creating a more inclusive world. The lessons learned from her experiences highlight the importance of intersectionality, dialogue, and authenticity in the ongoing struggle for justice.

Learning and growing from mistakes and missteps

In the journey of activism, mistakes are not merely setbacks; they are invaluable lessons that pave the way for growth and deeper understanding. For Paula Lupi, the road to becoming a prominent voice for LGBTQ and disability rights was littered with challenges and missteps, each serving as a catalyst for personal and professional development.

At the core of Paula's evolution was the recognition that no activist operates in a vacuum. Each action, each statement, and each campaign has implications that extend beyond the immediate context. This realization is grounded in the theory of *Reflexivity*, which posits that individuals must continuously reflect on their own positionality and the power dynamics at play in their advocacy efforts. Reflexivity requires activists to critically analyze their motivations, the impact of their actions, and the broader societal structures that inform their work.

A notable example from Paula's journey occurred during a high-profile campaign advocating for inclusive healthcare policies for LGBTQ individuals with disabilities. Initially, Paula's messaging inadvertently sidelined the voices of those who were most affected by the policies she aimed to change. This oversight sparked backlash from community members who felt their specific needs and experiences were being overlooked. Instead of becoming defensive, Paula embraced the criticism as an opportunity for learning. She convened a series of focus groups with LGBTQ disabled individuals to gain insights into their lived experiences and to better understand the nuances of the issues at hand.

This approach exemplifies the concept of *Participatory Action Research* (PAR), which emphasizes collaboration between researchers and community members to address social issues. By actively involving the community in the decision-making process, Paula not only rectified her previous missteps but also fostered a sense of ownership among community members regarding the outcomes of the campaign. This shift not only strengthened the campaign but also deepened Paula's understanding of the intersectionality that characterizes the experiences of marginalized groups.

Moreover, the process of learning from mistakes is inherently tied to the concept of *Growth Mindset*, a term popularized by psychologist Carol Dweck. A growth mindset encourages individuals to view challenges and failures as opportunities for development rather than as reflections of their abilities. Paula embodied this mindset when she faced criticism for her approach to activism. Instead of retreating in shame, she sought mentorship from seasoned activists who had navigated similar challenges. This willingness to learn from others not only enhanced her skills but also built a network of support that would prove crucial in her future endeavors.

One of the most significant lessons Paula learned was the importance of humility in activism. In a world where voices are often amplified based on privilege, it is essential for activists to recognize the limitations of their own perspectives. Paula's journey taught her that acknowledging one's mistakes is not a sign of weakness but a demonstration of strength and authenticity. By openly discussing her missteps in public forums, she created a space for others to share their experiences and learn from one another. This practice of vulnerability not only humanized her in the eyes of her supporters but also solidified her role as a trusted leader within the community.

Paula's experiences also highlight the significance of adaptability in activism. The landscape of social justice is constantly shifting, influenced by cultural, political, and technological changes. Activists must remain agile, ready to reassess strategies and approaches based on new information and feedback. For instance, when social media emerged as a powerful tool for mobilization, Paula recognized the need to adapt her outreach strategies to engage younger activists who were more comfortable with digital platforms. By embracing new technologies and methodologies, she was able to expand her reach and connect with a broader audience.

In conclusion, the journey of learning and growing from mistakes and missteps is an integral part of Paula Lupi's legacy. Through reflexivity, participatory approaches, a growth mindset, humility, and adaptability, Paula transformed her challenges into stepping stones for greater advocacy. Her story serves as a reminder that the path of activism is not linear; it is a complex tapestry woven with threads of triumph and failure, each contributing to a richer understanding of the fight for justice. As future activists look to Paula's example, they are encouraged to embrace their own missteps as opportunities for learning and growth, fostering a more inclusive and effective movement for change.

Rebuilding trust and reconciling with critics

In the tumultuous landscape of activism, trust is a currency that can be easily spent and, once spent, can be incredibly difficult to regain. For Paula Lupi, the journey of rebuilding trust and reconciling with critics was not just a personal endeavor; it was a necessary step in her broader mission to advocate for LGBTQ and disability rights. The challenges she faced were deeply intertwined with the complexities of intersectionality, privilege, and representation within activist spaces.

Understanding the Landscape of Distrust

Distrust often arises from perceived betrayals, miscommunications, or failures to represent a community authentically. In the case of Paula, some critics within the LGBTQ and disability communities felt that her approach sometimes overshadowed the voices of those who were not part of the dominant narrative. This criticism was rooted in the historical context where marginalized voices were often sidelined in favor of more palatable, mainstream representations.

$$D = \frac{M - R}{M} \times 100 \tag{110}$$

Where:

- D is the distrust index,
- M is the perceived marginalization of voices,
- R is the representation of those voices in advocacy.

A high distrust index indicated a significant gap between the representation of marginalized voices and the mainstream narrative, which Paula had to address head-on.

The Path to Reconciliation

Rebuilding trust necessitated a multifaceted approach. Paula recognized that reconciliation was not merely about addressing grievances but about actively engaging with her critics. This involved several key strategies:

1. **Listening Sessions:** Paula organized a series of listening sessions where community members could voice their concerns and share their experiences. This initiative was crucial in creating a safe space for dialogue and understanding. It allowed her to hear firsthand the impact of her actions and decisions.

2. **Public Acknowledgment:** Acknowledging past mistakes publicly was another significant step. Paula issued statements that recognized the criticisms and validated the feelings of those who felt marginalized. This act of vulnerability was essential in demonstrating her commitment to growth and accountability.

3. **Collaborative Initiatives:** Paula initiated collaborative projects with critics, focusing on shared goals. By working together on campaigns that prioritized the voices of those who felt sidelined, she fostered a sense of unity and purpose. This not only helped to mend relationships but also strengthened the community's collective advocacy efforts.

4. **Education and Training:** Understanding the importance of intersectionality in activism, Paula invested in training programs for herself and her team. These programs focused on privilege, representation, and the nuances of LGBTQ and disability rights, ensuring that future initiatives would be more inclusive and representative of diverse experiences.

5. **Mentorship and Support:** Paula also recognized the need to uplift emerging leaders within the LGBTQ and disability communities. By providing mentorship and support to those who felt overlooked, she not only rebuilt trust but also empowered a new generation of activists to take the reins of advocacy.

The Role of Transparency

Transparency played a pivotal role in Paula's journey of reconciliation. By openly sharing her decision-making processes and the rationale behind her actions, she cultivated an environment of trust. This transparency was not without its challenges; it required Paula to be vulnerable and to accept that not everyone would be satisfied with her choices. However, the act of being open about her intentions and the complexities of her role as an activist helped to bridge the gap between her and her critics.

Learning from Criticism

Criticism, while often painful, can serve as a catalyst for growth. Paula learned to view criticism not as an attack but as an opportunity to reflect on her practices and beliefs. This shift in perspective allowed her to engage more constructively with her critics.

For example, after receiving feedback on her approach to disability rights, Paula collaborated with disabled activists to reframe her messaging and advocacy strategies. This collaboration not only improved her outreach efforts but also demonstrated her commitment to inclusivity.

Building a Culture of Inclusivity

Through her efforts to reconcile with critics, Paula aimed to foster a culture of inclusivity within her advocacy work. This culture emphasized that all voices matter, and that activism is most effective when it is a collective effort.

$$I = \frac{C + D + E}{3} \qquad (111)$$

Where:

- I is the inclusivity index,
- C is community engagement,
- D is diversity in representation,
- E is education on intersectionality.

A higher inclusivity index indicated a stronger, more unified movement that could advocate effectively for the rights of all marginalized groups.

Conclusion: The Ongoing Journey

Rebuilding trust and reconciling with critics is an ongoing journey, not a destination. For Paula Lupi, this process was integral to her identity as an activist and her commitment to advocating for LGBTQ and disability rights. By embracing criticism, fostering dialogue, and prioritizing inclusivity, Paula not only mended relationships but also strengthened the very fabric of the activist community.

As she moved forward, Paula understood that reconciliation is not a one-time effort but a continual practice of listening, learning, and evolving. The lessons learned from this journey would not only shape her future endeavors but also inspire countless others to engage in the vital work of building trust and unity within their communities.

The impact of unauthorized biographies on public perception

Unauthorized biographies, by their very nature, can significantly shape public perception, often in ways that are both positive and negative. These narratives, which are created without the subject's consent or collaboration, can lead to a complex interplay between the subject's intended self-representation and the author's interpretation. This section explores the multifaceted impact of unauthorized biographies on public perception, delving into relevant theories, potential problems, and notable examples.

Theoretical Framework

At the core of understanding the impact of unauthorized biographies is the concept of *narrative identity*, as articulated by Paul Ricoeur. Ricoeur posits that individuals construct their identities through the stories they tell about themselves. Unauthorized biographies disrupt this process, as they often present a narrative that the subject may not endorse. This dissonance can lead to a skewed public perception, where the subject's true identity is misrepresented or oversimplified.

Moreover, the *social construction of reality* theory, proposed by Peter L. Berger and Thomas Luckmann, suggests that our understanding of the world is shaped through social interactions and shared narratives. Unauthorized biographies can introduce new narratives that challenge existing perceptions, potentially altering public opinion about the subject.

Problems Arising from Unauthorized Biographies

One of the primary issues with unauthorized biographies is the potential for *misrepresentation*. Authors may lack a comprehensive understanding of their subject, leading to inaccuracies that can perpetuate stereotypes or reinforce biases. For example, unauthorized biographies of LGBTQ activists may focus disproportionately on sensational aspects of their lives, overshadowing their contributions to social justice.

Additionally, these biographies can create a sense of *disempowerment* for the subjects. When individuals are not given the opportunity to narrate their own stories, they may feel stripped of agency over their identities. This can lead to public perceptions that are not only inaccurate but also harmful, as they may fail to acknowledge the complexities of the subject's experiences.

Examples of Impact

A notable example of the impact of unauthorized biographies can be found in the case of *The Unauthorized Biography of Steven Spielberg* by Marc Eliot. While the biography aimed to provide an in-depth look at Spielberg's life, it faced criticism for its sensationalized portrayal of the filmmaker's personal struggles. Critics argued that the biography misrepresented Spielberg's intentions and contributions to cinema, leading to a skewed public perception that focused more on controversy than on his artistic achievements.

THE CONTROVERSIES AND BACKLASH 275

In the realm of LGBTQ activism, the unauthorized biography of Marsha P. Johnson, a pivotal figure in the Stonewall uprising, has sparked debate. While the biography aimed to highlight Johnson's contributions, some activists criticized it for failing to capture the nuances of her identity as a Black transgender woman. This oversight led to discussions about the importance of representation and the need for narratives that honor the complexities of marginalized identities.

Positive Outcomes

Despite the challenges associated with unauthorized biographies, they can also serve as catalysts for discussion and awareness. When an unauthorized biography sheds light on underrepresented voices, it can provoke public interest and inspire further exploration of the subject's life and work. For instance, unauthorized biographies of lesser-known activists can bring attention to their contributions, prompting a reevaluation of their significance in the broader context of social movements.

Furthermore, unauthorized biographies can challenge dominant narratives, encouraging readers to question established perceptions. By presenting alternative viewpoints, these works can foster critical engagement and promote a more nuanced understanding of complex issues, such as intersectionality within the LGBTQ rights movement.

Conclusion

In conclusion, unauthorized biographies wield considerable influence over public perception, often straddling the line between empowerment and disempowerment. While they can misrepresent individuals and perpetuate harmful stereotypes, they also have the potential to challenge dominant narratives and inspire greater awareness. As society continues to grapple with issues of identity and representation, the impact of unauthorized biographies will remain a vital area of exploration, particularly in the context of marginalized communities. It is essential for readers and critics alike to approach these works with a critical eye, recognizing the power of narrative in shaping our understanding of the world and the individuals within it.

Supporting and uplifting marginalized voices in the LGBTQ and disability communities

In the vibrant tapestry of activism, the importance of supporting and uplifting marginalized voices within the LGBTQ and disability communities cannot be overstated. As Paula Lupi navigated her journey, she recognized that true advocacy is not merely about raising one's own voice, but rather about amplifying the voices of those who have historically been silenced or overlooked. This principle is foundational in intersectional activism, a theory that seeks to understand how various forms of discrimination overlap and impact individuals differently based on their unique identities.

Understanding Intersectionality

Intersectionality, a term coined by legal scholar Kimberlé Crenshaw, posits that individuals experience oppression in varying configurations and degrees of intensity based on their intersecting identities. For instance, a queer disabled woman like Paula faces distinct challenges that differ from those encountered by a cisgender, able-bodied LGBTQ individual. This concept is crucial for activists as it encourages a more nuanced understanding of the diverse experiences within the LGBTQ and disability communities.

Challenges Faced by Marginalized Voices

The challenges faced by marginalized voices in these communities are multifaceted. For example, individuals with disabilities may encounter barriers not only in physical accessibility but also in social acceptance within LGBTQ spaces. Similarly, LGBTQ individuals from racial or ethnic minorities may face compounded discrimination, leading to a sense of isolation even within their own communities.

These challenges are often exacerbated by systemic issues such as poverty, lack of access to healthcare, and societal stigma. According to a report by the Human Rights Campaign (HRC), LGBTQ individuals with disabilities are more likely to experience discrimination in healthcare settings, which can lead to significant health disparities. This highlights the urgent need for advocates like Paula to create inclusive spaces where all voices can be heard and valued.

Strategies for Uplifting Voices

To effectively support and uplift marginalized voices, activists must adopt several key strategies:

1. **Creating Inclusive Spaces:** Activists should strive to create environments where individuals feel safe and empowered to share their stories. This includes ensuring that events and organizations are accessible to people with disabilities and actively promoting the participation of marginalized groups.

2. **Amplifying Stories:** Sharing personal narratives is a powerful tool in advocacy. By amplifying the stories of individuals from marginalized backgrounds, activists can foster empathy and understanding within broader communities. Paula often utilized storytelling in her speeches and writings to highlight the unique experiences of queer disabled individuals.

3. **Collaborative Advocacy:** Building coalitions between various advocacy groups can strengthen efforts to uplift marginalized voices. For instance, partnerships between LGBTQ organizations and disability rights groups can lead to more comprehensive advocacy strategies that address the unique needs of their constituents.

4. **Education and Awareness:** Educating the broader community about the intersectional nature of oppression is crucial. Workshops, seminars, and social media campaigns can help raise awareness about the specific challenges faced by marginalized voices, thereby fostering greater understanding and support.

5. **Mentorship Programs:** Establishing mentorship programs can provide guidance and support to emerging activists from marginalized backgrounds. Paula often emphasized the importance of mentorship in her own journey, recognizing that having a supportive network can empower individuals to take on leadership roles.

Examples of Effective Advocacy

Several organizations exemplify the commitment to uplifting marginalized voices within the LGBTQ and disability communities. The *National LGBTQ Task Force* has been instrumental in advocating for policies that address the needs of LGBTQ individuals with disabilities. Their initiatives focus on ensuring access to healthcare, housing, and employment opportunities, recognizing the intersectional challenges faced by their constituents.

Another notable example is the *Disability Rights Education and Defense Fund (DREDF)*, which actively works to promote the rights of individuals with disabilities, including those within the LGBTQ community. Their efforts to educate policymakers and the public about the unique challenges faced by disabled LGBTQ individuals have helped to elevate these voices in critical conversations about rights and representation.

The Role of Allyship

Allyship plays a vital role in supporting marginalized voices. Allies are individuals who may not share the same marginalized identity but actively work to support and uplift those who do. Effective allies listen, learn, and take action to address inequities. Paula often collaborated with allies in her advocacy work, emphasizing that allyship is not a passive role but requires active engagement and commitment to social justice.

Conclusion

In conclusion, supporting and uplifting marginalized voices in the LGBTQ and disability communities is essential for creating a more equitable and inclusive society. Through understanding intersectionality, addressing challenges, implementing effective strategies, and fostering allyship, advocates can ensure that all voices are heard and valued. Paula Lupi's legacy serves as a reminder that the fight for equality is a collective effort, one that requires the strength and courage to stand together in solidarity. By amplifying the voices of the marginalized, we not only honor their experiences but also enrich the broader movement for justice and equality.

Focusing on reconciliation and unity in the face of adversity

In the realm of activism, particularly within the LGBTQ and disability rights movements, the need for reconciliation and unity often emerges as a fundamental challenge. Paula Lupi's journey exemplifies how focusing on these principles can transform adversity into a powerful catalyst for change. This section explores the theoretical frameworks, practical implications, and real-world examples that underscore the importance of reconciliation and unity in the face of adversity.

Theoretical Frameworks

Reconciliation in activism can be understood through various theoretical lenses, including conflict resolution theory and social identity theory. Conflict resolution theory posits that addressing underlying grievances and fostering dialogue can lead to peaceful resolutions and collaborative efforts. This theory is particularly relevant in the context of LGBTQ and disability rights, where intersecting identities can lead to tensions within the community itself.

Social identity theory, on the other hand, emphasizes the significance of group identity in shaping individual behaviors and attitudes. Activists like Paula Lupi recognize that fostering a collective identity among diverse groups can enhance solidarity and promote a unified front against discrimination and injustice. By embracing the multiplicity of identities within the LGBTQ and disability communities, activists can create an inclusive environment that values every voice.

THE CONTROVERSIES AND BACKLASH

Challenges to Reconciliation

Despite the theoretical frameworks that support reconciliation, several challenges persist. Internal conflicts within the LGBTQ and disability rights movements often arise from differing priorities and experiences. For instance, the intersection of race, gender, and disability can create divisions, as individuals may feel that their specific issues are sidelined in favor of more dominant narratives. These tensions can lead to fragmentation, undermining collective efforts.

Moreover, the backlash against marginalized groups can exacerbate these divisions. Paula faced significant challenges in her advocacy, particularly when addressing the complexities of intersectionality. Critics from within the community sometimes questioned her commitment to inclusivity, which made it essential for her to engage in self-reflection and dialogue. It was through these difficult conversations that Paula sought to bridge gaps and foster understanding among her peers.

Examples of Unity in Adversity

One notable example of reconciliation and unity in the face of adversity is the collaboration between LGBTQ and disability rights organizations during the annual Pride celebrations in Lisbon. Historically, Pride events have been criticized for prioritizing certain identities over others, leading to feelings of exclusion among disabled LGBTQ individuals. In response, Paula and her allies initiated a series of workshops designed to bring together diverse voices within the community. These workshops focused on shared experiences of discrimination and the need for a united front.

Through these efforts, activists were able to develop a comprehensive agenda that addressed both LGBTQ and disability rights. The collaboration resulted in a more inclusive Pride event, where accessibility measures were prioritized, and the narratives of disabled LGBTQ individuals were amplified. This example illustrates how reconciliation efforts can lead to tangible outcomes that benefit the entire community.

Another instance of unity emerged during the campaign for inclusive healthcare policies in Portugal. Paula recognized that healthcare access was a critical issue for both LGBTQ and disabled individuals. By forming coalitions with other activists and organizations, she was able to advocate for comprehensive reforms that addressed the needs of all marginalized groups. This collaborative approach not only strengthened the movement but also demonstrated the power of unity in overcoming systemic barriers.

The Role of Dialogue

At the heart of reconciliation lies the importance of dialogue. Paula Lupi emphasized the need for open conversations among activists, policymakers, and community members. By creating safe spaces for dialogue, individuals can share their experiences, express their concerns, and work toward common goals. Paula often facilitated discussions that encouraged participants to listen actively and engage empathetically with one another.

The use of restorative justice practices within activist communities has also proven effective in fostering reconciliation. These practices emphasize accountability, healing, and the restoration of relationships. For instance, when conflicts arose within the LGBTQ community regarding representation, Paula advocated for restorative circles where individuals could voice their grievances and collaboratively seek solutions. This approach not only addressed immediate concerns but also laid the groundwork for a more unified movement moving forward.

Conclusion

In conclusion, focusing on reconciliation and unity in the face of adversity is essential for the progress of LGBTQ and disability rights movements. By embracing theoretical frameworks that promote dialogue and understanding, activists can navigate internal conflicts and foster a sense of collective identity. Paula Lupi's commitment to these principles serves as a powerful reminder of the potential for healing and collaboration within marginalized communities.

As the movements continue to evolve, it is imperative that activists prioritize reconciliation and unity to address the complex challenges that lie ahead. By doing so, they can create a more inclusive and equitable future for all individuals, regardless of their identities or experiences. The legacy of Paula Lupi and her unwavering dedication to these ideals will undoubtedly inspire future generations of activists to embrace reconciliation as a fundamental pillar of their advocacy efforts.

The Unfinished Life of Paula Lupi

Reflecting on a life well-lived

In the tapestry of human existence, few lives shine as brightly and impactfully as that of Paula Lupi. Her journey from the vibrant streets of Lisbon to the global stage of activism is not merely a personal narrative; it is a testament to the power of resilience, love, and the relentless pursuit of justice. To reflect on a life well-lived is to engage with the complexities and triumphs that define Paula's legacy.

From her childhood in Lisbon, Paula's early experiences were marked by the dual challenges of navigating her identity as a queer disabled woman in a society that often marginalized both aspects of her being. The formative years of her life were characterized by a quest for belonging and acceptance, which she found through the supportive embrace of her family and a diverse circle of friends. These relationships served as the bedrock of her self-acceptance and fueled her burgeoning sense of justice. The formative moments of Paula's life illustrate the theory of intersectionality, as coined by Kimberlé Crenshaw, which posits that individuals experience multiple, overlapping identities that shape their experiences of oppression and privilege. Paula's journey exemplifies how these intersecting identities can catalyze a profound commitment to advocacy.

As she transitioned into adulthood, Paula's educational journey was fraught with challenges, yet it was within the academic environment that she discovered her passion for human rights. The struggles she faced at school, including discrimination and the fight for inclusive policies, were not just obstacles; they were transformative experiences that solidified her resolve to advocate for change. The power of education, as theorized by Paulo Freire, highlights the importance of critical consciousness—an awareness of social, political, and economic contradictions and the ability to take action against oppressive elements in one's life. Paula embodied this principle, using her education as a platform to amplify the voices of the marginalized.

The emergence of Paula as an activist was a natural progression from her personal journey. Witnessing the injustices faced by the LGBTQ community galvanized her into action. Her decision to join local LGBTQ organizations was not merely a step into activism; it was a declaration of her commitment to equality and justice. The significance of grassroots organizing cannot be overstated, as it creates spaces for collective action and solidarity. In this regard, Paula's activism was deeply rooted in the principles of community organizing, which emphasizes the importance of mobilizing individuals to effect change from the ground up.

However, with prominence came challenges. Paula faced backlash and hostility, both from external forces and within her communities. The complexities of her identity often placed her at the intersection of various struggles, leading to critiques regarding her approach to activism. Yet, it is essential to recognize that these challenges did not deter her; rather, they served as opportunities for growth and learning. The concept of resilience, as articulated by psychologists like Ann Masten, underscores the ability to adapt and thrive in the face of adversity. Paula's journey reflects this resilience, as she continually sought to learn from her experiences and rebuild trust with her critics.

As we reflect on Paula's life, it is crucial to acknowledge her role as a bridge-builder. Her advocacy extended beyond the LGBTQ community, encompassing the rights of disabled individuals and other marginalized groups. This intersectional approach is vital in contemporary activism, as it recognizes the interconnectedness of various social justice issues. Paula's legacy is one of inclusivity, reminding us that true advocacy cannot exist in silos; it must be a collective effort that uplifts all voices.

Moreover, Paula's impact transcends borders. Her international advocacy work positioned her as a global figure in the fight for LGBTQ and disability rights. By representing Portugal on the world stage, she not only raised awareness of these issues but also fostered collaboration among activists from diverse backgrounds. The importance of global solidarity in social movements cannot be overstated, as it enhances the collective power to challenge systemic injustices. Paula's legacy, therefore, is not just a reflection of her individual achievements but a call to action for future generations to continue the fight for a more inclusive world.

In conclusion, reflecting on a life well-lived, we celebrate Paula Lupi not only as an activist but as a beacon of hope and resilience. Her journey teaches us that activism is not a destination but a continuous process of learning, growing, and advocating for those who are often silenced. As we honor her memory, we are reminded that the fight for justice is far from over. Paula's life serves as an enduring inspiration, urging us to carry forward her legacy of love, acceptance, and unwavering commitment to equality for all.

Paula's vision for a more inclusive world

Paula Lupi's vision for a more inclusive world is deeply rooted in her personal experiences as a queer disabled woman and her extensive work in activism. Her philosophy encompasses the belief that true inclusivity transcends mere tolerance; it requires active engagement, understanding, and systemic change across all levels of society. This vision can be articulated through several key principles that guide her advocacy efforts.

Intersectionality as a Framework

At the heart of Paula's vision lies the concept of intersectionality, a term coined by legal scholar Kimberlé Crenshaw. Intersectionality recognizes that individuals experience overlapping social identities, which can lead to unique experiences of discrimination and privilege. For Paula, this framework is essential in understanding the complexities of both LGBTQ and disability rights. She posits that to create a truly inclusive society, it is imperative to address the specific needs of individuals at the intersections of various identities.

$$I = \sum_{n=1}^{N} P_n \tag{112}$$

where I represents individual identity, and P_n represents the various intersecting identities such as race, gender, sexuality, and disability. This equation illustrates that one's identity is not a singular experience but rather a composite of multiple factors that must be considered in advocacy and policy-making.

Empowerment through Education

Paula advocates for education as a transformative tool for empowerment. She believes that an inclusive world begins with educational systems that embrace diversity and teach students about the importance of acceptance and understanding. By integrating LGBTQ and disability studies into curricula, schools can foster environments where all students feel valued and respected.

$$E = C + D \tag{113}$$

In this equation, E represents the overall educational experience, while C is the curriculum and D is the diversity of the student body. A robust educational experience requires both a comprehensive curriculum that reflects diverse voices and an inclusive environment where all students can thrive.

Access to Healthcare

A critical component of Paula's vision is the right to accessible healthcare for all individuals, particularly those within the LGBTQ and disabled communities. She emphasizes that healthcare systems must be equipped to address the unique needs of marginalized populations. This includes not only physical health but also mental health support, which is often overlooked.

$$H_a = H_p + H_m \tag{114}$$

Here, H_a represents accessible healthcare, H_p is physical healthcare, and H_m is mental healthcare. Paula argues that a comprehensive approach to healthcare must integrate both aspects to ensure that individuals receive holistic support.

Creating Safe Spaces

Paula's vision also emphasizes the importance of creating safe spaces for marginalized communities. These spaces are essential for fostering dialogue, support, and empowerment. Whether through community centers, online platforms, or advocacy groups, safe spaces allow individuals to express themselves freely without fear of judgment or discrimination.

$$S = C + A \qquad (115)$$

In this equation, S represents safe spaces, C is community engagement, and A is advocacy efforts. Paula believes that the synergy between community involvement and active advocacy is crucial for cultivating environments where inclusivity can flourish.

Legislative Change

Finally, Paula underscores the necessity of legislative change to institutionalize inclusivity. She advocates for policies that protect the rights of LGBTQ individuals and people with disabilities, ensuring that discrimination is not only addressed but actively dismantled.

$$L_c = R + P \qquad (116)$$

In this equation, L_c signifies legislative change, R represents rights protection, and P stands for policy reform. Paula envisions a future where laws reflect the values of equality and justice for all, creating a framework that supports marginalized communities.

Conclusion

In summary, Paula Lupi's vision for a more inclusive world is multifaceted and deeply interconnected. Through the lens of intersectionality, education, healthcare access, safe spaces, and legislative change, she articulates a comprehensive approach to advocacy that seeks to uplift and empower marginalized voices. Paula's unwavering commitment to these principles serves as a guiding light for future generations, inspiring a collective movement towards a world where inclusivity is not just an aspiration, but a reality.

Continuing the fight for LGBTQ and disability rights

In the wake of Paula Lupi's impactful activism, the fight for LGBTQ and disability rights continues to evolve, presenting both challenges and opportunities for advocates around the globe. The intersectionality of these movements is crucial, as they share common goals of equality, acceptance, and justice. To understand the ongoing struggle, it is essential to explore the theoretical frameworks that underpin these rights, the persistent issues faced by marginalized communities, and the examples of contemporary activism that illustrate the path forward.

Theoretical Frameworks

One of the foundational theories in the fight for LGBTQ rights is Queer Theory, which challenges the binary understanding of gender and sexuality. As Judith Butler posits, gender is performative, meaning it is not an inherent quality but rather a series of actions and behaviors that society enforces. This perspective allows for a more inclusive understanding of identity, recognizing the fluidity of gender and sexual orientation.

Similarly, Disability Studies emphasizes the social model of disability, which argues that disability is not merely a medical issue but a result of societal barriers and discrimination. This model aligns with the principles of the social justice movement, advocating for the removal of obstacles that prevent disabled individuals from fully participating in society. By applying these theoretical frameworks, activists can better articulate their demands for change and highlight the interconnectedness of LGBTQ and disability rights.

Persistent Challenges

Despite the progress made, significant challenges remain in the fight for LGBTQ and disability rights. One of the most pressing issues is the stigma and discrimination that individuals face in various aspects of life, including healthcare, employment, and education. For instance, LGBTQ individuals, particularly those with disabilities, often encounter barriers to accessing appropriate healthcare services. A study by the National LGBTQ Task Force found that 30% of LGBTQ individuals reported being denied healthcare based on their sexual orientation or gender identity.

Additionally, the lack of inclusive policies in educational institutions continues to marginalize LGBTQ students with disabilities. Many schools fail to provide adequate support, leading to higher rates of bullying, mental health issues, and dropout rates among these students. The need for comprehensive anti-discrimination policies and inclusive curricula is paramount to ensure that all students feel safe and valued.

Contemporary Activism

Contemporary activists are employing various strategies to continue the fight for LGBTQ and disability rights. Grassroots movements, such as the Disability Justice movement, emphasize the importance of intersectionality, advocating for the rights of disabled individuals within the broader LGBTQ community. Organizations like Sins Invalid and the Disability Justice Collective are at the forefront of this movement, promoting the idea that disability is a natural part of human diversity and should be embraced rather than stigmatized.

Moreover, social media has become a powerful tool for advocacy, allowing activists to amplify their messages and connect with a global audience. Hashtags like #DisabilityTooWhite and #TransIsBeautiful have sparked discussions about representation and inclusivity within both movements. These platforms provide a space for marginalized voices to share their experiences, fostering solidarity and collective action.

Examples of Ongoing Initiatives

Several initiatives exemplify the ongoing fight for LGBTQ and disability rights. The "We the 15" campaign, launched by the International Paralympic Committee, aims to promote visibility and inclusion for the 15% of the world's population living with disabilities, including LGBTQ individuals. This campaign seeks to challenge stereotypes and advocate for equal opportunities in sports and beyond.

Additionally, the establishment of the "Queer and Disabled" project highlights the need for intersectional representation in media and culture. By showcasing the stories and experiences of queer disabled individuals, this initiative aims to challenge societal norms and foster greater understanding and acceptance.

Conclusion

Continuing the fight for LGBTQ and disability rights requires a multifaceted approach that embraces intersectionality, challenges systemic barriers, and amplifies marginalized voices. As Paula Lupi's legacy inspires new generations of activists, it is crucial to recognize that the struggle is far from over. By building on theoretical frameworks, addressing persistent challenges, and engaging in contemporary activism, advocates can work towards a more inclusive and equitable society for all.

The journey ahead may be fraught with obstacles, but the collective strength of the LGBTQ and disability rights movements holds the promise of a brighter future. As we reflect on Paula's contributions, let us remember that the fight for justice is a shared responsibility, and it is up to each of us to carry the torch forward.

The influence of Paula's legacy on future generations

Paula Lupi's legacy serves as a powerful beacon for future generations of activists, particularly within the LGBTQ and disability rights movements. Her life exemplifies the transformative impact that one individual's commitment to justice can have on society. By examining the various dimensions of her influence, we can understand how her legacy shapes the aspirations, strategies, and identities of emerging activists.

Inspiration and Empowerment

At the core of Paula's legacy is the inspiration she provides to young activists. Her journey from a child questioning societal norms to a prominent advocate demonstrates that change is possible, regardless of one's background or circumstances. This narrative resonates deeply with youth who may feel marginalized or voiceless. Paula's story illustrates that activism is not reserved for the privileged; it is accessible to anyone willing to fight for justice.

The empowerment drawn from Paula's legacy can be encapsulated in the concept of *social capital*, which refers to the networks of relationships among people who live and work in a particular society, enabling that society to function effectively. Paula cultivated a robust network of allies, mentors, and supporters, which future activists can emulate. By fostering connections within their communities, young advocates can build their own social capital, enhancing their ability to effect change.

Intersectionality in Activism

One of the most significant aspects of Paula's influence is her commitment to intersectionality. She recognized that the struggles faced by LGBTQ individuals are inextricably linked to issues of disability, race, and class. This understanding is crucial for future generations, as it encourages a more holistic approach to activism.

For example, the theory of *intersectionality*, coined by Kimberlé Crenshaw, posits that individuals experience overlapping systems of oppression. Paula's advocacy for inclusive policies within the LGBTQ community serves as a model for young activists to adopt an intersectional lens. By acknowledging the diverse identities and experiences within the movement, future leaders can create more effective strategies that address the unique challenges faced by marginalized groups.

Mentorship and Education

Paula's legacy also emphasizes the importance of mentorship in activism. Throughout her career, she actively engaged with younger activists, providing guidance and support. This mentorship model is critical for nurturing the next generation of leaders.

The educational component of Paula's legacy cannot be overstated. She championed inclusive education policies, advocating for curricula that reflect diverse perspectives. Future activists can draw from this example, recognizing that education is a powerful tool for social change. By promoting awareness of LGBTQ and disability rights in educational settings, they can cultivate a more informed and empathetic society.

Mobilizing Community Action

Paula's ability to mobilize community action is another vital aspect of her legacy. She demonstrated that grassroots organizing is essential for enacting change. Future generations can learn from her strategies, employing community engagement as a means to amplify their voices and drive collective action.

The principles of *community organizing*—building relationships, identifying shared goals, and mobilizing resources—are integral to effective activism. Paula's legacy encourages young advocates to harness these principles, fostering solidarity and collaboration within their communities. For instance, organizing local events, such as pride parades or disability rights forums, can create a sense of belonging and empowerment among participants.

Advocacy in the Digital Age

In an era dominated by technology and social media, Paula's legacy is particularly relevant. She understood the importance of leveraging these platforms to amplify marginalized voices. Future activists can utilize social media to raise awareness, share stories, and mobilize support for their causes.

The concept of *digital activism* encompasses various online strategies, including hashtag campaigns, virtual protests, and online petitions. By adopting these tools, young activists can reach a global audience, transcending geographical barriers. Paula's legacy serves as a reminder that the fight for LGBTQ and disability rights is not confined to physical spaces; it can thrive in the digital realm.

Continuing the Fight for Equality

Finally, Paula's legacy instills a sense of responsibility in future generations to continue the fight for equality. Her unwavering commitment to justice serves as a call to action, urging young activists to confront the ongoing challenges faced by LGBTQ and disabled individuals.

As they navigate the complexities of contemporary activism, future leaders can draw inspiration from Paula's resilience and determination. The struggles she faced—whether in the political arena, within the LGBTQ community, or in advocating for disability rights—serve as a testament to the importance of perseverance in the face of adversity.

In conclusion, Paula Lupi's legacy profoundly influences future generations of activists. Through inspiration, empowerment, intersectionality, mentorship, community mobilization, digital advocacy, and a commitment to equality, her life and work provide a roadmap for emerging leaders. As they carry forward her torch, they do so with the knowledge that they are part of a larger movement, one that continues to strive for justice, inclusivity, and dignity for all.

Honoring Paula's memory and contributions

In the tapestry of activism, Paula Lupi's threads are woven with resilience, passion, and an unwavering commitment to justice. Honoring her memory and contributions means acknowledging not only her achievements but also the profound impact she had on the lives of countless individuals within the LGBTQ and disability communities.

The Legacy of Advocacy

Paula's advocacy was characterized by her ability to bridge gaps between marginalized communities, illustrating the importance of intersectionality in activism. As she often said, "We are stronger together." This philosophy guided her work and inspired others to embrace their unique identities while fighting for collective rights. To honor her memory, it is essential to continue this legacy of unity and inclusivity, ensuring that no voice is left unheard.

Commemorative Events and Initiatives

One way to honor Paula's contributions is through commemorative events that celebrate her life and work. Annual gatherings, such as the *Paula Lupi Memorial Activism Conference*, can serve as platforms for activists to share their stories, discuss current challenges, and strategize for the future. These events can feature workshops, panels, and keynote speeches from prominent figures in the LGBTQ and disability rights movements.

Furthermore, establishing scholarships in Paula's name for LGBTQ and disabled students pursuing careers in social justice can create a lasting impact. These scholarships would not only provide financial support but also foster a new generation of activists who embody Paula's spirit of resilience and advocacy.

Educational Outreach and Awareness

To truly honor Paula's memory, we must engage in educational outreach that addresses the intersectionality of LGBTQ and disability rights. This involves creating curricula that highlight Paula's contributions and the ongoing struggles faced by these communities. Schools and universities can incorporate her story into their programs, emphasizing the importance of advocacy and activism.

Moreover, public awareness campaigns can be launched to celebrate Paula's life and work. These campaigns can utilize social media platforms to share her story, highlighting her achievements and the lessons learned from her journey. By amplifying her voice, we can inspire others to carry on her work.

Artistic Tributes

Art has always been a powerful medium for expression and remembrance. Honoring Paula can also take the form of artistic tributes that celebrate her life. This could include murals in public spaces, poetry slams, or art exhibitions dedicated to her legacy. Such initiatives not only pay tribute to Paula but also foster community engagement and dialogue around LGBTQ and disability rights.

For example, a mural depicting Paula surrounded by symbols of love and acceptance can serve as a constant reminder of her contributions to the community. This mural could be accompanied by a plaque detailing her achievements, ensuring that her story is told for generations to come.

Continuous Advocacy

Finally, honoring Paula's memory means committing to the ongoing fight for LGBTQ and disability rights. This involves supporting legislation that aligns with her vision of equality and justice. Activists and allies must rally together to advocate for policies that protect the rights of marginalized communities, ensuring that Paula's work does not end with her passing.

Incorporating Paula's principles into current activism can be achieved through grassroots organizing, community-building efforts, and collaboration with other movements. By maintaining momentum and striving for progress, we honor Paula's legacy and continue her fight for a more inclusive world.

Conclusion

In conclusion, honoring Paula Lupi's memory and contributions is a multifaceted endeavor that requires reflection, action, and commitment. By celebrating her life through commemorative events, educational outreach, artistic tributes, and continuous advocacy, we can ensure that her legacy lives on. Paula's journey serves as a reminder that while the fight for equality is ongoing, the spirit of activism she embodied will forever inspire us to strive for justice and inclusion for all.

Celebrating the milestones and achievements of Paula's activism

Paula Lupi's journey in the realm of LGBTQ and disability rights is marked by a series of significant milestones that not only reflect her personal growth but also the broader evolution of societal attitudes towards these communities. Each achievement serves as a beacon of hope, illustrating the power of advocacy and the impact of individual voices in shaping public policy and cultural perceptions.

One of Paula's most notable achievements was her role in the passage of the *Equality and Non-Discrimination Act*, a landmark piece of legislation that aimed to protect the rights of LGBTQ individuals and those with disabilities in Portugal. This act not only provided legal protections against discrimination but also established frameworks for inclusion in various sectors, including employment, healthcare, and education. The passage of this legislation can be quantified by the increase in reported cases of discrimination being addressed through legal channels, showcasing a 40% rise in claims filed under the new protections within the first year of its enactment.

Paula's activism also extended to grassroots organizing, where she led initiatives that fostered community engagement and awareness. One such initiative was the *Pride in Diversity* campaign, which brought together LGBTQ individuals and allies to celebrate their identities while advocating for inclusivity. The campaign saw participation from over 10,000 individuals in its inaugural year, demonstrating the collective power of community action. The campaign's success was not merely in numbers but in its ability to create safe spaces for dialogue, education, and celebration, leading to a marked increase in visibility for LGBTQ issues in local media.

Moreover, Paula's commitment to education as a tool for change was evident in her establishment of the *Inclusive Education Fund*. This fund aimed to provide scholarships and resources for LGBTQ and disabled youth, empowering them to pursue higher education without the burden of financial constraints. The fund supported over 500 students in its first five years, with a graduation rate of 85%, significantly higher than the national average for marginalized groups. This initiative exemplified Paula's understanding of intersectionality, addressing the unique challenges faced by individuals at the confluence of multiple identities.

In addition to legislative and community-focused achievements, Paula's influence extended into the international arena. She represented Portugal at the *Global LGBTQ Rights Conference*, where she advocated for the inclusion of disability rights within the broader LGBTQ movement. Her speech, which emphasized the importance of intersectionality, resonated with global activists and led to the formation of the *International Coalition for Inclusive Rights*. This coalition has since mobilized resources and support for LGBTQ and disabled individuals in over 30 countries, illustrating the ripple effect of Paula's advocacy beyond national borders.

Paula's work has not gone unnoticed, as evidenced by the numerous accolades and recognitions she has received throughout her career. She was awarded the prestigious *Human Rights Advocate of the Year* by the *International LGBTQ Federation*, a recognition that not only celebrated her achievements but also highlighted the ongoing struggles faced by marginalized communities. This award served as a reminder of the importance of perseverance in the face of adversity and the need to uplift the voices of those who are often silenced.

In celebrating Paula's milestones, it is essential to acknowledge the challenges she faced along the way. Each achievement was hard-won, often met with resistance from various sectors of society. For instance, her advocacy for inclusive policies in education faced significant pushback from conservative factions, who argued against the need for such measures. However, Paula's resilience and unwavering commitment to her cause allowed her to navigate these challenges effectively, turning opposition into opportunities for dialogue and education.

As we reflect on Paula Lupi's milestones and achievements, it becomes clear that her activism was not just about personal accolades but about creating a legacy of hope and empowerment for future generations. Her story serves as a testament to the impact one individual can have in the fight for justice and equality, inspiring countless others to join the movement. The milestones achieved under her leadership are not merely historical markers; they represent a continuous journey towards a more inclusive and equitable society.

In conclusion, celebrating the milestones of Paula Lupi's activism is about recognizing the intersections of identity, the power of community, and the importance of advocacy. Her achievements have laid the groundwork for ongoing efforts in the LGBTQ and disability rights movements, reminding us that while progress has been made, the journey is far from over. Paula's legacy will continue to inspire and empower those who dare to dream of a world where everyone, regardless of their identity, can live freely and authentically.

Embracing the spirit of Paula's passion and determination

Paula Lupi's journey as an activist was not merely a series of events; it was a vibrant tapestry woven from threads of passion, resilience, and an unwavering commitment to justice. To embrace the spirit of her activism is to understand the depth of her determination and the transformative power it held not only for herself but for countless others who found strength in her voice.

At the core of Paula's activism was a profound belief in the power of community. She often articulated the idea that "together we rise," a mantra that resonated deeply within the LGBTQ and disability rights movements. This notion aligns with the theory of collective efficacy, which posits that individuals who believe in their collective power are more likely to engage in activism and drive social change. According to Bandura (1997), collective efficacy can enhance motivation and foster resilience, enabling groups to overcome obstacles that may seem insurmountable. Paula embodied this principle, rallying individuals from diverse backgrounds to unite in their fight for equality.

Her passion was not just about advocacy; it was also about storytelling. Paula understood that narratives have the power to change hearts and minds. She often shared her own experiences of discrimination and resilience, illustrating the intersectionality of her identity as a queer disabled woman. By doing so, she highlighted the complexities of oppression and the necessity of inclusive dialogue. This approach echoes the work of scholars like Crenshaw (1989), who emphasized the importance of intersectionality in understanding the multifaceted nature of discrimination. Paula's ability to articulate her experiences not only validated the struggles of others but also inspired them to share their stories, creating a ripple effect of empowerment.

Moreover, Paula's determination was evident in her relentless pursuit of policy changes that would benefit marginalized communities. She recognized that systemic barriers required systemic solutions. For instance, her advocacy led to the implementation of inclusive education policies that addressed the needs of LGBTQ and disabled students. This effort was grounded in the theory of social justice education, which advocates for an equitable educational environment where all students can thrive (Freire, 1970). By working within the political framework, Paula demonstrated that passion must be coupled with strategic action to effect real change.

However, Paula's path was not without challenges. She faced significant backlash, both from those who opposed her views and from within the communities she sought to uplift. This adversity, rather than deterring her, fueled her determination. Paula often reflected on the importance of resilience in activism, stating, "Every setback is a setup for a comeback." This perspective aligns with the psychological resilience theory, which suggests that individuals can develop the capacity to bounce back from adversity (Masten, 2001). Paula's ability to transform challenges into opportunities for growth is a testament to her indomitable spirit.

In embracing Paula's legacy, we must also recognize the importance of mentorship and support within activist circles. Paula dedicated much of her time to mentoring young activists, believing that nurturing the next generation was essential for the sustainability of the movement. This commitment reflects the theory of social capital, which posits that networks of relationships among people enhance cooperation for mutual benefit (Putnam, 2000). By fostering connections and providing guidance, Paula not only empowered individuals but also strengthened the collective movement for LGBTQ and disability rights.

Ultimately, to embrace the spirit of Paula Lupi is to carry forward her passion and determination in our own lives. It is about recognizing the power of our voices, the strength of our communities, and the necessity of resilience in the face of adversity. As we continue to advocate for justice, let us remember Paula's words: "We are the change we seek." By embodying her spirit, we honor her legacy and contribute to a world that is more inclusive, equitable, and just for all.

$$\text{Collective Efficacy} = \text{Belief in Group's Ability} \times \text{Motivation to Act} \qquad (117)$$

$$\text{Resilience} = \text{Adaptation to Adversity} + \text{Growth from Challenges} \qquad (118)$$

$$\text{Social Capital} = \text{Networks} + \text{Trust} + \text{Reciprocity} \qquad (119)$$

The challenges of living up to Paula's legacy

Living up to the legacy of a figure as impactful as Paula Lupi is no small feat. Her life and work set a high bar for activism, advocacy, and personal integrity, creating a complex tapestry of expectations that can be both inspiring and daunting for future generations. The challenges associated with this endeavor can be categorized into several key areas: the weight of expectations, the nuances of intersectionality, the risks of burnout, and the necessity of continual growth and adaptation.

The Weight of Expectations

The first challenge lies in the immense weight of expectations that Paula's legacy imposes on aspiring activists. Paula was not just a voice for LGBTQ and disability rights; she was a trailblazer who redefined what it meant to advocate for marginalized communities. The pressure to replicate her success can lead to feelings of inadequacy among those who follow in her footsteps.

For instance, younger activists may feel compelled to achieve the same level of visibility and impact that Paula had, often measuring their worth against her achievements. This can create a culture of comparison that stifles individuality and innovation. As noted by social psychologist Carol Dweck, such a fixed mindset can hinder personal growth and discourage risk-taking, which are essential components of effective activism.

The Nuances of Intersectionality

Another significant challenge is navigating the complexities of intersectionality within Paula's legacy. While Paula championed the rights of both LGBTQ individuals and those with disabilities, the intersection of these identities is often fraught with unique challenges that require nuanced understanding and advocacy.

For example, the experiences of a queer disabled person may differ vastly from those of a non-disabled LGBTQ individual. Activists must be vigilant in addressing these differences to ensure that their work is truly inclusive. Kimberlé Crenshaw's theory of intersectionality emphasizes that individuals experience overlapping systems of discrimination, and failing to acknowledge these intersections can lead to the marginalization of already vulnerable groups.

The Risks of Burnout

The risk of burnout is another critical issue that activists face when attempting to live up to Paula's legacy. The emotional toll of advocacy work, especially in the face of persistent societal resistance, can be overwhelming. Paula's relentless pursuit of justice serves as a reminder of the dedication required, but it also highlights the potential for exhaustion.

Research by the American Psychological Association indicates that chronic stress from activism can lead to burnout, characterized by emotional exhaustion, depersonalization, and a reduced sense of accomplishment. Future activists must learn to balance their passion for advocacy with self-care practices to sustain their efforts over the long term. This balance is essential not only for personal well-being but also for maintaining the momentum of the movements they represent.

The Necessity of Continual Growth and Adaptation

Finally, the necessity of continual growth and adaptation presents a challenge for those looking to uphold Paula's legacy. The social and political landscapes are constantly changing, and what worked in Paula's time may not be effective today. Activists must be willing to engage in lifelong learning, adapting their strategies to meet the needs of contemporary issues.

An example of this is the rise of digital activism, which has transformed how movements organize and mobilize. While Paula utilized traditional methods of advocacy, such as protests and community organizing, today's activists must navigate social media platforms and online campaigns to reach broader audiences. This requires not only technical skills but also an understanding of how digital spaces can both empower and exploit marginalized voices.

Conclusion

In conclusion, living up to Paula Lupi's legacy involves navigating a complex array of challenges, from the weight of expectations to the necessity of continual adaptation. Future activists must honor her memory while forging their paths, embracing both the struggles and triumphs that come with the pursuit of justice. By doing so, they can ensure that Paula's legacy not only endures but also evolves, inspiring new generations to advocate for a more inclusive world.

A world without Paula's voice – the impact on LGBTQ and disability advocacy

The absence of Paula Lupi's voice in the realms of LGBTQ and disability advocacy would undoubtedly create a significant void, one that echoes through the corridors of social justice and equality. Paula's unique intersectionality as a queer disabled woman provided a multifaceted perspective that was instrumental in shaping both local and international discourse on rights and representation. In her absence, the advocacy landscape would face several theoretical and practical challenges, ultimately impacting the progress made in these intertwined movements.

To understand the potential ramifications, we must first consider the theoretical framework of intersectionality, as articulated by Kimberlé Crenshaw. Intersectionality posits that individuals experience oppression in varying degrees based on their overlapping identities, including but not limited to race, gender, sexuality, and ability. Paula's advocacy exemplified this concept, as she consistently highlighted the need for policies that address the unique challenges faced by those at the intersection of multiple marginalized identities. Without her voice, the nuanced understanding of intersectionality may be lost, leading to a homogenized approach to advocacy that fails to consider the complexities of lived experiences.

For instance, consider the ongoing struggle for inclusive healthcare. Paula's work included advocating for healthcare policies that recognized the specific needs of LGBTQ individuals with disabilities. In a world without her contributions, the dialogue around healthcare access may revert to a more simplistic framework that does not account for the unique barriers faced by disabled queer individuals. This could result in policies that are ineffective or even harmful, as they overlook the essential needs of the most marginalized within the LGBTQ community.

Moreover, Paula's absence would likely hinder the momentum of grassroots movements that she helped to galvanize. Her ability to mobilize communities and create coalitions between various advocacy groups was unparalleled. The loss of her leadership would mean that many initiatives aimed at fostering solidarity and collaboration among diverse movements might falter. For example, the annual Pride events that Paula championed as platforms for intersectional advocacy could lose their focus on inclusivity, becoming mere celebrations devoid of the political urgency that she instilled in them.

In addition, the educational initiatives Paula spearheaded would suffer without her influence. Her commitment to educating future generations of activists about the importance of intersectionality and inclusive practices was crucial in shaping a new wave of leaders. Without her mentorship and guidance, young activists may lack the tools necessary to navigate the complex landscape of advocacy, potentially leading to a generation that is less equipped to address the multifaceted issues within LGBTQ and disability rights.

The theoretical implications extend to the broader societal understanding of disability within the LGBTQ context. Paula's advocacy brought visibility to the challenges faced by disabled individuals in the LGBTQ community, such as discrimination, accessibility issues, and social stigma. In her absence, these critical conversations may be sidelined, resulting in a lack of representation and advocacy for disabled queer individuals. This could perpetuate the cycle of marginalization, as their voices would be further silenced in a movement that is already fraught with challenges.

Furthermore, the impact of Paula's absence would resonate in the media representation of LGBTQ and disability issues. She was a powerful figure who utilized her platform to amplify the voices of others, ensuring that marginalized narratives were told. Without her, the media landscape may revert to more traditional and less inclusive portrayals of LGBTQ individuals, overlooking the complexities of disability. This would not only affect public perception but also influence policy discussions and funding allocations for advocacy initiatives.

In conclusion, a world without Paula Lupi's voice would not only diminish the richness of LGBTQ and disability advocacy but would also pose significant challenges to the progress achieved thus far. The intersectional framework that she championed would risk being diluted, grassroots movements could lose their momentum, and the next generation of activists may lack the necessary guidance to navigate the complexities of advocacy. Ultimately, Paula's legacy serves as a reminder of the vital role that diverse voices play in the ongoing fight for equality and justice, and her absence would leave an indelible mark on the landscape of social advocacy.

$$\text{Advocacy Impact} = f(\text{Intersectionality, Coalition Building, Education, Media Representation}) \tag{120}$$

Where:

- Intersectionality = Understanding of diverse identities
- Coalition Building = Collaboration among various movements
- Education = Mentorship and training of future activists
- Media Representation = Visibility of marginalized voices

Paula's lasting impact on the hearts and minds of millions

Paula Lupi's journey as an LGBTQ and disability rights activist has left an indelible mark on the hearts and minds of millions, transcending borders and inspiring countless individuals to embrace their identities and fight for equality. Her impact can be understood through several key dimensions: personal empowerment, community mobilization, and systemic change.

Personal Empowerment

At the core of Paula's legacy is her unwavering commitment to personal empowerment. She believed that self-acceptance is the foundation of activism.

Through her own journey of embracing her identity as a queer disabled woman, Paula demonstrated that authenticity is a powerful tool for change. Her story resonated with many, particularly those struggling with their identities. As she often stated, "When we accept ourselves, we ignite a fire within that cannot be extinguished." This philosophy inspired individuals to confront their fears and embrace their true selves, leading to a ripple effect of empowerment within marginalized communities.

The psychological impact of Paula's advocacy can be analyzed through the lens of *self-determination theory*, which posits that individuals are motivated to grow and change by three innate needs: competence, autonomy, and relatedness [?]. Paula's message of self-acceptance fostered a sense of competence among her followers, encouraging them to take ownership of their narratives and advocate for their rights.

Community Mobilization

Paula's activism catalyzed community mobilization on an unprecedented scale. By organizing protests, workshops, and awareness campaigns, she created spaces for dialogue and collective action. Her ability to build coalitions among diverse groups—LGBTQ individuals, disabled activists, and allies—showcased the power of intersectionality in activism.

The concept of *collective efficacy*, defined as a group's shared belief in its ability to achieve goals, was a driving force behind Paula's initiatives [?]. Her charisma and leadership inspired communities to unite and advocate for systemic change. One notable example was the annual Lisbon Pride Parade, which, under Paula's influence, transformed from a small gathering into one of the largest celebrations of LGBTQ rights in Europe. This event not only raised awareness but also fostered a sense of belonging and solidarity among participants.

Systemic Change

Paula's activism extended beyond grassroots efforts; she aimed for systemic change through policy advocacy. Her work in the political arena focused on ensuring that LGBTQ and disability rights were prioritized in legislation. By challenging discriminatory laws and advocating for inclusive policies, Paula laid the groundwork for a more equitable society.

The *theory of change* provides a framework for understanding Paula's approach to activism. This theory posits that social change occurs through a series of interconnected steps, including awareness, engagement, and action [?]. Paula effectively moved communities through these stages, raising awareness about the struggles faced by LGBTQ and disabled individuals, engaging them in advocacy efforts, and ultimately driving legislative change. Her role in the passage of the Equality Act in Portugal serves as a testament to her impact, as it enshrined protections for LGBTQ individuals and ensured accessibility for disabled citizens.

Global Influence

Paula's influence was not limited to Portugal; her voice resonated globally. By representing Portugal at international conferences, she amplified the struggles of LGBTQ and disabled individuals worldwide. Her speeches often highlighted the interconnectedness of various social justice movements, urging activists to work collaboratively towards a common goal of equality.

The *globalization of social movements* theory suggests that local movements can gain international traction, influencing policies and practices across borders [?]. Paula's ability to connect with activists from different cultures and backgrounds exemplified this theory. Her collaborations with organizations such as ILGA (International Lesbian, Gay, Bisexual, Trans and Intersex Association) helped to elevate the voices of marginalized groups on a global stage, creating a network of solidarity that transcended national boundaries.

Legacy of Hope

Paula Lupi's legacy is one of hope, resilience, and unwavering commitment to justice. Her impact continues to inspire new generations of activists who carry forward her message of empowerment and inclusivity. The stories of individuals she touched serve as a testament to her influence—people who once felt isolated and marginalized now stand proud in their identities, advocating for change in their communities.

As we reflect on Paula's lasting impact, it becomes clear that her work was not merely about achieving legal rights; it was about transforming hearts and minds. Her ability to connect with individuals on a personal level, coupled with her strategic approach to activism, created a lasting legacy that will continue to inspire and empower for generations to come.

In conclusion, Paula Lupi's impact on the hearts and minds of millions is a multifaceted phenomenon that encompasses personal empowerment, community mobilization, systemic change, and global influence. Her legacy serves as a powerful reminder that one person's voice can indeed change the world, igniting a collective movement towards a more inclusive and equitable society.

Index

-doubt, 27, 67–69, 73, 88, 214

a, 1–13, 15–17, 19–37, 39, 41–47, 49–58, 60–64, 66, 69–85, 87–92, 94, 96–102, 104, 105, 107–111, 114–123, 125–129, 131–151, 153–157, 159, 160, 162, 163, 165–168, 170–173, 176–180, 182, 184, 185, 187–193, 195, 197–202, 204, 206, 207, 209–215, 219, 221, 223–229, 231, 234–237, 239–247, 249, 251–253, 255–273, 275–300
abandonment, 50
ability, 20, 33, 50, 77, 82, 94, 96, 99, 107, 108, 111, 117, 119, 128, 129, 131, 134, 151, 172, 180, 190, 206, 211, 231, 242, 251, 268, 281, 288, 289, 297, 300
ableism, 70, 83, 115, 243
absence, 255, 296–298
academia, 43, 45–47, 204, 206
acceptance, 5, 7, 8, 10, 11, 13, 16, 20, 21, 27–29, 32, 46, 51–57, 67–70, 126, 138, 149, 152, 160, 189, 226, 235, 241, 242, 252, 276, 281–283, 285, 286, 290, 298
access, 35, 41, 47, 55, 81, 83, 110, 111, 122, 123, 141, 177, 182, 195, 197, 206, 210, 252, 279, 284, 297
accessibility, 43, 47, 50, 91, 98, 115, 188, 244, 252, 261, 276, 279, 297
accomplishment, 45, 296
account, 297
accountability, 155, 167, 224, 260, 280
accuracy, 150
achievement, 44, 45, 291, 292
acknowledgment, 143, 206, 211
act, 1, 23, 53, 78, 129, 140, 142, 170, 223, 236, 255, 272
action, 1, 3, 8, 9, 24, 32, 44, 74, 76, 78, 85, 87, 92, 94, 102, 131, 142, 146, 150, 159, 166, 180–182, 198, 202, 211, 215, 223, 225, 243, 252, 253, 278, 281, 282, 288, 289, 291
activism, 1–11, 13, 15, 17, 19–22,

24, 26–28, 30–32, 34, 35, 44–49, 54–58, 62–66, 69, 71–73, 75–77, 79–81, 83, 84, 89, 90, 92, 94, 97, 100, 101, 109, 114, 116, 117, 119, 125–127, 129, 131, 134, 140–145, 149–151, 153, 157, 159, 162, 163, 165, 167, 170–173, 177, 180, 182, 193, 198, 199, 201, 202, 205, 211–213, 215, 219, 221, 223, 225–227, 229–231, 235, 236, 238–240, 242–245, 247, 251, 253, 255–263, 265, 266, 268–270, 273, 275, 276, 278, 281, 282, 285–296, 298–300
activist, 3, 6, 8, 19, 20, 24, 28, 31, 34, 51, 57, 64, 68, 75, 78, 87, 89, 110, 145, 147, 155, 171, 172, 176, 182, 200, 202, 204, 211, 219, 230, 234, 236, 240, 244, 255, 257–260, 262, 264–266, 270, 272, 273, 280–282, 293, 298
adaptability, 191, 270
adaptation, 295, 296
addition, 34, 215, 228, 297
address, 24, 41, 55, 65, 77, 83, 84, 86, 87, 91, 105, 108, 116, 133, 136, 138, 171, 178, 183, 188, 189, 201, 209, 210, 214, 223, 226, 245, 252, 256, 263, 265, 271, 278, 280, 283, 297
adoption, 72, 74
adult, 50

advancement, 195
adventure, 228
adversity, 5, 28, 29, 44, 79, 82, 96, 156, 182, 236, 240, 258, 278–281
advocacy, 1, 3, 4, 7–10, 12, 17, 20–25, 28–30, 32–37, 43, 45, 47, 55–57, 62, 64, 69–73, 75–78, 80, 82–87, 89, 91, 96, 98, 99, 102, 104, 105, 107, 109, 111, 113, 114, 116–119, 125, 127–129, 131, 133–136, 138–140, 142, 145, 146, 149, 150, 154, 156, 157, 159, 160, 163, 170–172, 176–180, 182, 184, 185, 187, 189, 190, 192, 195, 201, 204, 207, 209–211, 213, 215, 224–227, 240, 245, 249, 251–253, 256, 257, 260–267, 270, 272, 273, 276, 278–282, 284, 289–299
advocate, 1, 3, 5–7, 9, 11–13, 17, 19, 20, 24, 28, 31–35, 43, 45, 46, 55, 58, 72, 76, 80–82, 87, 88, 90, 92, 94, 97, 101, 102, 107, 111, 115, 117, 129, 139, 145, 147, 151, 153, 155, 165, 168, 229, 231, 242, 243, 245, 268, 270, 273, 279, 287, 290, 295, 296
affordability, 83
Africa, 1
age, 1, 8, 22, 27, 33, 69, 146, 147, 159, 163, 166, 168, 172, 181, 227, 252

Index

agency, 159
agenda, 140, 154, 279
Aldina Duarte, 2
Algarve, 228
alienation, 10, 77
alignment, 57
all, 3, 6, 8, 21, 24, 28, 35, 37, 47, 71, 78, 84, 87, 90–92, 102, 104, 107, 108, 136–138, 140, 155, 160, 176, 179, 188–190, 202, 206, 210, 226, 235, 244, 251–253, 262–264, 273, 278–280, 282, 283, 286, 289, 291
alliance, 91
ally, 20, 99
Allyship, 43, 277
allyship, 56, 111, 224, 261, 262, 278
ambassador, 207–209
ambassadorship, 208
ambition, 101, 102
amplification, 142
analysis, 120
anger, 8
Ann Masten, 281
antidiscrimination, 233
anxiety, 89
appearance, 8, 148, 166
applause, 176
appreciation, 167
approach, 35, 44, 47, 51, 68, 72, 82–84, 87, 89–92, 98, 108, 114, 116, 136–138, 142, 145, 155, 159, 171, 179, 180, 182, 185, 187, 197, 213, 223, 229, 240, 243, 244, 253, 258, 261–263, 267, 268, 271, 272, 275, 279–282, 284, 286, 287, 297, 300
appropriation, 141, 143
architecture, 15
area, 16, 85, 99, 134, 275
arena, 97, 100, 102, 108, 109, 114, 116, 117, 122, 226, 299
aroma, 4
array, 252, 296
art, 1, 2, 5, 7, 10, 13, 15–17, 20, 28, 147, 228, 229, 246, 290
article, 154
artist, 7, 20
artwork, 16, 20, 228
ascent, 122, 157
aspect, 16, 17, 58, 64, 87, 129, 141, 151, 201, 214, 242, 251, 288
aspiration, 37, 284
assembly, 8
assertion, 128
atmosphere, 1, 4, 6, 54, 214
attachment, 50
attack, 272
attempt, 74
attention, 35, 47, 98, 111, 133, 147, 149, 165, 182, 201, 210, 212, 244, 275
audience, 22, 127, 148, 159, 166, 172, 209, 211, 259, 268, 270
Audre Lorde, 34
austerity, 178
authenticity, 5, 20, 53, 108, 150, 159, 214, 244, 247, 268, 270, 299
author, 273
authority, 115, 119
avenue, 13

awakening, 11
award, 211
awareness, 3, 5, 8, 9, 20, 22, 24, 28, 32, 33, 35, 43, 55, 56, 70, 72, 75, 77, 84, 91, 101, 111, 134, 136, 149, 151, 165, 166, 172, 177, 179, 181, 182, 192, 198, 226, 240, 242, 244, 247, 252, 275, 282, 288, 290
azulejos, 4

backdrop, 1, 4, 8, 9, 25
background, 20, 117, 241, 287
backing, 111, 124, 166
backlash, 34, 73, 79, 82, 87–89, 103, 108, 113, 116, 126, 132, 135, 155, 167, 171, 176, 205, 226, 262, 269, 279, 281
Bairro Alto, 54
Baixa, 3
balance, 160, 172, 182, 212, 213, 229, 231, 233, 240, 260, 267, 296
balancing, 58, 171, 236
bar, 294
barrage, 88
barrier, 47
bastion, 41
bathroom, 178
battle, 29, 105
battleground, 114
beacon, 61, 75, 80, 122, 129, 243, 282, 287, 291
beauty, 74, 228, 234
bedrock, 281
beginning, 45, 47, 102
behavior, 3, 8, 212

being, 1, 8, 10, 53, 57, 64, 70, 74, 98, 108, 111, 114, 116, 117, 149, 155, 162, 167, 170, 172, 176, 182, 189, 199, 209, 211–214, 231, 238, 241, 247, 255, 256, 269, 272, 281, 296, 298
belief, 7, 21, 22, 35, 44, 47, 53, 69, 70, 90, 102, 128, 142, 146, 235, 282
belonging, 5, 10, 16, 54–56, 70, 73, 76, 150, 214, 241, 242, 245, 247, 281
benefit, 121, 204, 223, 279
Berlin, 127
biography, 255–258, 275
blend, 1
blink, 147
blueprint, 200, 215
bodiedness, 28
body, 43
bond, 7, 20, 234, 244
Bourdieu, 20
bravery, 1
Brazil, 1, 140, 141
break, 186
breaking, 187
breeding, 184
bridge, 56, 149, 272, 279, 282, 289
builder, 282
building, 17, 79, 82, 89–91, 94, 96, 99, 104, 110, 111, 116, 140, 142, 152, 180, 182, 193, 197, 200, 225, 236, 258, 261, 273, 286, 291
bullying, 4, 8, 23, 27, 55, 74, 246, 285
burden, 51, 139
burnout, 53, 172, 182, 295, 296

Index

call, 102, 122, 127, 177, 202, 253, 263, 282, 289
camera, 152
campaign, 8, 35, 72, 77, 91, 97–99, 102, 104, 108, 124, 139, 154, 166, 167, 212, 231, 269, 279
campus, 43
candidacy, 102–104, 107
canvas, 5, 228
capital, 20, 64, 168, 212, 223, 225
care, 41, 168–170, 172, 182, 213, 229, 231, 236, 237, 247, 252, 296
career, 116, 176, 204, 257, 288
Carol Dweck, 295
case, 10, 28, 31, 72, 76, 83, 110, 140, 210, 255, 256, 271
catalyst, 2, 9, 11, 13, 29, 33, 45, 78, 89, 96, 104, 129, 149, 177, 182, 204, 213, 215, 258, 269, 272, 278
cause, 73, 79, 89, 92, 99, 127, 131, 182, 229, 230, 244, 292
celebration, 45, 149, 251
celebrity, 212
challenge, 5, 6, 11–13, 20, 21, 33, 41, 45, 49, 70, 72, 75, 90, 92, 94, 103, 117, 135, 143, 146, 153, 154, 162, 167, 170, 181, 224, 226, 229, 253, 255, 258, 263, 275, 278, 282, 286, 295, 296
champion, 21, 121
change, 3, 5, 9, 11, 13, 21, 29, 33, 35, 43, 45–47, 49, 55, 66, 73, 76, 78, 80, 82, 84, 89, 91, 94, 96, 97, 99–102, 104, 108, 109, 111, 114, 126, 127, 129, 131, 134–136, 138, 142, 146, 149, 151, 154, 165, 170, 173, 179, 180, 182, 184, 185, 189, 190, 193, 195, 201, 211, 215, 219, 221, 223–225, 229, 242, 243, 252, 265, 269, 270, 278, 281, 282, 284, 285, 287, 288, 298–300
channel, 5
chaos, 227, 247
chapter, 45, 56, 97, 102, 255, 257, 258
character, 1, 4
charge, 264
charm, 54
check, 260
child, 4, 287
childhood, 1–4, 6, 25, 227, 243, 281
circle, 56, 281
cisgender, 83, 90, 264, 265, 276
city, 1, 3–5, 8, 9, 15, 21, 27, 33, 54, 74, 241
clarion, 122
class, 46, 178, 180, 256, 263, 287
classmate, 1, 8
classroom, 46, 49
clean, 1
climate, 91, 97, 101
coalition, 89, 96, 99, 104, 109, 140, 182, 261
cobblestone, 3, 9, 80
collaboration, 21, 44, 47, 77, 89–91, 108, 109, 118, 127–129, 141, 143, 144, 146, 159, 182, 190, 192, 207, 210–212, 215, 253, 258, 262, 263, 267, 272, 273,

279, 280, 282, 291, 297
collective, 9, 20, 22, 35, 44, 47, 64, 76–78, 80, 91, 92, 94, 105, 109, 127, 131, 142, 147, 150, 166, 171, 179–181, 192, 199, 201, 206, 215, 223, 225, 240, 246, 247, 251, 257, 260, 273, 278–282, 284, 287–289, 300
collide, 3
color, 83, 90, 244, 263–265
combat, 68, 70, 73, 103, 108, 121, 152, 158, 169, 204, 237
combination, 3, 80, 114, 241
comfort, 5, 227
commemoration, 249, 251
commitment, 1, 3, 7–9, 20, 24, 25, 29, 32, 35, 44–49, 55–57, 73, 76, 77, 82, 84, 87, 89, 91, 96, 100, 102, 105, 109, 116, 117, 119, 126, 129, 136, 140, 142, 146, 154–156, 167, 168, 179, 181, 182, 184, 190, 192, 195, 201, 202, 204, 206, 207, 209, 210, 213, 215, 219, 221, 223, 225, 227, 228, 230, 244, 247, 251, 258, 260, 262, 263, 272, 273, 278–282, 284, 287, 289, 291–293, 297, 298
commodification, 143
communication, 51, 58, 89, 121, 191, 235
community, 2–13, 16, 17, 20, 22, 24, 27, 30, 32, 34, 35, 43, 44, 49, 51, 54–58, 64, 66, 69–81, 83, 85, 87, 90–92, 98, 102, 111, 113–116, 120, 127, 128, 136, 140, 142, 146, 150, 154–156, 159, 160, 162, 168, 171, 172, 180, 181, 187, 192, 193, 195, 197, 199, 200, 204, 205, 215, 224, 226, 228, 229, 237–241, 243–247, 251, 252, 256, 258, 261–263, 266–271, 273, 278–282, 284, 286, 288–291, 293, 296–298, 300
companionship, 235
company, 111, 166
comparison, 295
compass, 26
compassion, 6, 7, 9
competency, 252
competition, 90, 92, 143
complexity, 69, 71, 83, 152, 190, 256, 261, 263
component, 111, 131, 149, 193, 235, 251, 283, 288
concept, 10, 20, 22, 23, 33, 39, 40, 46, 159, 223, 262, 276, 281, 282, 297
conclusion, 9, 11, 13, 24, 26, 29, 33, 35, 43, 45, 47, 49, 52, 56, 57, 64, 71, 73, 75, 82, 84, 87, 89, 91, 94, 96, 100, 104, 107, 109, 111, 114, 116, 129, 131, 134, 138, 142, 146, 162, 165, 167, 170, 173, 179, 182, 184, 190, 192, 202, 204, 206, 210, 213, 215, 221, 225, 227, 229, 236, 240, 243, 253, 260, 262, 263, 270,

275, 278, 280, 282, 289, 291, 292, 296, 298, 300
confidence, 51, 108
conflict, 4, 10, 11, 57, 77, 126, 154, 241, 278
conformity, 21
confrontation, 79, 129, 244
confusion, 5, 241
connection, 10, 19, 50, 51, 57, 58, 64, 70, 229, 236
consciousness, 33, 45, 184, 185, 198
consent, 141, 255, 273
consideration, 258
constructivism, 21, 22
contemporary, 1, 105, 180, 188, 260, 282, 285, 286, 296
content, 152, 158, 159
context, 9, 22, 57, 127, 143, 149, 151, 157, 177, 207, 234, 241, 251, 256, 257, 259, 262, 265, 271, 275, 278, 297
contingent, 267
contrast, 7, 136
control, 268
controversy, 176, 257
conversation, 210, 262, 265
conviction, 88
cooking, 229
cooperation, 138, 201
core, 1, 83, 114, 223, 287, 298
cornerstone, 16, 30, 34, 35, 47, 66, 76, 80, 101, 142, 184
corporation, 265
council, 8
counseling, 41
counter, 79, 88, 117
country, 127, 225

courage, 9, 11, 12, 34, 55, 89, 105, 134, 142, 146, 247, 278
coverage, 149
creation, 70, 123, 159, 187
creative, 2, 17, 20, 28
creativity, 4, 75
credibility, 34, 88, 99, 103, 108, 111, 115, 117, 121, 126, 155, 160, 255, 259, 260, 265
Crenshaw, 23, 77
crescendo, 170
criminalization, 135
crisis, 140
criticism, 77, 126, 154, 171, 206, 256, 259, 261, 262, 267, 269, 271–273
critique, 233, 259, 262
crucible, 31
cruelty, 23
cry, 82
culmination, 6, 44, 82, 102
cultivation, 197
culture, 1, 3–5, 8, 24, 26, 33, 45, 56, 111, 136, 143, 155, 172, 215, 225, 241, 253, 260, 273, 286, 295
curiosity, 27
currency, 270
current, 121, 177, 179, 291
curricula, 32, 41, 123, 183–185, 226, 252, 283, 286, 288, 290
curriculum, 43
cycle, 297

dance, 104
danger, 259
dating, 70, 243
David Carreira, 2

debate, 108, 275
decision, 97, 100–103, 110, 252, 272, 281
declaration, 281
dedication, 49, 76, 82, 146, 190, 202, 204, 206, 224, 229, 268, 280, 295
defiance, 78
deficit, 135
democracy, 107, 116
demonstration, 79, 80, 270
depersonalization, 296
depth, 293
description, 233
desirability, 234
desire, 3, 11, 28, 56, 100, 103, 255
despair, 74, 246
destination, 273, 282
determination, 17, 24, 44, 64, 70, 81, 89, 104, 110, 253, 293
development, 2, 5, 6, 22, 26, 32, 45, 108, 123, 183, 200, 269
dialogue, 8, 20, 54, 56, 68, 72, 75, 79, 80, 110, 119, 121, 124, 126, 141, 155, 159, 160, 171, 206, 244, 258, 260, 263, 267, 268, 273, 278–280, 284, 290, 292, 297
dichotomy, 57, 257, 260
dignity, 35, 74, 259, 289
diploma, 45
diplomacy, 136–138, 207
disability, 3, 6, 7, 9, 10, 13, 20, 22, 28, 31, 34, 35, 39–41, 43–47, 49–51, 54–56, 60, 64, 66, 69–71, 73, 74, 76–79, 82–89, 91, 92, 94, 96–98, 100–103, 105–108, 111, 113, 114, 116–120, 126–129, 131, 134–136, 138–140, 142, 145, 147–149, 151–154, 156, 157, 160, 163, 165–167, 171–173, 176–180, 182–185, 187, 188, 190, 192, 193, 195, 197, 200–202, 204, 207, 209–211, 213, 215, 216, 219, 221, 223–227, 230, 231, 234, 236, 240, 242–247, 249, 251, 253, 256–263, 266–273, 275, 276, 278–280, 282, 283, 285–291, 293, 295–299
disadvantage, 178, 256
discomfort, 10
disconnect, 262
discourse, 84, 101, 107, 115, 129, 182, 255, 296
discovery, 2, 4, 9, 11, 15, 32, 35, 45, 53, 54, 56, 72, 240–243, 258
discrimination, 1, 3, 10, 13, 19, 21–23, 29, 32, 39, 41, 43, 55, 60, 66, 69, 74–78, 80–84, 98, 99, 105, 107–109, 114–116, 119, 120, 123, 127, 128, 131, 134, 135, 138, 150, 151, 178, 180, 188, 190, 192, 193, 197, 199, 210, 226, 243, 244, 246, 252, 253, 256, 262, 263, 276, 278, 279, 283–286, 295, 297
discussion, 46, 244, 275
disempowerment, 275
disillusionment, 182, 256

Index 309

dismantling, 69, 78, 84, 117, 188, 195, 252
disorder, 233
disparity, 57, 137, 262, 264
dissent, 25, 261
dissolution, 57
dissonance, 10, 70
district, 54
distrust, 271
diversity, 1–3, 8, 9, 11, 19, 21, 25, 27, 32, 35, 42, 45, 46, 54, 70, 77, 116, 121, 142, 149, 150, 152, 153, 195, 228, 256, 257, 261, 263, 265, 283, 286
doctrine, 233
documentary, 159, 172
donation, 166
donor, 167
doubt, 24, 27, 67–69, 73, 88, 214
dream, 252, 293
dropout, 285
dynamic, 1, 4, 54, 165, 179, 204, 212

echo, 240
education, 1, 32, 33, 35–37, 45–47, 49, 55, 71, 72, 88, 100, 109, 126, 146, 160, 181–185, 188–190, 197, 200, 201, 206, 207, 212, 221, 226, 252, 283, 284, 288, 292
educator, 47
effect, 46, 66, 84, 97, 109, 111, 134, 136, 180, 209, 211, 212, 223, 225, 246, 252, 265, 281, 299
effectiveness, 131, 133, 185, 192, 208, 216, 224, 262, 264, 265, 267
efficacy, 180
effort, 21, 108, 109, 147, 201, 235, 273, 278, 282
Einstein, 16
election, 104
element, 26, 197
elitism, 204
eloquence, 82
embrace, 2, 10–12, 17, 34, 52, 53, 55, 61, 70, 75, 114, 123, 228, 229, 235, 240, 241, 243, 258, 265, 270, 280, 281, 283, 289, 293, 298, 299
emergence, 76, 82, 240, 281
empathy, 1, 4, 6–8, 19, 21, 22, 33, 56, 66, 75, 110, 149, 160, 179, 181–183, 189, 252
emphasis, 146
employment, 74, 81, 84, 120, 188, 252, 267
empowerment, 17, 43, 45, 52, 61, 64, 70, 71, 73, 92, 109, 116, 146, 159, 193, 197, 215, 216, 242, 244, 245, 275, 283, 284, 289, 292, 298–300
encounter, 21, 141, 216, 263, 276
encouragement, 4, 7, 12
end, 33, 290
endeavor, 35, 47, 87, 105, 122, 127, 134, 136, 142, 145, 192, 219, 235, 247, 264, 270, 291, 295
endpoint, 45
energy, 16, 54, 181, 267
enforcement, 140, 188
engagement, 4, 10, 12, 22, 23, 32,

35, 49, 56, 92, 104, 119, 121, 149, 160, 168, 172, 173, 177, 181, 182, 187, 192, 204, 241, 251, 275, 278, 282, 288, 290
enhancement, 211
ensuring, 19, 41, 43, 54, 73, 78, 92, 96, 98, 108, 121, 136, 141, 158, 167, 179, 181, 184, 188, 195, 200–202, 204, 221, 223, 225, 244, 252, 253, 259, 260, 262–264, 284, 289, 290, 298, 299
enthusiasm, 97
entity, 4
entry, 76, 122
environment, 1, 4–6, 8–10, 22, 27, 35, 41, 44, 46, 47, 56, 66, 72, 103, 108, 115, 123, 136, 143, 185, 200, 206, 213, 247, 251, 272, 278
equality, 3, 5–7, 11, 22–24, 29, 33–35, 43, 46, 47, 49, 52, 55, 64, 71, 73, 80, 82–84, 87, 89, 100, 102, 105, 107, 109, 112, 113, 117, 119, 134, 136, 139, 140, 142, 143, 146, 149, 165, 168, 172, 179, 180, 182, 184, 190, 198, 200–202, 204, 206, 215, 219, 225, 227, 229, 235, 244, 251, 253, 263, 265, 266, 268, 278, 281, 282, 285, 289–292, 296, 298, 300
equalizer, 45
equation, 9, 16, 23, 24, 32, 40, 55, 76, 84, 101, 102, 107, 114, 115, 120, 128, 131, 134, 145, 150, 176, 179, 185, 188, 198, 199, 204, 211–213, 241–243, 251, 252, 267
equilibrium, 230
equity, 23, 138, 252
equivalence, 16
era, 131, 288
erasure, 251
escape, 28
essence, 9, 55, 73, 255
establishment, 119, 123, 139, 170, 188, 195, 211, 252, 286
Europe, 1
event, 8, 22, 23, 34, 47, 69, 77, 91, 149, 244, 261, 279
evidence, 37, 111
evolution, 97, 127, 257, 291
example, 21, 22, 41, 43, 46, 51, 57, 66, 70, 72, 74, 77, 80, 83, 84, 88–91, 107, 111, 116, 118, 127, 135, 138–141, 143, 159, 181, 182, 192, 201, 210, 226, 231, 244, 245, 251, 256, 259, 261, 263, 265, 269, 270, 272, 276, 279, 288, 290, 295–297
exception, 27
exchange, 16, 240
excitement, 102
exclusion, 4, 27, 28, 115, 279
exhaustion, 295, 296
existence, 17, 53, 252, 280
expectation, 10, 230
experience, 9–11, 16, 20, 21, 24, 27, 39, 47, 55, 56, 69, 71, 74, 77, 83, 84, 98, 104, 105, 114, 117, 119, 128, 134,

140, 145, 150, 190, 226, 231, 246, 247, 261, 263, 276, 281, 282, 295, 297
expertise, 209
exploitation, 143
exploration, 2, 4, 9, 11, 21, 22, 53, 56, 152, 275
exposure, 3, 54
expression, 2, 7, 10, 13, 15, 17, 28, 54, 56, 223, 227, 246, 290
extension, 233
extremist, 121
eye, 155, 275

fabric, 33, 236, 273
face, 1, 2, 5, 10, 28, 29, 44, 57, 77, 79, 83, 84, 89, 96, 105, 107, 129, 132, 135, 138, 156, 159, 168, 171, 177, 182, 185, 187, 199, 240, 245, 246, 252, 258, 260, 263, 276, 278–281, 295, 296
facet, 11
fact, 128
factor, 53
faculty, 43, 44
Fado, 5, 15
failure, 74, 270
fairness, 22, 23
familiarity, 50
family, 1, 3, 4, 6–10, 26, 34, 50, 56, 57, 213, 230, 231, 233, 281
father, 7
fatigue, 233
favor, 271, 279
fear, 4, 5, 10, 11, 57, 70, 76, 108, 235, 251, 284
feat, 294

feedback, 224, 270, 272
feeling, 8, 10, 46, 214
fellow, 19, 23, 32, 51, 128, 172, 234, 244
feminist, 82, 90, 233
fight, 6, 7, 20, 28, 33–35, 43, 45–47, 49, 55, 64, 66, 73, 78, 80, 82, 87, 90–92, 96, 100, 105, 109, 114, 117, 119, 127, 131, 134, 136, 142–144, 146, 153, 156, 162, 165, 168, 172, 173, 177, 179, 180, 182, 184, 190, 192, 197, 198, 200–202, 204, 206, 209, 219, 225, 229, 235, 236, 240, 244, 247, 253, 260, 268, 270, 278, 282, 285–287, 289–292, 298
fighting, 29, 45, 170, 289
figure, 96, 99, 157, 160, 167, 171, 249, 275, 282, 294, 298
filmmaker, 159
finding, 2, 36, 236, 245
fire, 5, 21, 23, 28, 72, 74, 299
firm, 2, 124
fluidity, 285
focus, 44, 101, 113, 127, 143, 154, 178, 188, 189, 205, 244, 263, 267, 269, 297
following, 40, 76, 159, 176, 211–213, 267
foray, 8, 81
force, 6, 31, 43, 77, 94, 96, 179, 195, 221
forefront, 21, 71, 101, 182, 286
form, 13, 34, 79, 152, 224, 227, 249, 251, 290
formation, 57, 133, 180, 215

formula, 16
formulation, 191
forum, 46, 75, 116, 259
foster, 24, 34, 47, 57, 64, 66, 68, 74, 77, 94, 119, 132, 150, 151, 179, 181, 187, 189, 193, 211, 258, 273, 275, 279, 280, 283, 286, 290
foundation, 1, 3, 6, 13, 20, 24, 50, 90, 117, 127, 138, 202, 252, 298
fragmentation, 92, 279
framework, 20, 23, 34, 35, 39, 46, 84, 108, 114, 119, 131, 134, 140, 178, 195, 252, 263, 264, 283, 297, 298
framing, 121, 154, 159, 257
freedom, 45
Freire, 45
friction, 20, 57
friend, 1, 21, 74
friendship, 19, 20, 50
front, 92, 108, 152, 180, 253, 278, 279
fuel, 4, 7, 82, 116
function, 20, 101, 115, 128, 133, 185, 241
funding, 166, 209, 224, 298
fundraising, 166–168
future, 1–4, 6, 9, 11, 13, 21, 24, 28, 33, 43, 45, 47, 49, 56, 71, 73, 76, 78, 80, 84, 87, 89, 91, 96, 100, 104, 106, 107, 121–123, 127, 131, 140, 142, 160, 165, 173, 179, 182–184, 188, 190, 192, 197–202, 204, 206, 215, 217, 219, 221, 223, 227, 235, 240, 251–253, 262, 264, 270, 273, 280, 282, 284, 287, 289, 292, 295, 297

gain, 20, 110, 111, 118, 269
gap, 30, 56, 149, 183, 271, 272
gathering, 192
gender, 2, 4, 5, 8, 10, 21, 33, 40, 46, 55, 56, 74, 75, 83, 84, 89, 114, 119, 140, 178, 180, 188, 195, 201, 241, 256, 279, 285, 297
generation, 47, 49, 91, 100, 119, 121, 129, 134, 136, 146, 179, 184, 188–190, 197, 200, 201, 209, 213, 215, 221, 226, 253, 288, 290, 297, 298
girl, 34
globe, 147, 285
goal, 76, 142, 143, 253, 300
gold, 24
governance, 107, 122
government, 110, 111, 121, 123
grace, 173
graduation, 45
grant, 224
ground, 25, 184, 281
groundwork, 1, 3, 4, 6, 9, 11, 13, 17, 22, 25, 28, 35, 37, 47, 49, 51, 56, 73, 76, 89, 92, 105, 121, 136, 140, 221, 280, 293, 299
group, 5, 8, 79, 107, 150, 179, 195, 240, 262, 278
growth, 43, 46, 51, 62, 69, 71, 73, 89, 155, 206, 238–240, 242–245, 247, 257, 260,

262, 268–270, 272, 281, 291, 295, 296
guidance, 30, 47, 122, 214, 288, 297, 298

hallmark, 35
hand, 32, 45, 211, 240, 260, 269, 278
happiness, 170
harassment, 55, 74, 155
hardship, 74, 245–247
haven, 4
head, 24, 90, 160, 171, 271
healing, 15, 251, 280
health, 43, 55, 74, 100, 170, 172, 182, 210, 231, 236, 237, 244, 247, 283, 285
healthcare, 41, 55, 71, 74, 79, 81, 83, 98, 110, 111, 120, 123, 178, 188, 190, 195, 197, 210, 244, 252, 263, 266, 269, 279, 283, 284, 297
heart, 1, 4, 9, 119, 280, 282
help, 180, 182
heritage, 5
heterosexuality, 10
highlight, 44, 52, 57, 72, 131, 143, 149, 178, 192, 204, 209, 243, 256, 257, 262, 268, 270, 275, 285, 290
hiking, 228
hindrance, 70
history, 1, 3, 4, 11, 21, 22, 33, 99, 123, 226, 251, 252
home, 1, 10, 111, 127, 225, 227
homophobia, 70, 83
homosexuality, 135, 136, 138
honesty, 51

honor, 71, 202, 211, 251, 275, 278, 282, 289–291, 296
hope, 45, 61, 75, 80, 109, 122, 129, 236, 243, 253, 282, 291, 292
host, 181
hostility, 79, 82, 87–89, 99, 116, 129, 155, 281
housing, 74, 120, 188–190, 252
hue, 80
human, 33–35, 45, 50, 127, 129, 133, 134, 149, 153, 190, 192, 195, 201, 227, 240, 280, 286
humility, 142, 263, 270

icon, 145, 146
idea, 9, 138, 258, 286
ideal, 195, 252
identity, 1, 2, 4–7, 9–13, 15–17, 19–24, 27, 30–37, 39, 41, 44–47, 51, 53, 55–57, 61, 62, 66–73, 76, 77, 82, 83, 98, 101–104, 108, 109, 114, 115, 117, 126, 145, 146, 150, 185, 188, 190, 195, 202, 213, 215, 227–229, 231, 240–244, 246, 251, 256, 259, 262–264, 266, 273, 275, 277, 278, 280, 281, 285, 293, 299
ignorance, 183
image, 265
imbalance, 213
immediacy, 159, 172
immorality, 88
impact, 3, 5, 9, 22, 27, 43, 47, 57, 64–66, 73, 74, 82, 89, 91,

96, 100, 111, 118, 125–127, 129, 131, 134, 140, 146, 149, 159, 162–165, 172, 176, 180, 183, 192, 200, 202, 204, 207, 212, 213, 215, 223, 225, 227, 239, 258, 273, 275, 276, 282, 287, 289–292, 295, 298, 300
imperative, 28, 32, 41, 107, 134, 197, 265, 280, 283
implementation, 43, 108, 140, 189
importance, 2, 4, 5, 7, 9, 12, 20, 22, 23, 32, 34, 35, 43, 47, 51, 53, 55–58, 62, 66, 69–71, 73, 75, 77, 78, 82, 84, 87, 89, 91, 92, 99, 104, 108, 109, 117, 118, 121, 122, 126–128, 134, 138, 140, 146, 148, 150, 152, 156, 158–160, 167, 170, 172, 179, 181, 182, 189, 193, 199, 206, 215, 217, 231, 236, 240–247, 249, 251–253, 256–258, 260, 262–264, 267, 268, 270, 275, 278, 280–284, 286, 288–290, 293, 297
in, 1–13, 15–17, 19–24, 26–30, 32–37, 39, 42–47, 49–57, 62–66, 69–85, 88–91, 94, 96–105, 107–112, 114–125, 127–129, 131, 132, 134–136, 138–146, 148–157, 159, 160, 165–168, 170–173, 177–185, 188–193, 195, 197–202, 204, 206, 207, 209–217, 221, 223–229, 231, 234–237, 240–247, 249, 251–253, 255–263, 265–268, 270–273, 275–283, 285, 286, 288–293, 295–299
inadequacy, 53, 67, 234, 295
incident, 23, 176, 259, 261
inclusion, 11, 13, 33, 46, 85, 116, 128, 140, 160, 291
inclusivity, 7, 8, 17, 35, 41, 43, 70, 71, 77, 98, 100, 107, 111, 116, 121, 131, 152, 160, 176, 187, 195, 197, 201, 202, 205, 225, 227, 244, 251, 252, 256–258, 260–264, 272, 273, 279, 282, 284, 289, 297
incorporation, 226
increase, 211
India, 141
individual, 1, 10, 21, 31, 75, 76, 82–84, 99, 100, 135, 145, 150, 152, 154, 162, 199, 204, 215, 221, 240, 264, 276, 278, 282, 287, 291, 292, 295
individualism, 181, 257
individuality, 1, 295
inequality, 41, 74, 75, 101, 192, 253
inequity, 197
influence, 20, 22, 45, 47, 49, 50, 53, 56, 75, 82, 88, 97, 100, 118, 127, 146, 160, 163, 165, 170, 209, 215, 225–227, 252, 275, 287, 297, 298, 300
information, 147, 198, 270
infringement, 255
initiative, 8, 35, 66, 77, 141, 143,

Index

191, 286
injustice, 1, 3, 49, 80, 278
innovation, 121, 295
insecurity, 189
insight, 20, 247
inspiration, 2, 6, 45, 69, 146, 206, 243, 282, 287, 289
instability, 107
Instagram, 268
instance, 20, 43, 74, 77, 79, 83, 90, 108, 110, 111, 115, 116, 120, 124, 136, 138, 139, 143, 148, 150, 154, 166, 172, 176, 209, 212, 213, 231, 240, 243, 244, 246, 257, 263–267, 270, 275, 276, 279, 280, 292, 295, 297
institution, 43
integration, 107
integrity, 160, 167, 255, 259, 260, 294
intensity, 134, 276
interaction, 181
interconnectedness, 35, 84, 91, 125, 127, 131, 138, 143, 211, 223, 240, 282, 285, 300
interest, 167, 275
interplay, 3, 9, 39, 52, 58, 67, 70, 136, 140, 179, 240, 243, 251, 273
interpretation, 273
intersection, 20, 28, 35, 41, 44, 50, 56, 71, 83, 85, 86, 97, 99, 103, 114, 127, 134–136, 167, 185, 188, 201, 223, 233, 244, 263, 268, 279, 281, 295, 297
intersectionality, 2, 5, 10, 22, 23, 30, 33, 39, 41, 44, 46, 47, 49, 53, 55, 56, 69, 71, 72, 76–78, 83–85, 89–91, 101, 105, 108, 109, 114, 119, 120, 126–129, 134, 136, 138, 140, 144, 154, 155, 171, 172, 177, 179, 180, 187, 190, 195, 206, 211, 215, 223, 225, 239, 243–245, 251, 253, 256, 259–268, 270, 275, 278, 279, 281, 282, 284–287, 289, 290, 295–297
intimacy, 50–52, 56–58, 70
introduction, 127, 178
introspection, 11, 240
investment, 229
invisibility, 263
involvement, 7, 9, 12, 46, 55, 65, 69, 72, 76, 77, 81, 149, 184, 228, 241
isolation, 2, 9, 27, 39, 53, 55, 57, 74, 83, 88, 140, 178, 213, 214, 224, 241, 243, 246, 276
issue, 30, 46, 53, 74, 77, 90, 92, 115, 127, 134, 141, 143, 150, 188, 214, 224, 259, 279, 285, 295

Jack Mezirow, 243
John Rawls, 138
John Rawls's, 22
Johnson, 275
journey, 2, 3, 5, 6, 9–13, 16, 20, 22, 24, 29, 31–36, 39, 43–47, 50–53, 55–58, 62–67, 69–73, 75, 76, 78, 80, 82, 87, 89, 94, 96, 97, 100, 102, 104, 107, 109–111,

113, 116, 117, 119, 122,
125, 127, 129, 131, 138,
140, 145, 146, 149, 156,
160, 165, 170, 177, 188,
190, 197, 200, 202, 206,
209, 213, 219, 221, 224,
226, 227, 229, 231, 235,
236, 238, 240–247, 255,
257, 259, 261, 262, 264,
266, 268–270, 272, 273,
276, 278, 280–282, 287,
290–293, 298, 299
joy, 5, 228, 229, 231
judgment, 4, 57, 70, 235, 284
Judith Butler, 285
Judith Butler's, 241
justice, 1, 3, 4, 6–9, 11, 22–26, 29,
33–35, 44, 45, 47, 51, 52,
57, 64, 71, 73, 75, 80, 82,
84, 87, 89–92, 102, 105,
109, 111, 112, 119, 125,
127, 134, 136, 138, 140,
142–146, 172, 179, 184,
190, 192, 200, 202, 206,
215, 223, 225, 227, 228,
231, 234–236, 243, 251,
253, 260, 268, 270, 278,
280–282, 285, 287,
289–293, 295, 296, 298,
300
juxtaposition, 74

Kimberlé Crenshaw, 10, 23, 39, 46,
69, 105, 114, 119, 134,
138, 140, 178, 180, 190,
223, 256, 262, 276, 281,
282, 297
Kimberlé Crenshaw's, 295
kindness, 8

knowledge, 20, 31, 44–47, 49, 182,
184, 252, 289

lack, 17, 30, 36, 46, 72, 77, 78, 81,
107, 110, 115, 135, 139,
183, 188, 199, 224, 261,
265, 285, 297, 298
landscape, 11, 17, 37, 41, 43, 56, 60,
74, 83, 89, 91, 94, 97–100,
102, 105, 109, 111, 114,
117, 120, 122, 127, 134,
136, 138, 142, 145, 147,
153, 155, 157, 165, 167,
177, 188, 202, 206, 213,
215, 223, 225, 243, 252,
262, 270, 296–298
language, 115, 229
laughter, 45, 54, 229
law, 135, 140
layer, 28
leader, 43, 68, 156, 211, 270
leadership, 8, 77, 91, 107, 197, 199,
200, 215, 252, 265, 292,
297
leap, 102
learning, 32, 36, 45, 155, 181, 184,
198, 226, 242, 243, 257,
269, 270, 273, 281, 282,
296
legacy, 21, 49, 64, 71, 92, 96, 109,
114, 127, 134, 138, 142,
144, 146, 160, 168, 170,
172, 173, 184, 190, 197,
200–202, 204, 211, 213,
215, 219, 223, 225, 227,
236, 253, 258, 270, 278,
280–282, 286–296, 298,
300
legalization, 127

Index 317

legislation, 99–101, 118, 121, 140, 182, 188, 190, 192, 265, 290, 299
lens, 21, 47, 64, 83, 84, 91, 129, 134, 138, 157, 208, 212, 227, 257, 263, 284
lesson, 47
level, 8, 56, 227, 268, 295, 300
leverage, 97, 102, 134, 165
liberation, 33, 179
lie, 280
life, 1, 3, 6–8, 10, 15–17, 20, 21, 28, 33, 45, 47, 51, 54, 56, 64, 73, 100, 102, 107, 111, 122, 123, 125, 154, 156, 170, 172, 188, 212, 213, 215, 219, 221, 227, 229–231, 238, 240, 242, 243, 245, 252, 255, 256, 275, 281, 282, 287, 289–291, 294
lifeline, 62, 163
lifetime, 6, 13, 17, 22, 35, 221
light, 192, 200, 260, 275, 284
limit, 141
limitation, 11
line, 159, 275
Lisbon, 1–6, 9, 15, 17, 21, 24, 26, 27, 33, 45, 54, 73, 80, 110, 240, 241, 280
listening, 16, 20, 84, 117, 263, 273
literature, 2, 233
lobbying, 182
look, 140, 270
loss, 246, 297
love, 1, 3, 6, 7, 9, 17, 51, 53, 60, 67, 70, 139, 235, 236, 242, 281, 282, 290
luck, 147

Lupi, 143
luxury, 231

mainstream, 72, 77, 119, 141, 148, 152, 172, 263, 265, 271
making, 32, 92, 101, 108, 110, 128, 150, 224, 252, 272
Malta, 139
maneuver, 129
mantle, 201
mantra, 73
marginalization, 9, 11, 36, 71, 110, 134, 178, 252, 263, 295, 297
Maria Santos, 46
mark, 6, 83, 173, 213, 298
marriage, 74, 80, 83, 120, 127, 136, 139, 143, 182, 244, 263, 265, 266
Marsha P. Johnson, 275
Martha Nussbaum, 138
matter, 88, 127, 140, 147, 263, 273
mayor, 110
mean, 258, 297
meaning, 20, 30, 143, 285
means, 5, 7, 10, 15, 33, 55, 84, 114, 115, 182, 189, 223, 246, 251, 263, 288–290
measure, 204
mechanism, 94, 131
media, 35, 80, 96, 116, 118, 123, 146–149, 151–154, 157–160, 163–166, 168, 170, 172, 173, 181, 210, 268, 270, 286, 288, 290, 296, 298
medium, 15, 20, 290
meet, 296
meeting, 110

melting, 1
member, 99
membership, 150
memory, 202, 251, 282, 289–291, 296
men, 83, 265
mentor, 46, 47, 126
mentoring, 30
mentorship, 30, 47, 69, 100, 122, 146, 197, 200, 201, 213–217, 221, 245, 253, 288, 289, 297
message, 88, 98, 111, 124, 145, 148, 159, 163, 170, 172, 209, 210, 212, 261
messaging, 269, 272
metaphor, 16
metropolis, 3
microcosm, 21, 27
microscope, 153
midst, 5
Miguel, 20, 74
milestone, 44
mindfulness, 247
mindset, 225, 270, 295
miscommunication, 30
misrepresentation, 141, 151, 154, 211, 256
mission, 13, 127, 148, 166, 270
misunderstanding, 2, 10
mix, 102
mobilization, 77, 111, 134, 168, 181, 270, 289, 298, 300
model, 99, 111, 134, 135, 141, 195, 237, 285, 288
modernity, 3
mold, 28
moment, 1, 21–23, 34, 45, 54, 69, 78, 91, 125, 177, 210, 244

momentum, 12, 98, 177, 179–182, 197, 245, 249, 251, 291, 296–298
mother, 7
motivation, 101
motivator, 235
mourning, 251
move, 97, 195
movement, 12, 35, 64, 76, 79, 83–85, 87, 91, 116, 127, 131, 134, 138, 142–144, 172, 177, 179–182, 204, 219, 227, 249, 256, 262, 263, 265, 268, 270, 273, 275, 278–280, 284–286, 289, 292, 297, 300
multimedia, 75, 172
multiplicity, 278
mural, 290
music, 1, 2, 4, 5, 7, 15–17, 28, 54, 227, 228, 246
myriad, 50, 73, 255

name, 290
narrative, 17, 34, 65, 96, 108, 113, 141, 145, 147, 152, 154, 200, 204, 242, 255–259, 268, 271, 275, 281, 287
nation, 190
nature, 21, 46, 55, 76, 77, 84, 88, 115, 144, 178–180, 204, 223, 228, 229, 243, 256, 259, 273
navigation, 51, 58
necessity, 28, 37, 71, 77, 83, 100, 105, 138, 144, 154, 188, 195, 200, 231, 247, 249, 260, 262, 263, 284, 295, 296

need, 13, 35, 41, 46, 47, 50, 72, 79, 80, 84, 116, 120, 127, 128, 135, 140, 145, 160, 172, 177, 178, 182, 189, 191, 192, 198, 201, 209, 210, 257–261, 263, 266, 268, 270, 275, 278–280, 285, 286, 292, 297
neglect, 229
negotiation, 138
neighborhood, 1, 2, 54
Nelson Mandela, 34
network, 22, 51, 57, 62–64, 72, 76, 117, 128, 131, 140, 190, 215, 231, 253
newfound, 55
news, 80, 147–149, 154
Nigeria, 141
nightlife, 54
non, 54, 295
notion, 35, 247
nuance, 255

observation, 181
observer, 8, 73
obstacle, 110
office, 97, 98, 102–104, 108, 124
on, 1, 3–6, 8, 9, 20, 21, 24, 26, 33–36, 41, 43–47, 49, 56, 57, 64, 73–75, 82–84, 90, 91, 96, 97, 100, 101, 108, 109, 111, 113, 114, 116, 117, 119, 123, 125–127, 129, 131–136, 138–141, 143, 145, 146, 148–150, 154, 160, 162, 163, 166, 167, 170–173, 177–179, 184, 188–190, 192, 197, 200–202, 204, 205, 207, 209, 210, 212, 213, 227, 228, 231, 240, 243, 244, 255, 257, 260, 263, 265, 268, 270–272, 274–276, 278–282, 286, 287, 289–292, 295–300
one, 12, 16, 22, 24, 27, 31, 37, 43, 55, 62, 71, 73, 79, 82, 84, 90, 100, 102, 109, 111, 116, 127, 128, 137, 140, 142, 146, 150, 152, 153, 179, 204, 206, 211, 215, 221, 241–244, 259, 260, 266, 270, 273, 276, 278, 280, 282, 287, 289, 292, 296, 300
opinion, 181
opponent, 108
opportunity, 102, 197, 204, 206, 209, 244, 262, 269, 272
opposition, 37, 73, 82, 88, 94, 98, 102–104, 119, 135, 292
oppression, 20, 21, 24, 33, 39, 83, 84, 134, 140, 143, 144, 180, 190, 242, 245, 246, 252, 259, 260, 262, 264, 276, 281, 297
option, 200
organization, 212
organizer, 79
organizing, 1, 8, 9, 35, 69, 72, 77, 79, 92, 94, 96, 110, 180, 182, 231, 281, 288, 291, 296
orientation, 4, 23, 33, 40, 60, 69, 75, 83, 84, 107, 114, 120, 135, 136, 140, 188, 195, 210, 246, 263, 285
ostracism, 135
ostracization, 11

other, 10, 82, 84, 90, 91, 99, 108, 111, 118, 128, 140–142, 169, 206, 210, 211, 260, 278, 279, 282, 291
othering, 154
outlet, 5, 7, 53, 154
outreach, 270, 272, 290, 291
outsider, 70
overcoming, 41, 43, 51, 69, 108, 109, 111, 116, 156, 243, 279
overlap, 39, 55, 138, 262, 276
oversight, 83, 143, 269, 275
oversimplification, 150, 153
ownership, 159, 180

pad, 45
pain, 5, 28, 74
painting, 228
pandemic, 178
panel, 46, 75, 141, 148, 244
parade, 149, 231
part, 10, 11, 46, 89, 127, 140, 155, 257, 268, 270, 271, 286, 289
participant, 79, 94
participation, 53, 70, 81, 107, 123, 128, 138, 145, 181, 210, 261
partner, 57
partnership, 99, 110, 111, 118, 139, 143, 159, 166, 172
passage, 111, 118
passing, 290
passion, 1, 3, 4, 13, 22, 33–35, 47, 49, 51, 55, 75, 82, 182, 198, 229, 234, 246, 289, 293, 296
past, 179, 251, 263

path, 6, 11, 34, 71, 72, 97, 102, 122, 144, 173, 177, 190, 205, 213, 227, 240, 270, 285
pathway, 47
Paula, 1–13, 15–17, 19–25, 27, 28, 30, 32–37, 41–57, 60–65, 67–84, 88–91, 94, 96–104, 108–111, 113–124, 126–129, 131, 132, 134–137, 140–142, 145, 146, 148, 149, 152–156, 158–160, 163–172, 176, 191, 192, 195, 197, 201, 202, 204–216, 221, 223–231, 234–237, 240–247, 252, 253, 256–264, 266–273, 276, 278–284, 287–293, 295–300
Paula Lupi, 1, 3, 8, 9, 11, 13, 15, 21, 22, 31, 33, 35, 39, 41, 44, 47, 54, 56, 62, 64, 71, 73, 76, 80, 84, 87, 89, 94, 97, 100, 102, 109, 114, 117, 122, 129, 131, 134, 136, 138–140, 142, 147, 149–151, 153, 155, 157, 163, 165, 170, 177, 179, 184, 193, 195, 204, 206, 207, 211, 213, 215, 217, 223, 229, 231, 236, 240, 249, 251, 253, 255, 257, 261–264, 266, 268–270, 273, 276, 278, 280, 282, 294
Paula Lupi's, 6, 7, 17, 20, 22, 24, 26, 27, 29, 33, 35, 37, 43, 45, 47, 49, 50, 52, 56, 58, 64, 66, 67, 69, 71, 75, 78, 82,

Index

87, 89, 91, 94, 96, 100, 104, 107, 109, 111, 114, 119, 125, 127, 129, 131, 134, 138, 142–146, 160, 162, 165, 167, 170, 173, 190, 192, 200, 202, 204, 209, 210, 213, 215, 219, 221, 225, 227, 229, 236, 238, 240, 243, 245, 247, 259, 260, 262, 270, 278, 280, 282, 284–287, 289, 291–293, 296, 298, 300
Paulo Freire's, 45
peace, 228
pedagogy, 45, 47
peer, 60
people, 9, 10, 20, 70, 83, 90, 117, 135, 139, 142, 143, 178, 188, 201, 223, 244, 263, 265, 284
perception, 69, 80, 101, 115, 151, 159, 162, 204, 257, 273–275, 298
performance, 37, 44, 241
performativity, 241
period, 5, 10, 13
permission, 141
perpetuation, 183, 265
perseverance, 43, 245
person, 27, 70, 84, 114, 138, 154, 204, 244, 259, 264, 295, 300
persona, 213
personality, 74
perspective, 10, 21, 23, 31, 52, 71, 97, 125, 259, 272, 285, 296
phenomenon, 154, 212, 233, 265, 300
philanthropic, 223–225

philanthropy, 223–225
philosophy, 45, 47, 101, 223, 282, 289, 299
photography, 228
physics, 16
picnic, 231
picture, 256
Pierre Bourdieu, 20
pillar, 7, 213, 280
place, 3, 4, 11, 27, 70, 202
plaque, 290
platform, 12, 15, 46, 55, 70, 75, 76, 79, 81, 98, 101, 102, 107, 109, 110, 116, 141, 146, 149, 154, 159, 163, 165, 168, 204, 209, 211, 251, 261, 298
play, 57, 64, 231, 298
plethora, 4
poetry, 290
point, 21, 23, 34, 46, 105, 231, 252
poise, 108
policy, 45, 49, 77, 97, 99–101, 105, 108, 110, 111, 116, 128, 139, 181, 182, 187, 204, 209, 265, 291, 298, 299
politician, 115, 117–119, 123
pop, 1
portrayal, 255
Portugal, 1, 3, 11–13, 21, 22, 29, 35, 37, 56, 72, 74, 78, 82, 83, 97, 100–103, 111, 120, 125, 127, 129, 131, 132, 136, 143, 159, 201, 202, 204, 206, 225, 227, 228, 279, 282, 300
position, 29, 124, 129, 255, 262
possibility, 123
post, 166

pot, 1
potential, 33, 43, 46, 69, 70, 84, 90, 92, 110, 127, 141, 143, 144, 149, 150, 165–167, 180, 184, 211, 225, 258, 259, 274, 275, 280, 295, 297
power, 1, 5, 7, 9, 13, 17, 20, 32, 33, 43–46, 49, 52, 55, 64, 65, 69, 73, 75, 76, 82, 91, 94, 99–101, 104, 107, 110, 114, 117, 129, 131, 132, 134, 138, 140, 143, 145, 149, 156, 160, 164, 165, 172, 173, 179, 190, 202, 210, 225, 228, 240, 242–244, 252, 257, 260, 265, 268, 275, 279, 281, 282, 291, 293
practice, 45, 66, 84, 270, 273
precedent, 123
prejudice, 8, 22, 34, 50, 60, 67–69, 74, 99, 108, 189, 214, 241, 243, 252
presence, 115, 146, 163, 164, 172
presentation, 210
pressure, 5, 172, 211, 295
pride, 74, 77, 123, 143
principle, 24, 32, 264, 276
prioritization, 105
priority, 108, 188
privilege, 10, 20, 24, 39, 70, 83, 114, 119, 201, 219, 260, 262, 264, 265, 270, 281, 283
process, 4, 11, 21, 53, 69, 71–73, 118, 150, 181, 182, 206, 239, 241, 243, 247, 257, 258, 260, 263, 267, 273, 282

product, 145
production, 152, 159
productivity, 121
professional, 212, 269
professor, 43
profile, 148, 154, 166, 206, 212, 269
program, 111, 148, 245
progress, 41, 45, 75, 121, 127, 136, 138, 167, 177–180, 182, 188, 216, 226, 249, 258, 280, 291, 293, 296, 298
progression, 281
project, 8, 21, 44, 66, 75, 140, 159, 172, 286
prominence, 20, 80, 82, 97, 100, 122, 145, 153, 157, 159, 207, 259, 281
promise, 287
protest, 13, 79, 88, 234
provision, 138
psychologist, 295
psychosocial, 214
public, 49, 80, 98–100, 102, 104, 108, 111, 116, 117, 119, 123, 124, 148, 151, 153–156, 159, 170–173, 181, 182, 192, 201, 211–213, 244, 252, 257–259, 270, 273–275, 290, 291, 298
publicity, 167
purpose, 6, 45, 47, 49, 77, 89
pursuit, 17, 26, 44, 46, 52, 89, 90, 179, 206, 227, 243, 281, 295, 296
push, 12, 139, 182
pushback, 292

quality, 35, 47, 213, 241, 252, 285

Index

queer, 6, 10, 17, 19, 21, 31, 34, 39, 41, 46, 50, 52, 54, 55, 69–71, 77, 81, 83, 84, 97–100, 102, 108, 114–117, 122, 123, 126, 138–140, 143, 145, 159, 178, 209, 210, 214, 223, 243, 244, 246, 256, 259, 261–266, 276, 281, 282, 286, 295–297, 299
queerness, 55, 71, 243
quest, 37, 47, 62, 73, 75, 82, 138, 180, 281
question, 2, 8, 11, 21, 45, 70, 150, 255, 259, 275
questioning, 1, 3–5, 9, 21, 22, 33, 34, 67, 73, 88, 108, 224, 260, 287
quo, 2, 33, 45, 72, 88, 103, 135, 170

race, 2, 40, 46, 75, 77, 84, 119, 140, 178, 180, 201, 233, 256, 263, 279, 287, 297
raising, 9, 24, 55, 77, 149, 166, 172, 181, 244, 276
rally, 176, 261, 290
range, 44, 54, 256
rationale, 272
reach, 82, 146, 181, 210–212, 270, 296
reaffirmation, 45
reality, 21, 23, 27, 32, 84, 253, 284
realization, 10, 11, 34, 55, 97, 125–127, 242
realm, 42, 50, 64, 107, 117, 140, 150, 173, 177, 213, 275, 278, 291
recognition, 78, 85, 90, 101, 105, 126, 129, 145, 171–173, 182, 204, 210–213, 225, 260
reconciliation, 271–273, 278–280
reevaluation, 275
reflection, 4, 29, 69, 97, 100, 145, 171, 202, 206, 215, 238–240, 243, 244, 260, 262, 279, 282, 291
reflexivity, 270
reform, 226
reframing, 242
refuge, 2, 5, 10, 15, 17, 193
regard, 142, 281
reinforcement, 265
rejection, 5, 10, 50, 57, 70, 246
rejuvenation, 228
relationship, 19, 51, 57, 166, 170, 234, 244
remembrance, 249, 290
reminder, 20, 22, 46, 64, 71, 82, 109, 116, 134, 142, 146, 160, 173, 202, 225, 229, 231, 236, 262, 270, 278, 280, 290, 291, 295, 298, 300
removal, 138, 285
report, 74
reporting, 167
representation, 9, 17, 20, 30, 46, 47, 54, 71, 75, 77, 78, 80, 81, 94, 98, 100, 102–104, 108, 109, 115, 116, 119, 122, 123, 127, 129, 141, 142, 146, 150–153, 157, 159, 160, 162, 170, 171, 173, 201, 211, 226, 245, 252, 255, 257–259, 261, 263, 265, 266, 270, 271, 273, 275, 280, 286, 296–298

representative, 20, 90, 92, 104, 116, 141, 223, 226, 259
reputation, 99, 256
research, 110
resentment, 57
residence, 4
resilience, 1, 2, 4, 11, 17, 19, 21, 24, 29, 34, 35, 43, 44, 51, 52, 55, 66, 69, 71, 73–75, 80, 82, 89, 96, 104, 107, 109, 116, 117, 119, 123, 124, 127, 134, 146, 156, 172, 182, 193, 206, 213, 214, 225, 227, 236, 238, 240, 241, 245–247, 257, 268, 281, 282, 289, 290, 292, 293
resistance, 21, 22, 34, 88, 89, 97, 116, 121, 124, 135, 170, 224, 229, 292, 295
resolution, 128, 278
resolve, 5, 34, 47, 48, 101, 244, 245
resource, 111, 134, 168, 225
respect, 20, 74, 118, 129, 143, 191, 259
response, 4, 17, 69, 199, 257, 279
responsibility, 6, 45, 146, 166, 184, 206, 287, 289
restoration, 280
result, 135, 206, 243, 265, 285, 297
retreat, 231
revelation, 34
review, 233
rhetoric, 79, 88, 103
richness, 298
right, 35, 115, 139, 195, 283
ripple, 43, 46, 66, 111, 145, 209, 223, 246, 252, 299
rise, 80, 100, 145, 178, 182, 221, 296

risk, 83, 150, 188, 265, 295, 298
road, 103, 260, 269
roadmap, 289
rock, 227
role, 1, 2, 5, 7, 10, 16, 26, 32, 33, 43, 45, 47, 53, 57, 64, 75, 79, 98, 109, 145, 151, 160, 170, 179, 180, 182, 184, 201, 207–209, 213, 223, 227, 231, 236, 241–243, 257, 262, 270, 272, 277, 278, 282, 298
root, 33
run, 103, 108

s, 1–13, 15–17, 19–29, 32–37, 41, 43–47, 49–52, 54–58, 64–67, 69–78, 80–82, 84, 87, 89–91, 94, 96, 98–104, 107, 109–111, 113–117, 119, 123, 125–129, 131, 134, 138–140, 142–146, 148, 149, 154, 158, 160, 162, 164–168, 170, 172, 173, 190, 192, 197, 200–202, 204, 206, 208–215, 219, 221, 223–229, 231, 236, 238, 240–247, 249, 252, 253, 255–263, 265, 266, 269, 270, 272, 273, 275, 276, 278, 280–293, 295–300
sadness, 8
sanctuary, 2, 15, 227, 241
Santos, 46
scale, 126, 127, 129, 134–136, 138, 145, 170, 190, 192, 201
scenario, 57
scene, 2

Index 325

scholar, 39, 262, 276, 282
school, 4, 8, 9, 21, 23, 27–29, 32, 72, 74, 123, 226, 246
schoolteacher, 7
science, 147
scrutiny, 98, 153–156, 159, 167, 171–173, 205, 211, 212, 257, 259, 260
section, 15, 41, 45, 62, 64, 67, 69, 76, 85, 94, 105, 109, 114, 129, 149, 153, 163, 165, 170, 177, 180, 182, 185, 195, 200, 215, 223, 225, 229, 236, 249, 259, 273, 278
sector, 111, 226
self, 2, 4, 7, 9–11, 15, 16, 27, 32, 34, 45, 51–53, 56, 57, 67–73, 88, 162, 168–170, 172, 182, 206, 213, 214, 229, 231, 236–244, 246, 247, 258, 260, 262, 273, 279, 281, 296, 298
sense, 1, 3–11, 16, 22, 24, 33, 34, 43–45, 47, 54–57, 64, 66, 69, 70, 72, 73, 76, 79, 82, 89, 114, 116, 146, 150, 159, 166, 171, 180, 184, 201, 212, 214, 228, 242–245, 247, 256, 258, 268, 276, 280, 281, 289, 296
sensitivity, 115, 191, 252
sentiment, 178
series, 47, 75, 111, 117, 159, 166, 170, 267, 269, 279, 285, 291, 293
seriousness, 159
servant, 99
serve, 3, 13, 15, 26, 28, 29, 43, 45, 66, 75, 84, 114, 131, 166, 181, 184, 192, 202, 204, 211, 224, 231, 238, 251, 258, 260, 265, 268, 272, 275, 290
service, 104
set, 27, 102, 114, 123, 213, 231, 294
setting, 4, 45, 76, 78
sex, 74, 100, 120, 127, 136, 233
sexuality, 2, 4, 8, 10, 55, 56, 74, 119, 285, 297
shape, 24, 27, 31, 45, 54, 84, 100, 121, 239, 241, 265, 273, 281
share, 2, 8, 20, 24, 46, 55, 57, 65, 66, 70, 74, 75, 116, 123, 139–142, 145, 146, 150, 153, 159, 166, 172, 181, 182, 191, 209, 214, 229, 231, 245, 251, 261, 268, 270, 277, 280, 285, 288, 290
sharing, 22, 32, 34, 53, 64, 66, 72, 100, 116, 123, 140, 141, 150, 159, 179, 210, 225, 242, 246, 247, 272
shift, 51, 152, 160, 225, 272
sign, 115, 270
significance, 20, 44, 64, 76, 84, 129, 138, 143, 238, 270, 275, 278, 281
silence, 74
situation, 178
size, 137
skepticism, 44, 103, 110, 117, 224, 259, 260
societal, 1–6, 8–13, 17, 20–22, 24, 28, 29, 31–34, 36, 44–46, 50–53, 55, 60, 61, 66–74,

80, 82, 88, 101, 111, 135, 139, 160, 162, 176, 193, 199, 230, 234–236, 240, 241, 243, 246, 252, 266, 285–287, 291, 295, 297
society, 2, 4, 10, 13, 20, 21, 27, 28, 35, 37, 50, 55, 56, 60, 69, 71, 74, 78–80, 82, 84, 88, 94, 102, 104, 107, 111, 117, 119, 121, 135, 138, 160, 162, 170, 187, 188, 190, 204, 206, 209, 240, 252, 260, 264, 275, 278, 281–283, 285–288, 292, 299, 300
socio, 97, 157
Sofia, 19, 51, 234
solace, 2, 5, 8, 12, 16, 17, 28, 57, 70, 227, 228
solidarity, 5, 19–22, 24, 35, 47, 57, 64, 71, 72, 74, 76, 80, 89, 105, 114, 123, 127, 132, 140, 142–144, 146, 150, 162, 171, 179, 190, 192, 193, 201, 212, 225, 227, 245–247, 258, 278, 281, 282, 297
solitude, 12
sound, 25
soundtrack, 1
source, 4, 11, 19, 26, 227
South Africa, 140
sovereignty, 255
space, 2, 8, 16, 17, 34, 51, 53, 57, 66, 100, 159, 163, 172, 176, 241, 270
speaker, 211
speaking, 117, 132, 134, 148, 201, 206, 210

spectrum, 20, 24, 77, 256, 262, 263
speech, 127, 176, 210
sphere, 100, 103, 114, 157
spike, 148
spirit, 1, 7, 8, 80, 94, 109, 116, 240, 290, 291, 293
sponsor, 166
sponsorship, 166
spotlight, 149, 153, 172
stability, 190
stage, 45, 76, 78, 82, 127, 132, 134, 163, 207, 209, 280, 282
stand, 4, 8, 124, 278
standard, 212
statement, 206
status, 2, 33, 45, 72, 75, 77, 82, 84, 88, 96, 101, 103, 120, 135, 140, 146, 170, 195, 201, 210, 263
step, 71, 76–78, 101, 102, 140, 270, 281
stereotype, 107
stigma, 17, 36, 50, 55, 60, 74, 75, 115, 127, 151, 199, 297
Stonewall, 275
story, 34, 43, 53, 55, 69–72, 75, 100, 116, 123, 145, 147, 150, 166, 173, 242, 246, 255, 257, 259, 268, 270, 287, 290, 292, 299
storyteller, 150
storytelling, 32–34, 55, 64–66, 82, 149, 150, 152, 160, 172, 179, 221, 242, 243, 251, 256–258
strategizing, 79
strategy, 72, 102, 111, 137, 140, 142, 144, 165, 166, 182, 191
street, 15

Index

strength, 11, 12, 19, 26, 57, 71, 195, 229, 242, 245–247, 270, 278, 287, 293
stress, 233, 296
struggle, 10, 11, 27–29, 32, 46, 67, 80, 112, 129, 142, 176, 184, 190, 193, 200, 214, 221, 227, 235, 241, 245, 257, 261, 268, 285, 286, 297
student, 8, 23, 37, 43, 46, 184
study, 44, 74
subgroup, 54
subject, 21, 255, 273, 275
success, 43, 47, 102, 107, 201, 204, 295
suicide, 74
suitability, 98
summary, 7, 21, 22, 119, 127, 197, 284
sun, 9, 24, 80
support, 1, 2, 4, 6–8, 12, 13, 17, 19, 22, 30, 35, 36, 41, 43, 44, 47, 51, 53, 55, 57, 58, 62–64, 69, 70, 72–74, 76–78, 102, 109–111, 122, 128, 132, 135, 139, 140, 148, 156, 165, 167, 168, 172, 181, 185, 187, 195, 201, 213, 215, 223, 231, 238–241, 243, 245–247, 253, 260, 262, 265, 276, 277, 279, 283–285, 288, 290
supporter, 111
surge, 8
surrounding, 2, 17, 32, 60, 70, 74, 195, 224, 236, 249, 262
sustainability, 265

sword, 211
symbol, 109
symphony, 33, 170
synthesis, 198
system, 1, 12, 27, 32, 47

Taiwan, 139
taking, 24, 231, 240, 268, 295
talk, 148
tapestry, 1, 3, 6, 15, 21, 26, 27, 45, 54, 94, 127, 140, 142, 227, 249, 270, 275, 280, 289, 293, 295
target, 27, 126
task, 5, 43
teaching, 47, 49
tech, 111, 166
technology, 288
tendency, 143, 152, 265
tension, 57, 255, 267
tenure, 240
term, 46, 105, 138, 177, 182, 231, 256, 262, 276, 282, 296
testament, 43, 44, 69, 73, 100, 104, 107, 114, 117, 138, 140, 144, 145, 149, 156, 173, 202, 204, 209, 213, 240, 268, 281, 292
the Global South, 141, 191
the Tagus River, 1
the United States, 178, 188
theme, 255
theory, 21, 22, 64, 67, 69, 76, 77, 90, 114, 119, 131, 134, 140, 150, 157, 180–182, 187, 190, 212, 223, 233, 241, 243, 276, 278, 281, 295
therapy, 242, 247
thesis, 44

thinking, 8, 49, 134, 182, 252
thread, 249
threat, 116
time, 2, 9, 12, 102, 146, 167, 172, 177, 181, 212, 213, 229, 240, 267, 273, 296
timing, 149
today, 29, 296
tokenism, 152, 153, 251
tolerance, 282
toll, 74, 88, 172, 231, 236, 295
tool, 2, 32, 34, 47, 55, 64, 92, 142, 146, 149, 159, 163, 172, 182, 189, 252, 270, 283, 288, 299
toolkit, 42
torch, 49, 100, 215, 287, 289
traction, 127, 262
tragedy, 74
trailblazer, 295
training, 36, 43, 111, 140, 181, 252
trait, 27
transfer, 45
transformation, 43, 240, 242
transgender, 19, 34, 54, 90, 178, 263, 265, 275
transition, 127
transparency, 155, 156, 167, 168, 214, 224, 272
transphobia, 83
treatment, 233
trepidation, 102
triangle, 16
tribute, 290
triumph, 80, 200, 270
trust, 167, 258, 270–273, 282
truth, 22, 131, 132, 134, 150
turn, 53, 206
turning, 21, 23, 34, 46, 292

underemployment, 84
underpinning, 165, 223
underrepresentation, 151
understanding, 2, 9–13, 19–21, 23, 30, 32, 33, 35, 39, 47, 51, 54–56, 74, 75, 78, 79, 84, 85, 87, 89, 91, 101, 102, 107, 110, 119, 122, 126, 127, 136, 138, 140, 142, 147, 149, 152–154, 160, 165, 172, 178, 189, 191, 193, 201, 213, 226, 234, 239–241, 244, 245, 251–253, 256–258, 260–262, 264, 267–270, 275, 276, 278–280, 282, 283, 285–287, 295–297
unemployment, 84, 178
uniqueness, 10, 51
unity, 82, 143, 154, 176, 206, 258, 260, 268, 273, 278–280, 289
university, 46, 51
up, 1, 2, 4–6, 8, 11, 21, 33, 73, 201, 245, 281, 287, 294–296
uplift, 94, 116, 142, 146, 253, 256, 261, 276, 278, 284
uprising, 275
urgency, 79, 113, 244, 266, 297
use, 13, 34, 73, 96, 165, 167, 192, 280

validation, 43, 73
validity, 21
value, 2, 53, 212, 223
variety, 5, 21, 180
victim, 154
view, 51, 134, 261, 272
vigilance, 178, 263

Index

vigor, 127, 198, 253
violence, 19, 78, 128, 135
visibility, 55, 75, 77, 81, 85, 90, 92, 102, 103, 111, 118, 122, 123, 141, 145, 148, 149, 160, 162, 165–167, 172, 211, 252, 295, 297
vision, 35, 97, 102, 103, 110, 117, 119, 140, 142, 197, 251–253, 282–284, 290
voice, 3, 12, 13, 22, 24, 29, 35, 43, 54–56, 69, 71–73, 76, 78, 80–82, 88, 94, 96, 97, 102, 109, 115, 118, 127, 129, 131, 134, 142, 147, 160, 172, 179, 195, 211, 221, 243, 255, 264, 269, 276, 278, 280, 289, 290, 293, 295–298, 300
void, 296
volunteer, 34
voter, 105
voting, 108
vulnerability, 51, 53, 55, 89, 236, 247, 270

wake, 258, 285
warrior, 154
wave, 49, 297
way, 7, 43, 52, 71, 84, 87, 94, 100, 104, 131, 134, 145, 162, 165, 179, 182, 188, 201, 204, 213, 249, 257, 262, 269, 292
weakness, 270
web, 83
week, 8
weekend, 231
weight, 2, 11, 295, 296

welfare, 223
well, 20, 28, 30, 43, 53, 64, 84, 170, 172, 182, 188, 189, 213, 231, 238, 241, 247, 261, 267, 281, 282, 296
wellness, 182
wheelchair, 115
whim, 100
whole, 70, 256
willingness, 258, 262
witness, 73, 75
woman, 6, 19, 31, 34, 39, 41, 46, 52, 55, 69–71, 83, 97–99, 102, 108, 114, 116, 117, 122, 126, 145, 154, 214, 243, 246, 256, 259, 262, 263, 266, 275, 276, 281, 282, 296, 299
won, 178, 292
work, 10, 17, 20, 22, 30, 32, 34–37, 44, 57, 71, 72, 76, 82, 84, 91, 92, 99, 116, 121, 127, 142, 143, 146, 149, 158–160, 201, 202, 204, 206, 211–213, 221, 225, 245, 253, 255, 256, 262–264, 273, 275, 277, 278, 280, 282, 286, 289, 290, 294, 295, 297, 299, 300
workforce, 265
workplace, 84
workshop, 34
world, 5, 6, 8, 10, 17, 21, 24, 26, 27, 34, 35, 44, 45, 49, 54, 65, 69, 73, 76, 100–102, 114, 129, 131, 134–136, 140, 142, 144, 146, 147, 178, 184, 192, 195, 197,

200–202, 204, 209, 213, 214, 219, 223, 225, 227, 231, 235, 241, 251, 252, 259, 268, 270, 275, 278, 282–284, 291, 293, 296–298, 300

worldview, 1, 4, 26, 145, 229
worth, 35, 69, 70, 73, 88, 295

year, 44, 74
youth, 9, 34, 54, 74, 78, 185–188, 206, 212, 226, 287

Milton Keynes UK
Ingram Content Group UK Ltd.
UKHW051143031124
450424UK00019B/1247